Political
Monopolies
in
American
Cities

Jessica Trounstine

Political
Monopolies
in
American
Cities

The Rise and Fall of Bosses and Reformers

The University of Chicago Press

Chicago and London

JESSICA TROUNSTINE is assistant professor of politics
and public affairs at Princeton University.

The University of Chicago Press, Chicago 60637
The University of Chicago Press, Ltd., London
© 2008 by The University of Chicago
All rights reserved. Published 2008
Printed in the United States of America

17 16 15 14 13 12 11 10 09 08   1 2 3 4 5

Library of Congress Cataloging-in-Publication Data

Trounstine, Jessica.
   Political monopolies in American cities : the rise and fall of bosses and
reformers / Jessica Trounstine.
      p. cm.
   Includes bibliographical references and index.
   ISBN-13: 978-0-226-81281-6 (cloth : alk. paper)
   ISBN-13: 978-0-226-81282-3 (pbk. : alk. paper)
   ISBN-10: 0-226-81281-2 (cloth : alk. paper)
   ISBN-10: 0-226-81282-0 (pbk. : alk. paper)
   1. Incumbency (Public officers)—United States.   2. Local elections—
United States.   3. Municipal government—United States.   4. Power (Social
sciences)—United States.   5. Political culture—United States.   6. Patronage,
Political—United States.   7. Political corruption—United States.   I. Title.
   JS395 .T76   2008
   320.8'50973—dc22

                                                            2008007421

⊚ The paper used in this publication meets the
minimum requirements of the American National
Standard for Information Sciences—Permanence of
Paper for Printed Library Materials,
ANSI Z39.48-1992.

For my (many) parents

CONTENTS

ILLUSTRATIONS

Figures

Tables

ACKNOWLEDGMENTS

AN ENORMOUS DEBT of gratitude is owed to a great many individuals who have offered me their time, knowledge, and support as I tackled this project. My advisor, mentor, and dear friend Amy Bridges first kindled my interest in urban politics, gracefully guided me though graduate school, and then walked me through the writing of my first book. Without hesitation she shared with me her data, her brilliance, and her excitement for academia. She provided unyielding support. There are no adequate words to thank her.

In addition to my advisor, I was lucky to be surrounded by wise and supportive faculty and peers in my graduate program. Zoltan Hajnal taught me to tie city politics to larger questions of democracy and how to quantify my arguments. He kept his door open to me on a daily basis for advice and coauthorship, and has continued to do so even now that our doors are across the country. Elisabeth Gerber guided my research designs, clarified my theories, and has unflaggingly introduced me to networks of social scientists. Steve Erie and Bruce Cain offered invaluable comments and generous enthusiasm. I also received helpful feedback from Gary Cox, Kathleen Cunningham, Gary Jacobson, Mike Kelly, Thad Kousser, Sam Popkin, Chris Shortell, Tony Smith, Melody Valdini, and the participants at the Consortium for Qualitative Research Methods second annual institute.

After leaving UC San Diego, I was lucky to find an equally important academic support system at Princeton University. David Lewis has allowed me to bother him frequently. He read many of the chapters in the book and offered terrific advice. Chuck Cameron read an early draft of the book and laid out for me a detailed set of recommendations for making it more persuasive and rigorous. I am grateful for his data-collection suggestions in particular. I also received extremely helpful feedback on research design, data analysis, drafts of chapters, and the publishing process from Chris Achen, Doug Arnold, Larry Bartels, Brandice Canes-Wrone, Matt Cleary, Josh Clinton, Martin Gilens, Fred Greenstein,

Kosuke Imai, Karen Jusko, Jason Lyall, Nolan McCarty, Adam Meiro-witz, Tali Mendelberg, Tasha Philpot, Markus Prior, Julie Taylor, Josh Tucker, Rick Valelly, and Robert Willig.

In the spring of 2006 the Princeton Department of Politics and the Center for the Study of Democratic Politics funded a manuscript confer-ence so that I might be given formal feedback on the draft of the book. The comments I received from the conference participants were trans-formative. Amy Bridges, Douglas Massey, David Mayhew, John Mollen-kopf, Rebecca Morton, and Paul Peterson dissected the manuscript. The amount of time these scholars invested and the degree of detail they of-fered for my revisions improved my project immensely. The two review-ers selected by the University of Chicago Press to review the manuscript offered similarly invaluable recommendations. John Tryneski has been an amazing editor. From the beginning he has been enthusiastic, patient, approachable, and incredibly insightful. I have trusted him completely. Rodney Powell provided extremely helpful advice as well.

Countless city and county registrars and bureaucrats aided my quest for data. Those in the San Jose city clerk's office, the Santa Clara coun-ty registrar, and the San Jose Department of Public Works were espe-cially helpful. Robert Lineberry mailed me a precious data collection for Chicago. Richard Simpson shared his vast knowledge of Chicago's city council and political underbelly. Kristen Badal, Zach Epstein, and Shivani Gupta provided excellent research assistance. I am grateful for the openness and honesty of all my interviewees who collectively spent many hours helping me understand the structure of power in San Jose.

This book is dedicated to my parents Mary, Celine, Phil, and Deb-bie, because they are without a doubt the reason it exists. They offered me profound love, critiques of my writing, and incredible insight into urban politics. I am also lucky to count my siblings among my very best friends in the world. David, Amy, Ryan, and Patrick, and my almost-sister Gemma have been my oldest and most trusted confidants. My newest family member, Brian, has kept me focused and calm, made me laugh until I could no longer breathe, endured countless conversations about political monopolies, and adored me. To you all, I offer my most heartfelt thanks.

INTRODUCTION

IN MANY WAYS, Chicago, Illinois, and San Jose, California, are extremely different places. Politically they represent the stark distinctions between machine and reform governments examined by generations of urban scholars. Throughout the twentieth century, Chicago pulsed with life. Sordid links among a series of infamous political bosses and notorious crime lords ensured that the city never went dry, reelection came easy, and men like Al Capone became fabulously rich. Chicago housed millions of immigrants in an economy of factories and slaughterhouses. The very model of a political machine, Chicago's hierarchically organized political parties were characterized by corruption, patronage armies, and decades of single-party rule established by bosses and maintained by working-class constituencies.

Meanwhile, on the other edge of the nation, San Jose made its way into the world as a sleepy, agricultural community with a single square block downtown. Its most famous residents have been innovators of technology, not politicians or gangsters. In recent years San Jose has consistently been ranked among the safest and wealthiest big cities in America. Typically, reform governments, like San Jose's, have been defined only by their ideals and institutional structures: serving the good of the whole through efficient administration, dispassionate and removed from the gritty details of politics. Upper-class, middle-class, and business constituencies have been the strongest supporters of reformed systems. In this way, bosses and reformers have been placed in opposition to each other as representations of wholly different political worlds.

Yet, despite these vast differences, Chicago and San Jose share one conspicuous trait: a legacy of extraordinarily long tenure by political leaders. Richard J. Daley governed Chicago while Anthony "Dutch" Hamann managed San Jose. Both were political centralizers, leaders of phenomenally powerful coalitions. In cities more than 2,000 miles apart, Daley and Hamann each came to office in the early 1950s and went on to preside for a quarter of a century. But in the twilight of the 1970s, the regimes these men guided were eclipsed by rising political movements. So, given the differences between machine and reform regimes, why do these places share political patterns; how could Daley and Hamann have both governed for multiple decades in cities that were so different? The answer lies in the approach to reelection employed by politicians in both places: they biased the system in favor of incumbents.

In the past, scholars have placed the boss and the manager at opposite ends of a spectrum of healthy government with machines anchoring the antidemocratic side while reformers held up the better end. This characterization has obscured our ability to understand the process by which representative democracy functions and the process by which it fails. I argue that it is not whether a government is machine or reform that determines its propensity to represent the people, but rather its success at stacking the deck in its favor. When political coalitions successfully limit the probability that they will be defeated over the long term—when they eliminate effective competition—they achieve a political monopoly. In these circumstances the governing coalition gains the freedom to be responsive to a narrow segment of the electorate at the expense of the broader community.

Daley and Hamann both led coalitions that pursued and secured political monopolies. These types of organizations are not as rare in American politics as one might think. In approximately 30 percent of the nation's largest cities, a single coalition has controlled all branches of government for more than a decade at some point during the twentieth century. This book asks why and how coalitions establish political monopolies, it investigates the consequences monopolies have for the communities that house them, and it explores why they collapse.

There was a time when urban-politics scholarship led the discipline of political science; when theories of local systems informed our understanding of politics more generally. Today the study of cities is frequently the side effect of studying other topics—racial and ethnic politics, public administration, or economic development. For those who do focus on cities, a common theme is that cities are constrained and can do little to affect their own futures. As Douglas Rae (2003) put it, "most American cities are sitting ducks, unable to move out of the way when change comes roaring at them" (xvii). Such a perspective suggests that the last place we should look to understand important outcomes and explain causal forces would be the city government itself. This book unabashedly disagrees with this view; it is a conscious attempt to refocus the dialogue on cities, to bring back politics, and to make predictive claims.

In the simplest terms, I argue that many reelection strategies employed at the local level break the electoral connection between constituents and representatives, leaving voters with diminished opportunity to control their elected officials. Political science research asserts that reelection-seeking activity offers voters the best opportunity for a responsive and representative government (Key [1949] 1984; Downs 1957; Mayhew 1974). Through elections citizens select and empower their representatives. Ideally, the desire to keep their jobs ensures that politicians, in pursuit of larger vote shares, serve constituents. But amassing more votes is not the only way to secure reelection. Politicians have a more appealing alternative for ensuring victory—biasing the system. In other words, coalitions have incentives to take advantage of and implement structures that increase their probability of reelection regardless of the government's performance or the quality of representation. When politicians cease to worry about reelection, they become free to pursue government policy that does not reflect constituent preferences. They acquire the ability to enrich themselves and their supporters or pursue policies that would otherwise lead to their electoral defeat. Ironically, this behavior contributes to the coalitions' own political downfall. By limiting attention to narrow segments of the electorate and building rigid institutions to insulate their regimes from challenges, coalitions foster both the incentives and the means for the collapse of their monopolies. Over time, monopolists sow the seeds of their own destruction.

Given the presence and diversity of political monopolies at the local level in the United States, a comparative analysis of twentieth-century urban politics is the perfect place to begin. For each man (and they all have been men) who headed a political monopoly a different story can be told of his rise to the top. Some combination of luck, circumstance, and dogged perseverance enabled his success. The context in which these leaders lived and governed individualizes each tale, but none is entirely unique. Both machine and reform organizations presided over cities for multiple terms without significant threats to their power, both focused benefits on their supporters, and both collapsed when they could not adjust to a changing political world.

Another reason American cities offer a good focus for this investigation is that city electoral systems tend to be fairly flexible, leading to myriad variations in urban political institutions. Some cities have mayors, others have managers, and still others have both. City legislatures vary widely in size and form; some are elected by districts or wards while others are selected through at-large (citywide) systems. Because I argue that institutional changes can advantage the governing coalition, this variation offers the opportunity to study the effect of changing the rules for monopoly control.

Using this framework, I challenge a number of conclusions drawn in the literature. First, scholars have generally determined that political machines are a thing of the past, no longer necessary or possible in the modern age. By placing machine governments in a broader framework of political monopolies I suggest that this conclusion is incorrect. While politicians may no longer be able to dump ballots in the river with impunity, they continue to employ strategies to reduce electoral competition. The need for unity, power, and centralization is as great today as it ever was.

Filmmaker Marshall Curry (2003) documented the operation of a dying but still powerful machine in Newark, New Jersey, as he traced Cory Booker's 2002 campaign to unseat the incumbent mayor in the movie *Street Fight*. Time and again the film shows police officers working to protect the five-term incumbent Sharpe James while suppressing Booker's organization. Booker's signs were removed, his supporters intimidated with threats of losing their city contracts, his headquarters burglarized, and meeting locations shuttered by city agencies. Ultimately, Booker lost the election.[1] In the same year, newly elected Thomas Suozzi, Nassau County, New York's first Democratic executive in thirty years, asked the people to "dismantle the culture of machine politics," arguing that in his administration "workers [would] be rewarded based upon their performance, not their political connections." Two years later, Suozzi plead guilty to forcing a municipal employee into political service and remained under investigation for accepting quid pro quo campaign contributions (quoted in Lambert and Domash 2004, A1). In San Antonio, two council members were indicted for "running a corrupt political machine" in 2002 (Robbins 2004, 1B). The *New York Times* argues that New Jersey's Hudson County Democratic organization "is one of the most formidable political machines in the nation . . . and it is only becoming stronger" (Hernandez 2003, A2). As long as political coalitions continue to act strategically, monopoly remains a real possibility.

Understanding the effects of political monopolies has important implications for the study of city politics and democratic practice more broadly. The story of monopoly control over government is not the *typical* story of urban governance. Monopolies are difficult to establish and hard to maintain. Much more common are urban electoral systems that have responsive governing regimes, competitive parties, divided government, or factional politics. Yet monopolies do govern in many different types of cities and during a variety of time periods.[2] Twentieth-century monopolies arose during the Gilded Age in cities like Baltimore and Philadelphia, during the Progressive Era in places like Cincinnati and New York, between the two world wars in places as different as Chicago and Dallas, and in the years following the Second World War in cities like New Haven, San Antonio, and Berkeley. Further, monopolies have occurred in every region of the country during the twentieth century. There is evidence of twenty-five monopolies in the Northeast, twenty-two in the South, nine in the Midwest, and eight in the West. These cities have diverse demographic profiles and have varied widely in size over time. The smallest city hosting a monopoly had only 75,797 people (Pawtucket, Rhode Island) while the largest, New York City, had a population of over seven million (see tables A2 and A3).[3]

Given this variety, knowing when, why, and how monopolies dominate governance enables scholars and practitioners to evaluate the extent to which democratic institutions become compromised in the United States. Politicians in pursuit of monopoly attempt to structure electoral and governing institutions in a manner which will enhance their chances for reelection. This means that institutional changes frequently reflect political goals and compromises. Once a coalition is in power, the preservation of the monopoly structures decisions on expenditures and policy. Monopolies shape who is elected and appointed to office and when power is likely to be shared. They influence which residents are likely to participate in elections and whether or not participation affects political outcomes. Monopolies provide insight into the organization of local bureaucracies and patterns of decision making by local agencies. In order to know who governs and how cities operate, it is important to know whether or not a city is dominated by a monopoly, who the monopoly represents, and who it does not. Finally, understanding monopolies gets to the heart of democracy. If we expect people to be represented through the electoral system, we must ensure that the opportunity to exercise choice exists equally for all members of the community and that reelection is tied to the quality and performance of incumbents.

To date, there has been no general consensus on the extent to which city political systems remain competitive, representative democracies. Scholars debate the regularity with which bosses controlled cities. Some, like Munro (1933), argue that "there may be some large urban communities in the United States which have a right to call themselves unbossed, but they can be numbered on the fingers of a single hand" (12). More recently revisionist urban historians have suggested that city machines dominated the minds of Progressive reformers more frequently than they dominated cities (Shefter 1976; Teaford 1984; McDonald 1985). Stave et al. (1988) explains, "[T]here were remarkably few 'machines' that controlled city-wide political offices for long periods of time, and there is remarkably little evidence that political organizations either wanted or had the resources to be uncritical respondents to the needs of the urban masses" (300). Additionally, other than work by Bridges (1997), Davidson and Fraga (1988), and Fraga (1988) there has been little recognition that reformers operated as cohesive coalitions for an extended period of time. Many scholars have studied the effects of reform institutions (e.g., Welch and Bledsoe 1988), but have frequently seen these effects as unintended. In their introductory urban-politics textbook, Ross and Levine (2001) state "The resulting reforms helped clean up city politics and make municipal government more professional and efficient. Yet the reforms also produced unanticipated and undesirable effects" (159).

In this work I illustrate that although rare, machine and reform regimes *did* exist. I draw on new data to show that coalitions dominated city elections, that these coalitions were goal seeking, that the outcomes they wrought were intentional, and that they generated clear patterns of governmental expenditures. The rich case-study literature on city regimes has provided an excellent foundation for understanding political monopolies and yet causal explanations tend to be ad hoc, wholly dependent on individual contexts. I seek to systematize these descriptions to determine where and when the causal relationships provide predictive and explanatory power, to uncover empirical regularities, and to generalize the findings to apply to cities in particular and to democratically elected governments more broadly. I also strive to contribute to our understanding of local political institutions and to clarify the links between practices and outcomes—explaining, for instance, exactly why patronage produced a machine and why nonpartisan elections aided reformers.

The existing literature on city electoral systems is insufficient to explain why Chicago and San Jose have such similar political histories. It is generally accepted that machines are the epitome of monopoly, reform its antithesis. Early analyses of machines were written by the municipal reformers themselves, the general consensus being that dominance by local party organizations generated corrupt and inefficient government that was supported by ignorant immigrant masses, who were bribed into loyalty (Bryce 1888; Steffens 1902). This structure opposed that of the reformers, who sought clean government run by experts and supported by a knowledgeable, decisive electorate. Machines were "condemned as the weakest link in American democracy," an issueless politics in which the only goal was to win votes (C. Stone 1996, 446). Reformers were defined by their opposition to machines (Finegold 1995).

A second generation of scholarship sought distance from the normative claims and drew upon social-science theories to understand the operation and effect of machines. Theorists like Robert K. Merton (1957) argued that machines dominated for such extended periods of time because they offered integral social functions such as the provision of welfare, the creation of informal networks between business and government, and the centralization of power. The machines in this portrayal helped immigrants assimilate, softened the harshness of industrialization for the poor, and created stability for economic interests. Simultaneously, a new generation of scholarship on municipal reform had begun to argue that the reform movement was an effort by businessmen and the middle class to regain power in society. To achieve this goal reformers sought to disenfranchise poor, working-class, and immigrant voters (Hays 1964; Holli 1969). Today, scholarship has swung back in the direction of deriding machines, highlighting the holes in the functionalist accounts (Erie 1988; DiGaetano 1988) and reinterpreting reform as a more nuanced movement (Buenker 1973; Finegold 1995; Connolly 1998; Wyman 1974). However, even in these revisionist accounts machine and reform politicians are still analyzed separately.

The existing scholarly work has much to offer students of city politics, but leaves room for new developments. The argument in *Political Monopolies* is that our understanding of city politics should be revised to reflect the underlying similarities of these organizations; machine and reform were different versions of the same political phenomenon. The quest for power and the effects of dominance are comparable across time and place. By defining regimes through the goals and strategies of political leaders, rather than by their constituencies, this becomes clear. Studying political machines and municipal reform side by side allows us to see how alike they were.

In this context it also becomes clear that the debate over the functions of machines presents a false dichotomy. Were machine politicians greedy hacks after the spoils of office or did they truly aid the suffering masses? The distinction implies that politicians should not want to win votes. But the very structure of representative democracy channels the desire for reelection into successful governance. It was only after machines *stopped* doing things to win votes that the distribution of municipal benefits became more narrowly focused. This argument helps us to be more precise about the negative and positive effects of machines.

The research in *Political Monopolies* also speaks to the body of urban-politics research that has found no support for the claim that governments distribute benefits to political supporters and withhold benefits from political enemies (Mladenka 1980; Koehler and Wrightson 1987) or that elected political officials have only limited influence on spending priorities (Peterson 1981; Wolman, Strate, and Melchoir 1996). Evidence is presented here that dominance leads coalitions to target supporters at the expense of people outside of the governing organization. Regardless of the characteristics of the dominant regime, in each of these cities, spending declined and the distribution of benefits narrowed. Political coalitions *are* able to monopolize government, even in democracies, and choose to reward fewer constituents when they solidify control.[4]

Finally, the evidence and argument presented here speaks to debates in political science more generally. For instance, a central debate has been concerned with explaining the distribution of power within polities. In much of the work on institutions electoral systems are treated as fixed and scholars study their effects on the success of different interests. Recent work has begun to analyze the source of institutional structure and change (Boix 1999; Boix and Stokes 2003), but comparative work in this vein across cases and time is still rare. Without understanding the genesis of institutions we lack a complete understanding of their effects on the distribution of power and resources (see Benoit 2007 for a review). *Political Monopolies* offers a contribution to this literature by identifying factors that give rise to both institutional change and stability. It then uses this knowledge to analyze the effect of institutions on the distribution of government benefits.

Political Monopolies also contributes to our understanding of competitiveness. By identifying institutions that bias outcomes towards incumbents the book offers an alternative to relying on endogenous descriptors such as the share of seats or margin of victory won by a given party (e.g., Ranney and Kendall 1954; Koetzle 1998). Additionally, work by scholars like Zaller (1998) and Carson, Engstrom, and Roberts (2007), has argued persuasively that the source of the incumbency advantage in American politics is the high quality of incumbent candidates. Alternatively, I show that incumbents can increase their chances of winning regardless of their performance as representatives. Further, contrary to findings by scholars like Bennett and Resnick (1990), Norrander (1989), Wolfinger and Rosenstone (1980), and Dahl (1961), I argue that limited participation among subpopulations in a polity can have serious negative long-term consequences. When monopolies bias the system and depress turnout it not only affects elections at the local level, but has the potential to affect elections and institutions at all levels of government. For example, a resident who is dissuaded (or prohibited) from voting for mayor may also be disinclined (or disallowed) to cast a ballot for state or federal officials. Further, as Liazos (2006) has shown, efforts to reform local political institutions frequently led to state-level policy changes with regard to regulatory power, taxation, service provision, and home rule. As many cities won the right to enact and manage programs to provide for their populations, monopolies simultaneously limited the benefit of such programs to core members of their coalitions.

The remainder of this chapter discusses the rationale for seeking a monopoly over local government, details the research design, explains the case selection and the sources of evidence, and offers a short description of each chapter in the book.

Spoils of Urban Governance

There are a number of reasons scholars may be skeptical of the argument that political coalitions seek to monopolize local government. For one, it may seem counterintuitive for politicians to expend effort to control a political system that is severely constrained in its distributional and policy choices due to its subordinate status in the federal system and due to competition with other municipalities for population and investment.[5]

In other words, why would anyone waste time trying to capture power in a city if there are few important decisions to be made? Answering this question requires first recognizing what there is to control at the local level and who might seek to control it. Paul Peterson's (1981) famous policy typology summarizes much of what city governments do— redistribute income, engage in development, and manage the allocation of services. But these are abstract categories and might be said to apply at any level of government, so they do not illuminate the rationale behind seeking power at the city level. It is not clear that control over *local* government would be the best mechanism to promote goals in any of these arenas.

Many of the important and unique decisions that cities make have to do with space. Cities control the process of zoning; as a result local debates are frequently organized territorially. Even in cities that choose not to zone explicitly, the regulation of land use creates patterns of development. Residents whose material interests are geographically determined have reason to be concerned with these kinds of decisions. Land-based elites like developers, property investors, and real-estate financiers, assisted by lawyers, lenders, and brokers are the most visible type of residents with geographically determined material interests (Logan and Molotch 1987). Additionally, Logan and Molotch argue that businesses dependent on growth of the city, like newspapers and utility companies, focus on land-use decisions, particularly those that encourage development. Other residents may have an interest in land-use options to the extent that their community, home, or business is affected by a decision. It is not difficult to imagine a fiercely competitive local election centered on spending city funds to promote development versus a platform that urges funds be allocated toward services; or an election where zoning for commercial versus residential construction is the focus; or one in which the location of the development is at stake.

City governments also control various regulations imposed to maintain order and keep the peace like restrictions on loitering, building codes, and liquor licenses. Local governments may be called upon to negotiate culture wars among residents in areas such as domestic-partner rights, access to abortion clinics, and school dress codes (Sharp 1999). To the extent that voters and elites have interests in these policy arenas, these individuals may be motivated to compete for local control because higher levels of government and the private market are not the locus of power.

Perhaps most importantly, cities provide services like water, garbage, sewerage, and power. They build and maintain infrastructure such as roads, bridges, ports, public transit, libraries, parks, and schools. They manage and staff police, fire, and education forces. In some cases they spend municipal funds on health care and other welfare functions like low income housing and, frequently, on development projects like convention centers, waterfront parks, or stadiums. Every city has a unique mixture of the types and levels of services provided, and residents will have preferences regarding the ideal combination. Some preferences are driven by ability to pay for private versions of the municipal good, others are determined by the expense or tax required to supply the good, and still others are dictated by the long-term effect on growth, investment, and employment. Controlling local government translates to having the ability to determine these arrangements.

City politics has also been the locus of intense struggles over racial control and domination. Among other things, these fights have been about increasing or decreasing benefits to racially or ethnically identified groups, the protection of segregation, fights for integration, or achieving descriptive representation. Local politics, as opposed to state or federal politics, is especially important in this arena for a number of reasons. First, cities can have substantial populations of people who are nation-wide minorities. Groups like the Irish, African Americans, and Latinos may have a more vested interest or a better chance at control at the local level. Cities also have the ability to control and enforce the level of seg-regation by virtue of their land use powers. Finally much of what cities do is allocate benefits. As Kaufmann (2004) explains, "The essential questions that dominate many, if not most, local elections focus on the priorities and allocation of local government services: who will receive how much and at the expense of whom" (19). At times the important reference groups for these allocational decisions are defined by geogra-phy, party, or ideology; but particularly when racial conflict becomes palpable, group interests tend to be defined along racial and ethnic lines. Winning control of local government may mean the ability to ensure a group comes out ahead or does not fall behind in these battles.

The goals pursued by machine and reform organizations fit within these possibilities. According to urban-politics scholars, reformers were primarily policy seeking while political machines are believed to have sought economic benefits through the distribution of contracts and patronage without regard to policy goals or ideology. In this view the machine sought to control local government in order to distribute pa-tronage. But this argument confuses the goals of elites with their strate-gies. One must ask *why* machines wanted to distribute patronage.

It is possible that machine politicians were, in fact, policy seeking—that they sought to redistribute income using patronage.[6] Since local governments control vast numbers of public jobs, power at the city level would be a logical focus for such politicians. During the early twentieth century, when machines were most powerful (Brown and Halaby 1984), public jobs frequently paid better wages than private employment. Dur-ing this period in San Jose "persons in the public employ receive[d] a higher average rate of pay than any commercial or industrial group," (Thorpe 1938, 3). Furthermore, discrimination was pervasive in the pri-vate realm and could be overcome in the public arena if a group captured the levers of government.

Some scholars (Weber 1946; C. Stone 1996) indicate that the un-derlying drive of machine politicians was winning elections to achieve power for power's sake. But this argument does not get us any closer to understanding why machine politicians sought to win local elections and not other kinds of elections unless local elections were easier to win and keep winning. This is likely to be the case. Some local constituencies are more homogenous than state or federal constituencies, so turnover may be less frequent. Small electorates may also enable a politician to win without fame or fortune. As this work shows, local arenas, by virtue of their size and more malleable institutional structures, are easier to bias, so serving multiple terms may be more certain at the local level. Additionally, local elections can be insulated from all but the largest national partisan tides. Finally, local elections are much less visible than national or state elections, and so perhaps easier to win (Wolfinger 1972). It may also be that it is relatively more straightforward at the local level to define a platform that appeals to a majority of the electorate. As the famous boss of Kansas City, Tom Pendergast, once said:

> What's government for if it isn't to help people? They're interested only in local conditions—not about the tariff or the war debts. They've got their own problems. They want consideration for their troubles in their house, across the street or around the corner—paving, a water main, police protection, consideration for a complaint about taxes. They vote for the fellow who gives it to them. (Quoted in Larsen and Hulston 1997, 72)

For the machine politician interested in maintaining power for power's sake, control at the local level offered an additional benefit during at least the first half of the twentieth century. Due to the strength of partisan cues, winning control at the city level frequently translated into power and influence at the state and federal levels as well. Many machine politicians were dual office holders, and many were active in their state and federal party organizations. Further, at the time many machines were consolidated; big city governments were frequently more important and powerful than state governments. They had larger budgets, greater patronage, and paid higher salaries.

Scholars have also argued that some machine politicians sought personal wealth through trading favors or by taking advantage of inside information (McDonald 1994). For this to incentivize *local* control it must be true that earning a profit from one's political position is easier or more certain at the local level than at other levels of government. Reid and Kurth (1988) make an argument along these lines. They suggest that machine politicians sought to tax the profits of the wealthy. To do this they needed to hold power; the cheapest route to which was purchasing votes from the poor through patronage. Since many machine politicians were the product of humble origins, it is possible, perhaps even likely, that local political positions represented one of the few options for socioeconomic advancement.[7]

Distilling the aims of reform organizations is equally difficult. One reason why is that many different types of political movements referred to themselves as reform. My focus is the structural reformers (as opposed to social reformers) who governed in the South and West through changes in electoral institutions.[8] Why did reformers seek to monopolize local government? According to a review of city manager government in Austin, reform proposals to change city government were "not made in a self-sacrificing spirit . . . their principal economic interest was the development of the city as a pleasant place in which to live" (H. Stone, Price, and K. Stone 1937, 4). Bridges (1997) presents extensive evidence that reformers in the Southwest sought increased development in terms of population and economic growth. Having power over local government would have been integral to the realization of this goal because cities controlled zoning, local tax rates, municipal services, and the structure of the bureaucracy.

Most scholars of the reform period have focused on a different set of goals—running cities like businesses by promoting clean and efficient forms of government. However, this only explains reformers' focus on the local level if cities (as opposed to state and federal governments) were particularly prone to corruption, a lack of efficiency, or decaying morality. This is reasonable given that many clashes between immigrants and native-born Americans were centered on issues controlled by local level governments like prohibition, neighborhood preservation, and schooling. However, this argument still fails to explain *why* reformers sought to place government in the hands of "better men," since few were motivated by moral salvation of immigrants.[9] One explanation is that many business owners (small business in particular) found city government unpredictable, bloated, expensive, and extortionist at the dawn of the twentieth century. The desire to create a more accommodating environment for business, prevent pork-barrel politics, and promote citywide development projects encouraged reformers to seek power at the local level. Since the founding, it has been the responsibility of state and local (as opposed to federal) government to spend public monies on development. Thus, reformers were not just strategic power seekers, but sought power as a means to a specific policy end. They tended to be keenly instrumental in this pursuit; many displayed an open disdain for public office, but realized nonetheless that control over government was necessary to promote the development they sought.

Efforts to reinvent government were supported by residents who sought low tax rates and high levels of services, the combination of which required efficiency. Famous reform advocate Andrew White (1890) argued, "In consideration of the fact that the city is a corporation, I would have those owning property in it properly recognized. I would leave to them, and to them alone, the election of a board of control, without whose permission no franchise should be granted and no expenditure should be made" (104). Reformers from the nativist tradition believed that "a crowd of illiterate peasants, freshly raked in from Irish bogs, or Bohemian mines, or Italian robber nests [were] not alive even to their own most direct interests" (White 1890, 104) and so could not be counted on to govern municipal affairs. This view of course did not reflect all of the reform platforms that were presented to voters, but it did reflect a dominant stream within the tradition.[10] Commonly reformers viewed popular democracy as problematic. One San Jose reformer explained, "If the charter required [voters] to elect a [city] manager they would most certainly make a botch of it" (quoted in Ellsworth and Garbely 1976, 16). The result was that reformers implemented changes to the electoral structure, which effectively disenfranchised portions of the population, particularly low-income and minority residents, in the name of more efficiently functioning cities.

At least one conclusion to draw from this discussion is that there are many reasons why an individual politician might seek local office. Members of monopoly coalitions need not share the same goals, only the desire to control local government. Thus, I make the simplifying assumption that politicians seek reelection. Some politicians who run for local office will see it as a stepping stone, but not monopolists. They see municipal affairs as an end in and of itself. These politicians (even reformers) do not strive to make good public policy per se except to the extent that it benefits their coalition or helps them achieve their electoral goals. When members of the coalition believe that their individual goals would be better served by a different organization or outside of government, they have an incentive to leave.

Research Design and Data

The evidence and analyses offered throughout the book draw on varied methodological traditions. I use a large number of cases to determine general patterns in city politics, rely on a subset of this data set to analyze electoral effects, and use a few selected cases to study the process of monopolization. I depend heavily on historical narrative to explain political contexts and choices, and to offer evidence of phenomena that are difficult to measure (like electoral fraud). Scholars of each methodological tradition may find aspects of my analysis objectionable. Historically oriented scholars may be frustrated by the lack of a neat chronological time line for monopolies and the mixing of time periods in my presentation. Other readers may be bothered by the number of characters I introduce and the weakness of some of my measures. In short, there is no element of the story that is persuasive with each type of data alone. But I hope that taken as a whole the body of evidence will convince even the most skeptical audiences. A detailed description of my case selection, data collection, and research design is included in the appendix, but a summary of my choices is useful here.

Historical city-level data is notoriously difficult to collect, with the best records available for large cities. Consequently, to provide evidence for my argument, I collected data on the 244 cities that made the list of the one hundred largest cities in the United States at any decennial census between 1790 and 1990 (Gibson 1998). I chose this time span in order to ensure that my collection would cover cities that have been sustained centers of populations, as well as those that had ceased to be important by the twentieth century, and those that rose to prominence only in recent decades. I collected data on these cities for the years 1900–85. I draw on narrative, historical, and statistical analyses, using subsets of the larger data set to answer my questions.

My large-N data analysis begins in chapter 4 with an investigation into the electoral effects of bias and coordination, the components I argue are necessary and sufficient for monopoly control. Here I determine years in which a single organization controls nominations for office, seeks to dominate government, and relies on or implements strategies of bias to win. I then show that during these years incumbents win by larger margins and are reelected at a higher rate. In this chapter I use data from four reform cities: Austin, Dallas, San Antonio, and San Jose; and five machine cities: Chicago, New York, New Haven, Kansas City, and Philadelphia. This group of nine cities represents diverse regions of the United States, and each was listed as one of the nation's fifty largest cities at some point during the twentieth century. These cities differ on important demographic characteristics, such as economic and racial makeup, and total population. Finally, the cities' monopoly periods represent a variety of time spans, reducing the possibility that some unidentified trend was the actual cause for the similar political patterns during the reign of dominant coalitions.

To understand the actual process of implementing bias in chapter 2, I present historical data from these nine cities collected from primary and secondary sources. I analyze two cases in depth, one archetypal of classic machine politics (Chicago, Illinois) and the other representing classic reform (San Jose, California). Throughout the manuscript I provide narrative evidence regarding additional machine and reform cities that followed the patterns I describe.

The broadest analyses (in chapters 4, 5, and 6) use the entire collection of 244 cities to establish trends in the rise and fall of monopolies. I determine time periods during which a single organization appeared to have strong control over government, citywide, for at least a decade during the twentieth century.[11] Ideally, I would have relied on my key characteristics of monopoly (bias and coordination) to define these periods. In order to do this, I would have needed detailed information about the coalitions in every city at each election, the relationships and alliances among all candidates for office and office holders, and their use of biasing mechanisms. These data are not available for such a large number of cities. Instead, I relied on the main comparative urban texts that discuss dominance. I used Mayhew's analysis in *Placing Parties in American Politics* (1986) and Erie's *Rainbow's End* (1988) to define periods of time when a city was dominated by a machine organization. Mayhew also reported on a select number of reform-dominated cities. I supplemented Mayhew's historical analysis with information on the development and dominance of reform coalitions from Bridges (1997), Davidson and Fraga (1988), and Childs (1965) for reform monopolies. In total, I determined that sixty-six of the 244 cities were governed by a monopoly for at least one decade. I was able to determine dates for the rise and fall of the monopoly in twenty-four of the sixty-six cities (see tables A1–A3). One city, San Antonio, hosted two monopolies, providing a total of twenty-five cases with clear start and end dates for the monopoly.[12] Eight of these cases are reform monopolies and seventeen are machines. To test my hypotheses regarding the effect of demographic shifts and institutional control on the emergence and collapse of monopolies, I analyze data collected from the United States Census before, during, and after the monopoly period. The analyses include information from all 244 cities.

In chapter 5, I analyze the distributional consequences of monopolies by comparing monopoly cities to nonmonopoly cities. Not surprisingly, the data on city expenditure is also limited. Data at the subcity level that would have allowed me to show precisely which groups and neighborhoods benefited (or suffered) from the dominance of municipal monopolies was not available.[13] For citywide financial figures I relied on the United States Census, which provides standardized measures beginning in 1945.

My analysis of spending patterns makes use of the twenty-five cases for which I could determine start and end dates of the monopoly period as well as the 178 cities that were never monopolized (see tables A3 and A1). This model allows me to treat the onset of monopoly like a quasi-experiment. The years in which the monopoly cities are not dominated as well as all years for cities that are never dominated act as the control group. Those years when a monopoly dominated are the treatment. I compare expenditure patterns during the treatment years with the patterns during control years to provide evidence that monopolies concentrated benefits on core constituents and the governing coalition.

The data that I collected are far from ideal. But they capture information from enough cities over a long enough time span to be both illuminating and helpful. Urban politics has suffered from a lack of data, making it difficult to conduct large-scale comparative research on political processes, institutions, and outcomes, particularly in historical periods. *Political Monopolies* takes a step toward cross-sectional time-series analysis of city politics.

Organization of the Book

The book is organized by the components of monopoly development: from establishing bias, to building an organization, to the electoral and distributional effects wrought by monopoly, and finally to the monopoly's decline. In each chapter, the similarities between machine and reform regimes are presented and evidence is provided that urban coalitions in different types of cities were reliant on similar political logic, yielding similar political results.

Chapter 1 presents a theory of political monopoly. I argue that politicians seek to secure reelection by eliminating their competition, thereby creating a monopoly over government. I suggest that a single group should be able to dominate the political market for an extended period of time if it is highly organized and able to implement institutional rules that advantage incumbents. Additionally, I explain the difference between my concept of political monopoly and the extensively studied political machine. I provide an overview of the types of mechanisms coalitions can use to advantage incumbents and discuss the conditions leading coalitions to select different structures. I then lay out the main argument for why political monopolies reduce the size of their coalition, narrow the beneficiaries of urban policy, and ultimately sow the seeds for their own destruction. Depending on the political, social, and economic contexts that the coalition faces, leaders will choose different strategies to accomplish dominance. Along with differing strategies come differing success rates for monopolization. I theorize that monopolies collapse in the face of rising discontent, a loss of bias, factions in their coalitions, and resource imbalances.

Chapter 2 begins the analysis of the development of monopoly by detailing the establishment of biased political structures. This chapter provides historical evidence asserting that dominant coalitions sought to tilt the electoral arena in their favor. I argue that all political systems favor some participants and skills over others and further define a biased system as one in which incumbent office holders are advantaged by limited information, barriers to entry or exit for voters or challengers, and non-neutral translation of votes to seats. For this end, I catalogue the strategies used to maintain power and reduce competition. The list of biasing mechanisms available to coalitions includes everything from gerrymandering districts to assassinating opponents. The mechanisms politicians use to tilt the system in favor of incumbents fall into three broad categories representing the points at which an electoral system might be biased: information bias, vote bias, and seat bias. I present historical evidence about how politicians in nine cities employed these strategies.

Chapter 3 focuses on the second component of monopoly—the coordination of the organization. In this chapter I explain why coalitions became consolidated, the strategies that they adopted, and who became part of the coalition (and who did not). I explain the timing of organization and the strategies for maintaining loyalty in the coalition. Additionally, I argue that coalitions consolidated when they faced threats to their desired outcomes, and were successful when their opposition endured moments of weakness. Further, I describe the internal organization of successful coalitions and the electoral context in which monopolies are built. To support this argument, I use historical evidence from the nine cities mentioned above.

In chapter 4 I begin my statistical analysis. I show first that the combination of bias and organization had identifiable electoral benefits for incumbent politicians. Then, I offer a series of analyses exploring the reasons monopolies develop in some political systems but not in others. I argue that political context offers opportunities and constraints for the establishment of monopoly. A changing environment threatening a coalition's political control or policy program provides the impetus for monopoly. Thus, strategies are determined by the demographic characteristics of the community and the extent of the coalition's control over the political system. I find that machine and reform cities were characterized by different political environments and demographics. I provide evidence that machine politicians, reliant on patronage to monopolize the system, had little institutional control and dealt with relatively large poor populations. I find that reform cities, where suffrage restrictions and vote dilution were the common forms of bias, had a high degree of institutional control and smaller poor populations. Finally, I analyze the environmental factors that increase the likelihood that a coalition would establish a monopoly. I show that changes in political context that threaten coalitions' electoral prospects or policy goals instigate the development of monopolies.

Chapter 5 analyzes the effects of monopolies. I provide quantitative and qualitative support for the theory that monopoly dominance depresses turnout and leads to concentrations of benefits for specific subgroups. When elections become noncompetitive for long periods of time and political coalitions establish dominant regimes, the distribution of government benefits is altered. Coalitions focus political goods on a group of core voters and elites, while providing others little or nothing. Politicians, no longer worried about reelection, become freer to pursue government policy that does not reflect constituent preferences. In this chapter, I analyze the beneficiaries of monopoly regimes and identify discontented community members. I find that during the monopoly period, turnout and spending decline, and fewer groups are rewarded.

Chapter 6 considers the causes of decline of long-reigning monopolies. I argue that dominant coalitions create a natural base for regime opponents by limiting benefits to constituents peripheral to the coalition. The timing of challenger emergence, mobilization of the discontented, and monopoly collapse are tied to losses of bias, fissures in the governing coalition, and periods of economic stress. Exogenous events and actors often feature prominently in changes to the levels of bias and economic stress, while diversity of elite goals frequently threatens organizational unity. Under duress monopolies can become responsive, co-opting the challenge or else increase their reliance on bias. The availability of resources often dictates which path monopolies choose. In this chapter I explore the makeup of opposition coalitions, analyze the factors that increase the probability of decline, and discuss the options monopolies have in responding to challenges.

Chapter 7 synthesizes the results and describes their implications for the study of elections, government responsiveness, and urban politics.

I discuss the ramifications of the study for the future of urban governance given that constraints for establishing a biased regime are continually in flux. I explore the ways in which the findings presented here can inform scholarship on authoritarianism, development, state and federal politics, as well as studies of representative democracy. I conclude with recommendations for limiting the development of monopolies in the future.

1 The Logic of Political Monopolies

DESPITE MANY MEANINGFUL differences between machine and reform cities, they share political patterns. The logic of political monopolies successfully explains these similarities. Threats to political goals inspired the development of monopolies in both types of cities. Politicians' desire to ensure reelection undermined the ability for all constituents to be represented in both types of cities. Choices incumbent coalitions made to preserve their power ultimately led to their defeat in both types of cities. This chapter explores these arguments in detail, describes how they apply in different contexts, and makes predictions that will inform the analysis of data in later chapters.

Political scientists argue that elections play a fundamental role in keeping representatives accountable. Reelection-seeking politicians attempt to maximize votes (Downs 1957) and organize institutions to allow them to do so (Mayhew 1974). When political elites, worried about reelection, mobilize large numbers of voters, turnout is high because groups are encouraged to enter the political process (Jackman 1987). Thus, participation in governance is broad, and the government provides benefits to many different groups in the community (Morton 1987; Bueno de Mesquita et al. 2003; Keiser 1997; Uhlaner 1995). Competitive elections provide an incentive for politicians to serve these goals. In short, the quest for reelection is the heart of representative democracy.

But not all elections motivate leaders in this way. Once elected, rational leaders not only have an incentive to win reelection but also have an incentive to reduce uncertainty about their future. In other words, they have an incentive to try to *guarantee* themselves reelection. What's more is that they may have the power to do so. We can expect that once a coalition wins election to office, it will take steps to increase the probability that it will retain control over government (Cox and Katz 2007). Such safety in office has the potential to affect the quality and effectiveness of governance. Similarly, a substantial literature in economics analyzes the relationship between the safety of incumbent firms and market performance (Posner 1975; Harrington 1984).

We do not find *perfect* competition in either economic or political markets. However, exploring ideal types allows us to understand the ways in which reality deviates from these models, and can offer insight into interventions that might improve social welfare. Economists have developed a set of conditions that describe perfectly competitive markets in which products are offered for the lowest possible price in the long run. One of the most (some say *the* most) important condition is that entry into and exit from the market be free and instantaneous for both buyers and sellers. This limits the ability of firms to raise the price of products above marginal cost. Additionally, buyers and sellers must have perfect information about the quality and price of the product. In a seminal book, Baumol, Panzar, and Willig (1982) argue that the *threat* of entry can be enough to prevent firms from extracting monopoly profits. They find that such markets remain "contestable" and that in these cases even firms with large market shares are compelled to keep prices competitive. Thus, the degree to which the market remains contestable determines the degree to which we can expect social welfare to be maximized.

Analogously for political incumbents, the threat of removal may be enough to inspire responsiveness and maximization of social welfare.[1] We can draw on this framework for thinking about political markets in a relative way, arranging systems along a spectrum of contestability. Contestability can be described by three indicators of bias: the degree to which constituents' information about governmental performance or available alternatives is limited; the degree to which the entry, exit, or behavior of candidates or voters is restricted; and the degree to which incumbents' control over government seats is insulated from their vote share.

In the (unrealizable) political market with perfect information, free entry and exit of voters and candidates, and a perfectly responsive and neutral translation of votes to seats, incumbents can only win by being responsive to voters and elites.[2] This idealized version of the world represents one end of the contestability spectrum. Institutions or strategies (e.g., bias) that move the political market away from this end increase the probability of reelection for incumbents without regard to the effectiveness of representation or the quality of the candidate. Thus, the opposite end of the spectrum can be described as an uncontestable political market in which reelection of incumbents is wholly disconnected from quality of candidates and representation of voters. These biased systems reduce electoral risk for the incumbent coalition, increasing its probability of retaining power at any given level of performance.

It is important to note that coalitions at both ends of this spectrum are likely to dominate government for multiple successive terms. Hence the difference between monopolies and responsive dominant coalitions can not be empirically detected through an analysis of reelection rates alone. It requires evidence of the presence of bias. Only then is there an incentive for the coalition to concentrate municipal resources on a minority of the population. Like economic monopolies, these coalitions can earn positive profits for the members of the coalition at the expense of the broader public.[3] In the absence of bias, dominant coalitions can only remain in power by being responsive to the electorate and elites. Thus, it is bias that sets political monopolies apart from responsive government and leads to the possibility of extortion by political leaders.

All political systems are biased to some degree. They feature barriers to entry and exit by making it difficult for new contestants to enter and by regulating who can vote, they feature voters and candidates with incomplete information, and they demonstrate varying degrees of neutrality and proportionality in the allocation of seats. Yet, some electoral arenas are more biased than others, creating more or less contestable markets. A system in which incumbents routinely raise more money than challengers, while perhaps not free, is closer to competitive than one in which the incumbent jails potential opponents. The latter is an uncontestable political market. The greater the degree of bias in the system, the greater incentive there is for the coalition to respond to a narrowly defined constituency.

However, bias is not sufficient for establishment of monopoly control. Political scientists have determined that gerrymandered districts have reduced competition for congressional seats, biasing the system in favor of incumbents (see, for example, Cain 1985; Cox and Katz 1999). But no monopoly exists so long as no single faction gains control over the entire government. This suggests a second component to the maintenance of a political monopoly—coordination. Coordination refers to the extent to which individuals and/or groups work together to nominate, elect, and control politicians in public offices in order to influence "government policies, policy stands, projects, graft, appointive government jobs, and other valued things officials. . . . have access to and give out" (Mayhew 1986, 4). A higher degree of coordination in the system translates to fewer groups competing for power and access to policy making. The coordination spectrum runs from totally atomistic, with each person for himself or herself, to a single dominant coalition managing the political system. A high degree of coordination requires organization in both the electorate and among elites. In other words political monopolies need to assemble a regime.

The concept of an organized regime is a common theme in studies of cities (Shefter 1976; Brown and Halaby 1987; C. Stone 1989; McCaffery 1992). A regime can be thought of as the collaborative arrangements through which the local governments and private actors assemble the capacity to govern. We can think of the organizational components for a regime as Stone does, as composed of the electoral coalition and the governing coalition.

The individuals (or groups) included in the electoral coalition might be determined by a range of factors including historical circumstances; economic considerations; race, class, or ethnic divisions; and compatibility with other members' preferences (Axelrod 1970; but cf. Wright and Goldberg 1985). The highest degree of coordination would mean that all individuals in the electorate belong to the same coalition.

The governing coalition is composed of a set of elites who control the resources necessary for maintaining power. Some elites control resources by virtue of being elected to office. Monopolies need power over a sufficient number of office holders in both the executive and legislative branches to make policy, direct the distribution of benefits, and manage the appointment of government officials. Controlling nominations and maintaining cohesiveness of elected officials are crucial components to preserving this level of coordination. The highest degree of coordination would mean that all elective office holders in the executive and legislative branches belong to the same organization. Other elites control resources exogenous to the city's political system but that are nonetheless necessary to make and implement governance decisions. These may be private actors or, in a federal system, public officials at higher levels of government. Private actors controlling important resources for governance might include business elites, labor leaders, religious leaders, or nonprofit organizations. Collectively, these elites make up the governing coalition—those people whose agreement is required for a change of the status quo or the implementation of policy. According to regime theorists, without the cooperation of these actors, either tacit or overt, elected officials remain severely constrained in their ability to govern (C. Stone 1989; Hunter 1953, 1980; Keiser 1997). For this reason, simply winning election to office, even winning a majority of the city council and the mayoralty, does not necessarily translate into control over city policymaking, and so does not equate to monopoly.

Thus, we can categorize political systems along two continuous dimensions: the degree of coordination and the degree of bias. A high

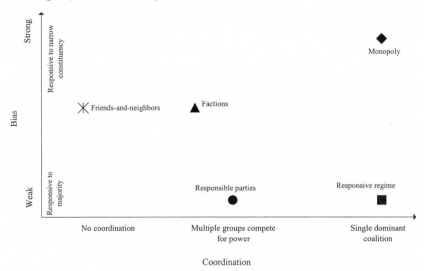

Fig. 1.1: Categorization of political systems

degree of coordination and bias are jointly sufficient conditions for a single coalition to dominate government for multiple terms. Figure 1.1 shows how different systems might be categorized according to these concepts.

As figure 1.1 indicates, monopolies and responsive regimes are both examples of single dominant coalitions, but only the former are characterized by strongly biased systems. The degree of bias in a system determines to how large a proportion of the population a coalition must be responsive in order to win reelection. The degree of coordination in the system determines how effective winners will be in implementing their preferred policies.

In arenas where multiple groups compete for power, the degree of bias in the system reflects the difference between "responsible" party government praised by 1950s political scientists and factional politics.[4] In both of these situations, divided government or turnover in office means that no one group dominates; the political market remains contestable. The term *factional politics* refers to systems like some of the states in V. O. Key's one-party South, where suffrage restrictions eviscerated the Republican Party, but a lack of organization limited the dominance of any one faction of the Democratic Party (though dominance by whites *was* ensured). This category also includes factional machine-style politics, in which patronage is used to organize voters and suppress opposition, but no single city-wide machine controls government. According to Brown and Halaby (1987) this was the most common form of machine-style politics to have existed in the United States. Politicians, working largely independently, engaged tactics like vote fraud or bribery, but failed to combine their efforts into a single organization that could dominate government. Powerful figures like Boston's James Michael Curly or New York's Robert Moses also represent this type of system in which one or a small number of leaders dominate areas of the city or portions of the city government. Similarly a powerful but uncoordinated bureaucracy as in historical Los Angeles (Erie 2004) might also lead to a factionalized system in which no centralized organization controls city policy. Finally, friends-and-neighbor politics is the kind of political system that emerges when organizations are ephemeral; no stable coalitions exist. Friends-and-neighbor systems may be characterized by bias, advantaging some political actors over others, but they need not be.

Given that machine and reform monopolies appear in only about 30 percent of cities, it is these other patterns of coordination and competition that define the remaining 70 percent. Although this project can not speak directly to these other forms, it is likely that the factional form is most pervasive. Gilbert and Clague (1962) find that not a single city in their twenty-four-city analysis could be described as having a truly organized and competitive system. Because a fractured political system, either one defined by factionalism or friends-and-neighbor politics, is characterized by a lack of control over the entire city or the entire city government, it is highly likely that voters are not provided responsive government in these scenarios either. In fact gridlock might be the over-riding feature of policy making. It is also plausible that in cities where a politician or coalition has captured a geographically or functionally de-fined portion of the city government a similar pattern of narrowing the constituency will occur within that realm. Thus, a responsive government is not implied by the lack of monopoly, but it might be. This sug-gests that maintaining competition that even begins to approach the ide-alized structure discussed above is likely to be quite rare. However, only in the case of monopolization, where the dominant coalition achieves success through bias, should we see the governing coalition have the opportunity and incentive to be responsive to a narrow portion of the electorate at the expense of the rest of the community on a citywide scale. While fractured systems might not be responsive to the broadest electorate, they are unlikely to have the extensive, negative consequences ascribed here to political monopolies.

Knowing that there are different ways that we might categorize politi-cal systems is helpful, but falls short of delineating where along the coordination and bias continua a city needs to fall in order to qualify as a monopoly. Theoretically we should be able to distinguish between levels of bias and degrees of coordination, and to use both to predict the presence or absence of monopoly. To carry out such an analysis we would need precise, continuous measures of bias and coordination as well as the degree of monopolization. While this would clearly be the ideal approach, a lack of specificity in the measures available leads me to take a less elegant tack. First, I use electoral dominance of a single coalition as an indicator of monopoly and show that at high levels of bias and coordination, the incumbents' reelection prospects improve. Then, to distinguish between monopolies and responsive regimes, I analyze changes in participation and policy outputs. If it were true that a coalition in power for a decade represented a responsive regime, declines in participation would likely be driven by those most content with the regime and we should see no systematic skew in policy output. Instead I show that where bias and coordination were present, groups peripheral to the monopoly were most likely to cease participating and government benefits to these nonmembers declined relative to expenditures in cities that lacked either a dominant coalition or severe bias. Thus monopolies are identified here as having a high degree of coordination and bias, which increases the incumbent coalition's probability of maintaining power, and leads to suboptimal government responsiveness. Where access to the political process was limited for some groups by bias, the result was reduced responsiveness.

This practice of identifying monopolies in part by their tactics and in part by their effects has precedent in both economics and political-science literatures. The legal determination of a monopoly firm takes into consideration the firm's market share and its ability to set profitable prices due to barriers to entry. Similarly, urban-politics scholars have defined political machines by their electoral success, their high degree of organization, and reliance on a strategy of rewarding supporters with material benefits in order to secure their loyalty. Erie (1988) argues that in mature machines "power was centralized in a single party boss," they "exhibited staying power, winning several municipal elections and remaining in power for at least a decade," and "trafficked primarily (but not exclusively) in divisible material benefits . . ." (19). Brown and Halaby (1987) specify "that to qualify as a dominant machine a political organization had to have controlled the election of the municipal executive and a majority of the legislative branch for an uninterrupted series of three elections," have been "sustained by patronage and favors," be "headed by a boss," and "based on identifiable grass roots organization" (597).

In sum, these authors use bias, coordination, and dominance to define a machine. Instead I show that bias and coordination lead to dominance and then, like Erie and Brown and Halaby, use the combined presence of these factors to signify monopolies. For the remainder of this book, the term *monopoly* will refer to only those dominant coalitions that achieve success through bias.

No doubt some readers will object to the hyperbole encapsulated in the term *monopoly*. No mayor or manager in this analysis ever governed as a dictator. Incumbents always faced challengers and voters continued to have the right to select their leaders. Violence was never used on a regular basis or a large scale to control political outcomes. Furthermore, no coalition included in this study was able to rely on biased reelection strategies alone. To the extent that monopoly means controlling the market without competition, it is indeed an overstatement in the political context. Like a competitive market, a political monopoly is an ideal type that rarely exists in the real world. For this reason it might be more appropriate to think of the coalitions under study here as relatively more like monopolists than competitive organizations. Indeed, all of the statistical analyses conducted provide evidence of *relative* differences in electoral and expenditure patterns. However, the term remains a useful analogy (if only relatively speaking); it is employed to represent coalitions that rely on strategies that limit competition and benefit narrow segments of the community *as compared to* coalitions that rely on classic strategies of reelection. The next section takes a closer look at distinguishing strategies of bias from other election-seeking behavior.

Strategies of Reelection

I assume that all democratic politicians desire to stay in office as long as possible. They seek reelection not just in the short term but for their entire careers.[5] But the road to election and reelection is paved with uncertainties. So politicians will do what they can to increase the probability of victory (Cain, Ferejohn, and Fiorina 1987). Many of these strategies form the base of the electoral connection. As Fenno ([1978] 2003) famously explained, to win office politicians develop a "home style" intended to build support among constituents and enhance the member's leeway in policy making. A member's home style encompasses the way in which he presents himself verbally and nonverbally to residents in his district. He works to establish that he is qualified to represent the people and that he empathizes and identifies with them. The member builds trust through regular contact, constituent service, by emphasizing "common denominator" issues, and through advertising his name and accomplishments. He also describes, interprets, and analyzes his activities in Washington. Fenno finds that members "know that they can not get too far away from the district" (144) because it would spell defeat at the hands of a challenger. Through these types of interactions constituents can come to know something about their member, what happens in government, and how their representative is (or is not) representing them. In sum, Fenno argues:

> [S]o long as representatives want to retain their office, the knowledge that they will later be held accountable at the polls will tend to make their representative behavior more responsive to the desires of their constituents. . . . On the whole they expend a great deal of time and effort keeping in touch with their various constituencies back home. . . . [M]embers of Congress feel uncertain and vulnerable—if not today then yesterday, if not yesterday then tomorrow . . . (233)

Fenno's politicians take positions, they mobilize supporters, and they provide policies favored by many of their voters. By so doing they make democracy function. However, there are a host of other strategies that can enhance incumbents' probability of victory and policy-making leeway without offering voters a representational link. These strategies might be preferable to politicians because they increase the chance that the politician will win regardless of the performance of the government. These are the structures and strategies of bias. There is, of course, no bright line differentiating these types of strategies; they lie along a continuum. A strategy which increases constituents' information about the candidate, the challenger, or the electoral or policy-making process will tend to fall toward Fenno's end of the spectrum. A strategy that enhances reelection while limiting constituents' information will tend to break the representational link. Similarly, strategies or structures which decrease the opportunity for challengers to enter the political fray or make it costly for them to exit (thereby decreasing the likelihood that they will enter) will fall toward the biased end of the spectrum.

If the political systems under analysis here were authoritarian regimes we might be able to find cases in which the maintenance of power were wholly based on strategies of bias. Since the focus is on democracies it is important to note that bias is never sufficient for winning reelection; all politicians and coalitions must be responsive to some constituents at some level. Nonetheless, systems can be more or less biased, relatively speaking.

If a coalition chooses strategies of bias over or in addition to conventional tactics, it selects from among a number of strategies for engineering the monopoly. Drawing on Cox (2001), strategies for biasing outcomes may be characterized by the decision points in a democratic electoral system. The points correspond to different stages of the voting process—generating preferences with regard to government performance (information bias), translating preferences into votes (vote bias), and transforming votes into seats (seat bias).

Information bias refers to a system in which the government has a systematic advantage in translating its record of performance into citizen's preferences. State-controlled media and low-information elections are mechanisms that can be used to enhance the prospects of the governing coalition regardless of the performance of the officeholders. In essence, information bias suggests an advantage for incumbents in the dissemination of information about government activity and available alternatives.

Vote bias describes a systematic advantage for the government in the way citizens' preferences are translated into votes as a result of barriers to entry or exit for voters or challengers. When a coalition uses government resources (for example, patronage employees) to promote the organization of its supporters or inhibit the organization of its opposition, it is engaging in vote bias. Mechanisms such as poll taxes, registration laws, and vote fraud can also advantage incumbents. This category includes barriers to competition that increase the costs of defeat or entry for a challenger, such as lowering officials' pay or physically intimidating candidates. If challengers are discouraged from entering the competition, the outcome will be biased toward the governing regime because voters have no other option.

The final step in the electoral process is the translation of votes into seats. The system's seat bias is determined by the degree to which the share of seats won exaggerates the share of votes won in favor of the incumbent coalition. Measures that create or increase malapportionment, gerrymandering, or reserved seats in the government's favor bias the system to increase the incumbent coalition's probability of retaining power. Seat bias has been extensively studied in the literature on apportionment and representation particularly with regard to the U.S. Congress and state legislatures (see, for example, Cox and Katz 2002; Gelman and King 1994). Scholars studying districted legislatures make a distinction between two different characteristics of the relationship between votes and seats—the extent of partisan bias and the degree of responsiveness

(King and Browning 1987). Partisan bias refers to the difference between the seat share a party wins with some proportion of the vote and the seat share the other party would be expected to win with the same share of the vote. This is particularly easy to see when a party wins 50 percent of the vote but not 50 percent of the seats. Responsiveness refers to the sensitivity of a party's aggregate seat share to increases or decreases in the party's aggregate vote share.

Whether an incumbent coalition is advantaged by having a more responsive system or a more biased system depends on the distribution of the incumbent's supporters and opponents (see Grofman, Koetzle, and Brunell 1997). Thus the vast majority of the literature on this topic uses the term *biased* to refer to an effect of political structures; here the term *biased* refers to the structure itself and is intended to capture both types of effects. A system is characterized by seat bias if the strategy selected increases the probability of the incumbent coalition maintaining power when votes are translated into seats.

In addition to strategies like gerrymandering and malapportionment, at the local level eliminating districts has been used to increase the probability of maintaining power.[6] When used in combination with voting restrictions, at-large elections can offer a substantial advantage to the incumbent coalition because all seats represent the same limited electorate. This means that a single median voter is the decisive voter for the entire legislature. Whereas district elections offer representation to geographically defined areas of the city, at-large elections represent only those who are able to participate in elections. As an added benefit, at-large elections reduce the hurdles of coordination for the governing coalition. Table 1.1 displays strategies that have been used to increase the probability of incumbents maintaining control of government in American cities.

Some institutional structures and strategic choices are unquestionably motivated by a desire to enhance the incumbents' probability of reelection. Electoral falsification is a clear example. But other structures and strategies may have alternative purposes, with reelection of the governing regime a welcome, but potentially unintended, consequence. It can be difficult to know the purpose of some actions, and whether or not they will bias the system in favor of the incumbent at the outset. If, for instance, we find a political coalition has implemented registration laws or limited voting to citizens, should researchers conclude that this is an effort to bias the system? Does the same strategy equate to bias in every system? There is no universal answer to these kinds of questions; case-by-case analysis is vital to understanding the biases (intended or

Table 1.1: Biasing strategies

Information bias	Vote bias	Seat bias
Media control (ownership, in regulation)	Vote bribery	Annexing or de-annexing government's favor
Suppression of voluntary associations	Obscure polling place sites	Gerrymandering
Control over judicial system/prosecutors	Use of government resources to prevent opponent organization or enhance incumbent organization	Malapportionment
Low-information elections (e.g., nonpartisan)	Impairment of election monitoring	Decreasing size of legislature
	Disqualification of candidates	At-large elections
	Candidate requirements (signatures, thresholds)	Increasing appointed offices
	Low pay for office holders	
	Violence keeping voters from polls or forcing vote choice	
	Electoral falsification (ghost/repeat voting, inflating totals, discarding ballots)	
	Registration requirements	
	Suffrage restrictions (literacy tests, poll taxes, language or race requirements, citizens only)	
	Assassinating/threatening/ imprisoning opponents	

not) in any one electoral arena. It is especially important to understand the makeup of the electorate in order to know whether a given strategy will bias the system in favor of incumbents in a particular case.

In this analysis it does not matter what the motivation behind the enactment was if the unintended consequence always works in favor of the incumbent organization. If, for example, the state government enacts a literacy test that disenfranchises most African Americans, and the white mayor and white city council in a heavily black city are advantaged by having this population eliminated from the electorate, I refer to this system as biased even if the mayor and council did not implement the strategy and even if the state legislature makes a compelling argument that only literate residents should participate in governance. Throughout the analysis information is presented on the motivations of the coalitions when available.

In any event it is worth noting that machines tended to rely on strategies that were clearly identifiable as bias, such as requiring police officers to work as political operatives, discarding ballots, and registering dead persons, while reformers frequently relied on strategies that had a separable purpose, like annexation and nonpartisan elections. This is part of the reason that scholars have seen machine and reform as so different from one another. It is also worth noting that machine and reform organizations were not monolithic; different coalitions selected different combinations of strategies. Which leads to the next question: how do coalitions determine which mixture of approaches to take?

Selecting Strategies of Bias and Reelection

Political coalitions are likely to prefer reelection strategies that maximize deterrence of challengers and minimize maintenance of the monopoly. Such mechanisms increase their probability of winning far into the future. But not all coalitions enjoy the conditions necessary for implementing such decisive strategies. Political coalitions operate in different social contexts that create varied costs of exclusion and hurdles for implementation. The way in which politicians can achieve their goals depends on the conditions that they face.

First, coalitions are constrained in implementing bias and selecting strategies by the extent of their institutional control and the stability of the institutions themselves.[7] The more control a coalition wields and the more malleable the institutions, the easier it should be for a political coalition to implement effective, nonneutral structures. Because U.S. cities are creatures of the states, biasing the system often requires either the consent of the state legislature or home rule. Without either, a coalition will be unable to alter the rules governing elections.[8] At the very least, in order to monopolize a system, the coalition must win access to both the legislative and executive components of government. In most cities, this means winning a majority of the seats on the council and control of the chief executive's office. More promising for the implementation of bias is control of county and state governments.

On the whole, the most effective and efficient strategies require the highest degree of institutional control. In other words, the better the strategy at eliminating competition over the long run, the harder it is likely to be to implement. All strategies of bias can be characterized by these tradeoffs. I argue that information bias tends to be easiest to implement, requiring little or no institutional control but also requiring costly, continuous long-term maintenance. Purchasing a newspaper outlet to promote the incumbent organization works so long as no other news organizations emerge. Vote bias frequently requires substantially more

institutional control because constitutions tend to make voting requirements difficult to change or evade, and violations can be characterized
as unfair or antidemocratic. Filling patronage posts with political appointees may require only winning the executive office, but ensuring
that these employees work for the organization, pay their dues, turn out
to vote, and operate the bureaucracy in the interest of the governing coalition requires tremendous oversight and policing and a high degree of
administrative skill. For a coalition to engage in election fraud, it needs
to control the elections board as well as election officials and the police
(and sometimes the courts). Another more complicated strategy for city
officials would be implementing a literacy test, which would require either state-level approval or changing the city charter. In keeping with
the tradeoff between maintenance and ease of implementation, election
fraud has a shorter life than literacy tests because it needs to be repeated
at every election. Seat bias, like malapportionment or gerrymandering,
also requires substantial institutional control and can be very effective at
providing a long-term advantage for the governing coalition.

Secondly, in determining which biasing strategy will work best for
the coalition, leaders are constrained by the characteristics of the coalition's core constituency and of its opposition. In general, coalitions in
American cities have relied on two dominant strategies: (1) the use of
government resources to mobilize supporters (e.g., machines) or (2) reducing the ability of opposition voters to voice dissent through suffrage
restrictions and vote dilution (e.g., reformers). Aside from assassinating
opponents, suffrage restriction is the most effective and efficient tool for
building monopolies as long as the group granted voting rights continues
to share the preferences of the monopolists. But not all coalitions can use
this strategy. In order to exclude opponents from the electorate, it is helpful if they are distinguishable by some politically exogenous but relevant
characteristic such as poverty, literacy, race, or ethnicity.[9]

If, for example, political divisions fall along class lines, and the coalition seeking a monopoly represents primarily wealthy residents while its
opposition represents poor residents, the coalition can enact property requirements for voting. The probability of reelection increases when opposition voters are excluded from the electorate. Property requirements
have the secondary benefit of guarding against potential redistribution.
Suffrage restrictions are also likely to be preferred if the core constituency is dominated by interests seeking an efficient bureaucracy. In this case
using government resources to mobilize support through a patronage
system is both unnecessary and an inefficient use of municipal revenue.

Alternatively, if the coalition's core constituency is relatively poor it cannot use property restrictions or poll taxes to manage electoral outcomes because it would exclude its own base of support. Poor coalitions cannot exclude wealthy residents because capital is mobile, and support from some middle- and upper-class residents is necessary to govern effectively and win reelection. Instead, the coalition might seek to bias the system by using government resources to its advantage. In other words, in cities with relatively large numbers of working-class voters, one should see patronage monopolies develop. This allows the leaders of a resource-poor coalition to put municipal largess to work for their political future. The strategy can also serve to redistribute wealth in the city by providing public employment for a larger proportion of the workforce.[10] In some cases patronage jobs will also be attractive to middle-class residents. Patronage regimes have secondary benefits as well. Once a coalition gains control over the bureaucracy, it can engage in fraudulent voting practices, selective enforcement of the laws, and discriminatory provision of city services.

In a hypothetical world in which personal income is the primary factor determining coalition membership and the electoral system is unbiased, I assume that the monopolist's core coalition will be determined by the socioeconomic group representing the largest share of the population. This stylized view leads to the prediction that in cities where low socioeconomic-status residents make up a large share of the population relative to middle- or high-status individuals, coalitions will seek monopoly control through patronage and the biasing mechanisms that come with control over the bureaucracy (e.g., selective application of laws, fraudulent voting, etc.). In cities where low socioeconomic-status residents make up a smaller share of the population, coalitions will seek monopoly control though suffrage restriction and biasing mechanisms that diminish opponents' ability to voice dissent through the electoral process.[11]

Thus, I draw on the caricatured differences between machine and reform coalitions to explore the role of context in monopoly building.[12] Some readers may question whether it is really possible or useful to dichotomize cities in this way. For one, there are innumerable combinations of strategies that a coalition might employ in order to solidify control. In the South, as Key ([1949] 1984) and Kousser (1974) have detailed, monopolies of racial exclusion were built using strategies that eviscerated access to the political system for nonwhite constituents and candidates. These regimes shared some strategies with those of the reformers, but were more clearly targeted to maintain racial supremacy. Additionally, machine and reform regimes were structured differently from city to city. Inevitably, some cities will not fall neatly into one category or the other. Kansas City, one of the cases in this analysis, is classified as a machine, but enacted a city-manager charter early in the twentieth century. Nonetheless there are unifying features within these categories that are useful here. All machines relied on patronage; all reform organizations employed nonpartisan, at-large elections, with city managers. The use of similar biasing mechanisms allows for an analysis of the context that gives rise to the selection of some strategies over others. The prevalence of the machine and reform monopolies makes this comparison statistically possible.

Monopolies Are a Response to Threats

All told, these conditions mean that political monopolies are extremely difficult to build and maintain, but certainly not impossible.[13] Given that monopolies are uncommon but attainable, what factors might lead to their establishment? In some cities the first step toward monopoly is the implementation of bias while others exhibit well-organized coalitions from the outset. Both components are necessary to increase the probability of winning without regard to the preferences of voters. Politicians learn these strategies through repeated interactions with each other and the voters. Coalitions may be especially inclined to undertake bias or take advantage of bias by coordinating effectively when they face threats to their desired outcomes. In particular, threats to political power and policy goals encourage leaders to organize coalitions to dominate government. Coalitions succeed in coordinating by mobilizing voters, defeating the opposition, disciplining politicians, and organizing governing coalitions.

In order to achieve a monopoly, a coalition needs a core group of supporters that favors its agenda. This core group of supporters is likely to be determined by the demographic characteristics of the community at the time the coalition rises to power. Many formulations of this core are possible. For instance, if a single ethnic or class group represents a majority of the voters, these individuals may form a natural core constituency for the coalition. In a heterogeneous population, the core constituency must be composed of different groups. These groups might share preferences for the distribution of municipal policies and benefits due to similar socioeconomic standing, geographic location, or ideological goals.

Once biased, I predict that systems will tend to display inertia until the benefits of returning to a nonbiased arena outweigh the costs of maintenance. This means that factors like institutional control and size of the core constituency may wane over the course of the coalition's life without introducing catastrophic consequences for the monopoly. These factors are most important at the inception of the monopoly. The presence of inertia also means that coalitions can be the beneficiaries of bias implemented by past incumbents or higher levels of government even if the coalition played no immediate role in orchestrating the bias.

Effects of Monopoly

After a coalition implements a biased system and coordinates voters and elites, its probability of reelection should increase. The electoral safety generated by bias can be expected to change the focus of the governing coalition; coalition leaders should be less likely to pay attention to the electorate in general and more likely to pay attention to their core constituency and powerful regime elites (Cox 2001; Cingranelli 1981; Lake and Baum 2001).

Once elected, coalitions face a scarcity of resources (benefits and policy options). Because they are driven to maximize their share of spoils (Riker 1962), coalitions should prefer to minimize the quantity of votes that they win to the smallest number that will retain their control of government. This is likely to be especially true at the local level, where restraints on government revenue and expenditure are heavy due to federal and state demands.[14] Since a large electoral coalition is more expensive to maintain than a small one, the most efficient strategy for maintaining low-cost reelection is to limit the number of coalition members to a minimum winning size, thereby minimizing the number to be rewarded. Politicians might trim their coalitions by repressing turnout of unwanted groups or paying selective attention to their supporters.

Aside from affording each member a greater share of government largess, smaller coalitions are also less expensive to maintain. Reducing or stabilizing expenditure on constituents' demands increases the likelihood of balancing city budgets (Fuchs 1992). Additionally, low-turnout elections are more predictable. Political leaders have an easier time ensuring that voters will cast ballots for their candidates if there are fewer voters to consider (Pinderhughes 1987). Having fewer groups in a coalition also reduces the potential for competing demands that may splinter the coalition in the long run. However, a minimizing strategy makes future elections riskier because it lowers the hurdle for a potential challenger (Hardin 1976; Hershey 1973; Shepsle 1974). So one should only see movement toward minimum winning size when coalitions are entrenched in government and competition has been severely reduced. I predict that during the monopoly period, turnout of eligible voters should decline as coalitions trim their membership.

There is an inverse relationship between the proportion of the electorate needed to stay in office and the extent of bias in the system (Bueno de Mesquita et al. 2003). The more biased a system, the fewer adherents the coalition needs in the electorate and the less time and energy the monopolists must spend mobilizing support. As coalitions become more secure, they can spend less time focusing on reelection and can devote more time and energy to increasing their share of the spoils of office (Key [1949] 1984; Cox 2001).

Although the probability of reelection is increased in a biased system, it is not guaranteed. Even political coalitions that bias the system need to mobilize support from some set of subgroup(s) in the population to legitimate their government. Thus, monopolists must be attentive to *some* voters. But given that resources are limited and many policy and funding choices at the municipal level are zero sum, some groups will win and others will lose. Consequently, politicians are most likely to provide better payoffs to those groups that reliably turn out to vote for the incumbent organization (Dixit and Londregan 1996; Cox and McCubbins 1986) and those who participate in the decision-making process (Banfield 1961). Groups that turn out less predictably should tend to receive fewer benefits than the incumbent's core coalition. The core group needed by the dominant coalition to maintain political control bargains for a share of government benefits. Other constituents may join the coalition (politicians prefer to have them), but only for the most inexpensive or symbolic benefits like holidays or parades honoring the group. Thus, dominance should have consequences for the distribution of government services, policies, jobs, and contracts. Decreased competition should mean that benefits become increasingly concentrated toward regime elites and core coalition members rather than to all electoral coalition members. If this theory is accurate, we should find that all voters, even all regime supporters, do not receive benefits in these political systems.

Decline Requires an Opposition Coalition

In a competitive electoral environment, a quality challenger should enter when the winning coalition is smaller than a majority of the eligible electorate. But in biased systems, dominant organizations have the luxury of winning even when attending to a narrow coalition. Once competition is reduced, coalitions should reduce the provision of goods for the broader public and increasingly concentrate rewards toward regime elites and core coalition members at the expense of peripheral groups. If this is the case, as a direct result of their maintenance strategies, dominant organizations will produce discontented residents. These constituents form a natural base for a challenger. This latent threat of dissatisfied constituents is most likely to be turned into real electoral losses when the coalition is unable to achieve bias or coordination, as well as during periods of economic stress.

The mobilization of residents against the regime may be no small task. Groups peripheral to the political process are likely to face serious collective-action problems (see Schneider and Teske 1993, for example). Mobilization is much more likely when constituents can learn about their situation relative to others. Thus, a lack of information bias offers a context in which voters can be mobilized against the regime in power if their preferences are not being met. A lack of vote bias encourages challengers to enter the political fray and decreases the probability that the incumbent will win if an opposition is mobilized. A lack of seat bias translates into smaller shares of government control for the incumbent coalition unless they are responsive to voters' demands. This effect feeds back into the mobilization of voters and challengers who are more likely to participate when they are more likely to win.[15] When a governing coalition faces a strong electoral challenge, even if the opponent does not win, the threat may increase organization against incumbents at the next election.

To avoid collapse, coalitions also must maintain unity. Monopolies are frequently weakened by internal fissures. Scholars of city politics (e.g., Munoz and Henry 1986; C. Stone 1989; Keiser 1997) have long noted the importance of divisions in the governing coalition to the rise of an alternative coalition. Also, V. O. Key ([1949] 1984) has argued that among elites, long-term, one-party politics can lead to factional infighting. When it does, renegade monopoly elites lead coalitions against the monopoly in pursuit of an alternative governing arrangement. Renegade elites have clear advantages over potential outside challengers because they may be able to bring some portion of the monopolist's vote base with them.[16] For this reason, I find that monopolies tend to see internal discipline as a higher priority than worrying about threats developing at the local level outside of their organizations. If the coalition factionalizes, one segment may be able to build a different power structure to govern the city. This is most likely to happen when the city has diversified, particularly when elites have diversified such that powerful members of the community have conflicting preferences with regard to the role or policies of government.

This means that changing demographics and economic structures have implications for the survival of monopolies. Demographic changes can alter the size or composition of the eligible electorate in favor of the opposition.[17] Additionally, threats to the city's economic health can also serve to mobilize voters and challengers. As is true in competitive systems as well as monopolies, voters may blame the incumbent organization for failure to prevent employment losses or inflation (Howell and McLean 2001) thereby focusing attention on the regime and alternative governance arrangements.

From Threats to Collapse

As protestors around the world can attest, organizing large numbers of angry people does not ensure the regime will relinquish power. A dominant coalition may be able to delay or prevent decline by increasing the level of bias or co-opting the opposition platform. In democracies, increasing the level of bias is frequently not an option. If monopolists choose the path of co-optation in order to maintain control, they must adjust their concentration of benefits to prevent challengers from entering or winning. Under these circumstances, monopolists may adopt reforms or open their systems in order to stave off collapse, transforming into responsive dominant coalitions.

However, there are a number of reasons why a regime in trouble may not be willing or able to make this kind of adjustment in the face of increased competition. As Erie (1988) has argued for machines, in many cases monopolies encounter problems of resource scarcity. Demands made by the challengers may create zero-sum conflicts with the core members of the regime's organization. These conflicts could be ideological, as in Chicago when Daley could not co-opt the rising African American opposition because its demands—integration, reduced institutional racism, etc.—were in direct conflict with the preferences of the party's white ethnic voters. To co-opt the black challenge would have meant the loss of the machine's base. Or, as is more frequently the case, the conflicts could be impossible to resolve because of a lack of resources or funds, e.g., increasing the supply of public housing means cutting back on police services. This should be most problematic during periods of declining resources (Erie 1988).

Perhaps the more interesting question here is why the coalition chooses not to abandon its base and shift policies toward the new voting power if it is clear that the coalition will lose. There is no simple answer to this question. One reason is that coalitions may be oriented toward the status quo and, thus, difficult to change. There can be negative repercussions associated with changing platforms given that the coalition has built a reputation for representing certain groups or policies. Further, there may be a high degree of uncertainty within the coalition over what constitutes a winning platform. Finally, the coalition may be unwilling to compromise if the leaders of the coalition have strong policy preferences that conflict with the new demands. In Chicago, for example, some scholars have argued that the white leadership of the Democratic organization was personally opposed to meeting black demands for integration and increased benefits.

Another, perhaps more interesting, reason a dominant regime refuses to co-opt a challenge is that it is not aware of the rising opposition. In a number of the cases reviewed here, dominant organizations fall because they are insulated from public preferences by the biased system and so miscalculate the danger from their opponents. Kuran's (1991) theory of regime collapse provides an elegant explanation for this phenomenon. Individuals frustrated with the regime in power choose not to express their discontent until enough people are organized against the regime to make it worth their involvement. Before joining the opposition, this latent coalition expresses a public preference for the monopolist that conflicts with the members' private preferences. Because the monopolist has no way to gauge how large the disconnect is between the public and private preferences, mobilization of opposition may happen too quickly for the monopolist to respond successfully. This final reason is another example of how monopolists, in pursuit of long-term power, become the architects of their own demise by insulating regimes from dissent.

When the opposition does succeed, the collapse of the monopoly is frequently followed by a period of factionalism and shifting coalitions. In some cases the pursuit of political monopoly can begin anew. But it is likely that each time an entrenched regime is displaced, it becomes more difficult to replicate the same system of dominance as new laws or changing public opinion limit use of the same strategies. However, political coalitions have proven themselves true chameleons in their ability to adapt to changing circumstances. In American cities as well as governments throughout the world, we continue to see politicians, driven by the goal of reelection, biasing the system in their favor, attending to a narrow coalition, and providing fodder for their own decline.

2 Foundations of Political Monopolies

As CHICAGO TRANSFORMED from a small merchant town in the early 1800s to a partisan, modern city after the Civil War, city officials gained power and city budgets expanded. These new resources offered politicians the opportunity to use public funds to increase their chances of reelection. Following the Chicago Fire of 1871, machine politics, the practice of exchanging benefits like city contracts or patronage jobs for votes, became common among aldermen, providing a head start in the next campaign to those who had already captured office (Simpson 2001). Once politicians gained control over city workers through patronage, they encouraged the bureaucracy to work for political purposes. When the patronage workforce was not sufficient to guarantee electoral victory, politicians of both parties were content to stuff ballot boxes, rig voting machines, and threaten and bribe voters throughout the twentieth century. These strategies biased outcomes in favor of those who were already in power.

In San Jose, politicians used a different set of strategies to enhance their probability of reelection. Starting in the late 1890s, a group of orchardists and fruit packers led a fight to implement California's first fully reformed city charter. Aided by their recent purchase of the city's newspapers, suffrage restrictions at the state level, and poll taxes in the county, by 1916 San Jose reformers achieved at-large elections for city council and replaced the elected mayor with an appointed executive. The new charter decreased the pay for council offices and made local elections nonpartisan. This created a political system in which incumbents had strong advantages going into elections because opportunities for opposition to arise were limited.

In any competition the relative skill, strategy, and luck of the contestants determine who will win and who shall lose. But the rules of the game define the competition itself. Rules dictate which skills and strategies will be most valuable, who may participate and who may not, and what constitutes victory versus defeat. Furthermore, changing the rules of the game can change who is likely to win. When the National Basketball Association added a three-point line, the new rule advantaged players who could successfully sink shots from more than twenty-two feet away, as opposed to the taller, larger players, who nearly always prevailed in fights closer to the basket. In anticipation of the rule change Detroit coach Dick Vitale explained that now "[a team] might have to draft a long shot specialist" (quoted in Dupree 1979, F5). Clearly, at least this observer believed that the new rule had the potential to change how the contributions and skills of various players would be evaluated in building a winning team.

Rules have the potential to advantage not only certain types of players and teams but also to advantage those who have already won. Professional sports leagues are so attuned to this possibility that they require that the most successful teams pick last in the next season's draft. Imagine instead that the winners of the World Series, the Super Bowl, the Stanley Cup, and the NBA playoffs were automatically granted first draft choice and that all other teams selected in order of their win/loss records. Such a rule would be very likely to increase the incumbency advantage for the winners, compounding the benefit of victory over time. So, although rules do not have any normative value per se, they do have consequences for the outcome of competitions. Thus, we should expect shrewd players and team owners to seek rules that benefit them, and once the rules are in place, to make decisions and select strategies that take advantage of the structure that the rules provide.[1]

Politicians, also engaged in competition, have incentives to do the same thing. They will tend to support rules and rule changes that enhance their chances for victory. All political systems are governed by sets of rules; and, just as in the sporting world, these rules determine which skills are most valued, which strategies are most useful, and who is most likely to win. However, the extent to which rules enhance or limit competition varies. Some systems are governed by rules that promote competition while others systematically advantage those who already control political power. In this work, biased systems refer to those political arrangements in which the rules limit information for constituents, make it costly for challengers or voters to enter or exit the political system, or disproportionately allocate seats, in effect advantaging incumbents over challengers regardless of government performance. Political systems do not fall neatly into two categories—biased or unbiased. They fall along a spectrum. Because of the infinite possible combinations of rules, it is impossible to rank systems precisely along a scale of bias. Furthermore, no single strategy is either necessary or sufficient for a coalition to dominate government for a long period of time. But it *is* possible to say that some rules increase bias compared to systems that lack such rules. Politicians in Chicago and San Jose were among the many that were advantaged by rules that increased the probability of victory for incumbent candidates.

In cities across the United States, politicians have enacted and relied on rules that increase their probability of reelection at all stages of the voting process—preference formation, casting votes, and translating votes into seats. Coalitions have used the strategies listed in table 1.1, which include information bias, vote bias, and seat bias, to advantage incumbent politicians. Two bundles of strategies have been common in American history: some coalitions achieved control primarily through the use of government resources for political ends (machines) while others monopolized government by relying on rules that limited the opportunity for dissenters and minority populations to participate in elections (reformers). The following sections provide a more in-depth analysis of each type of bias used by governing coalitions in nine cities: Chicago, New York, New Haven, Kansas City, Philadelphia, San Jose, Austin, San Antonio, and Dallas. The selection of these cities from the larger data collection was driven by the availability of electoral data as discussed in the introduction and in the appendix. The first five cities listed above are classified as machines and the last four are classified as reform. The following discussion is organized by biasing category (information bias, vote bias, and seat bias) and by coalition type (machine or reform). This chapter is meant to provide readers with a general understanding of how rules can enhance incumbents' reelection chances. It does not include a description of the context in which the strategies were selected, how the choices were made, who enacted the changes, and who opposed them. Additionally, evidence that a lack of biasing strategies limited incumbency advantage is only sparsely provided. These important details are covered in chapters 3 and 4.

Controlling Information

In order to shape the political preferences of residents, an organization must control information about government performance and available alternatives. Machines sought to control information using a number of different mechanisms. Perhaps the primary strategy of bias was to place organization loyalists in official positions that held investigative authority, such as local-level prosecutors, grand juries, or state attorney generals (Key 1935). When investigations did occur, machines used control over city agencies to destroy evidence, provide extended leaves to potential witnesses, and otherwise prevent people from cooperating with prosecutors (Key 1935). The machine's relationship to the criminal underworld was sometimes utilized to kill informants (Key 1935). In cases where machines failed to limit investigations, their ability to maintain control of government could be severely impeded. Throughout the latter half of the nineteenth century, Tammany was beset by state investigations into its strategies of fraud and the corrupt practices of its leaders (O'Conor 1871, 1). Such episodes were frequently followed by losing the mayoralty to reform forces (Finegold 1995).

Another mechanism of information control was influence over the news media. Machines attempted to achieve favorable news coverage by bribing editors or reporters, contributing heavily in advertising funds, or by offering publishers or editors public jobs (Key 1935). Key reports that bringing libel suits against papers was another tactic used to control the presentation of harmful information. In a few cases machines resorted to murdering investigative reporters (Key 1935). However, Gosnell (1933, 22) argues that machines often held power "in spite" of newspaper opposition. For some machines at least, this strategy of bias was not necessary to dominate elections.

Reformers had different and less obviously corrupt methods for controlling information and shaping the preferences of voters in favor of their incumbent organizations. At the turn of the century, many reform organizations secured the enactment of nonpartisan local elections, arguing that parties should be irrelevant to urban administration. Because reformers argued that they had identified the most appropriate approach to good government, political institutions that made governance conflictual, like parties, served to stymie progress. One reform leader in San Francisco argued that the purpose of the nonpartisan movement was "to unite decent voters in an effort to take the city government out of politics" (*Los Angeles Times* 1888, 1). By "politics" reformers meant "patronage and selfish intrigue of those who lived on the public payroll and were therefore considered hindrances to community development" (H. Stone, Price, and K. Stone 1940, 268). In converting elections to nonpartisan contests, reformers sought to minimize divisions in the electorate and among elites. In a similar vein, writing about authoritarian regimes, Przeworski (1986) explains, "If one set of policies is seen as superior for the welfare of the society and this set of policies is assumed to be known, then it seems irrational to introduce uncertainty as to whether this set of policies will be chosen" (59).

Nonpartisan elections also allowed reformers to build alliances across party lines more easily. In many cases reformers could not win without this bipartisan support. The lack of party cues to assist voters in the formation of preferences resulted in systems biased in favor of candidates with independent wealth or fame and incumbents (Adrian 1952, 1959; Schaffner, Streb, and Wright 2001), advantaging reform coalition members. Additionally, the less structured environment for competition in a nonpartisan system served to decrease interest and knowledge among constituents, making it difficult for challengers to activate opposition to the incumbent regime (Schaffner and Streb 2002; Lipset, Trow, and Coleman 1956). Without parties to train new leaders and teach voters political skills, nonpartisan elections also increased the probability that membership in the incumbent organization was the only path to access the system.

The most powerful reform weapon in shaping the preference of voters was control over the local media. Whereas machines were forced to persuade newspapers to refrain from investigative reporting or from printing attacks on their organizations, in reform cities newspaper editors and owners were the actual leaders of the reform movements. In San Jose, San Antonio, Dallas, and Austin, reform-owned newspapers refused to report stories that challenged the dominance of the local elites (Bridges 1997; P. Trounstine interview 2003). The local papers in all four reform cities endorsed reform charters, and news stories about city hall tended toward unabashed editorializing. According to a review of city manager government in Dallas, the publisher of the *Dallas News* "threw the full weight of his paper behind" the movement (H. Stone, Price, and K. Stone 1940, 267). Every day leading up to the charter election, the *Dallas News* published a front-page article explaining some aspect of the proposed change and urged its adoption. On the eve of charter reform in San Jose, the *Mercury-Herald* printed a front-page article that argued the election would reveal "whether the people of San Jose want boss rule or popular rule; whether the jobs of city hall shall go to henchmen who do nothing for their pay but politics for their master, or to clean capable men who are good citizens and are accustomed only to a fair wage for fair service" (quoted in Ellsworth and Garbely 1976, 14).

Newspaper owners and publishers supported reform coalitions at least in part because reformers promised to use public funds to help the cities grow, and growth translated into a larger market for news consumption. As an explanation for his pro-development stance, San Jose publisher Joseph Ridder was rumored to have remarked, "Trees don't buy newspapers" (Stanford Environmental Law Society 1970). Newspaper owners, with fixed assets, would also gain from an elimination of corrupt government and smaller tax bills. In some cities, newspaper owners and editors were the founders of the reform movement, like George Dealey in Dallas, who was the "initiator of the most up-to-date reforms in city government" (H. Stone, Price, and K. Stone 1940, 267). Many of these leaders also subscribed to the reform belief that there was only one good and right way to govern a city. Given that reformers had identified this right way, opposition to the reform agenda was viewed as unproductive for the community, and therefore not suitable for printing. Lipset, Trow, and Coleman (1956) explain that the Communist Party relied on a similar claim to justify suppression of dissent, arguing that "there is no legitimate basis for disagreement" (12).

Everywhere, local news organizations shared the vision of the common good that reformers proposed to enact. However, it took time to build this commonality of sentiment—especially when one or more papers were owned by an opposition party or faction. Strategic purchases of opposition newspapers aided reformers' pursuit of dominance. In Austin the leaders of the opposition owned the evening paper and reported anticharter speeches in great detail (H. Stone, Price, and K. Stone 1937). This changed after reform leaders purchased the paper in 1924. In 1896, the San Jose Good Government League was organized to win control of the city for the forces of reform but failed in part because the city's newspapers published articles critically analyzing the reform plan. Such problems were avoided when reform leaders J. O. and E. A. Hayes purchased two of the city's three newspapers and ended printed opposition to the reform charter and candidates. As publishers of the newly consolidated *San Jose Mercury Herald,* the Hayes brothers pushed the reform agenda in news articles and editorials. The editor of the *Herald* resigned after discovering that the new owners intended to impose an editorial policy with "political implications" (Arbuckle 1985, 42). The reform slate victory in 1902 was attributed to the news media support. The Hayes family completed their news monopoly in 1942 when they purchased the town's third and last independent newspaper, *The News.* Two years later the reform coalition finally achieved a monopoly. When the San Jose reform coalition lost power in the 1970s, it was only after the newspaper had again changed leadership and made public the diverse views and preferences of the San Jose community. By coordinating the support of papers, reformers were "shielded from criticism by enthusiastic and boosterish local mass media" (Bridges 1997, 140) and successfully biased the system in their favor.

Biasing Votes Using Government Resources

The second stage of the voting process requires voters to translate their preferences into votes on election day. Coalitions can take steps to ensure that incumbent office holders are advantaged when ballots are cast by limiting the ability for residents or challengers to enter or exit electoral contests. In order to bias outcomes toward their organizations, governing coalitions in many political systems focus on trading divisible benefits (like public jobs) for support, thereby using government resources to engender loyalty to the incumbent regime and pay political workers (Sorauf 1960). In one sense, jobs awarded through political connections represent a strategy of electoral mobilization that might be considered similar to providing supporters with targeted tax breaks. In both strategies benefits are awarded to a particular segment of the community rather than the public as a whole, and both strategies at least loosely connect political support to the receipt of the benefit.

Patronage and tax breaks are particularistic as opposed to programmatic policies, which benefit abstractly defined categories of citizens regardless of the individual's vote (Stokes 2007). Relying on particularistic benefits can enhance an incumbent's probability of victory relative to challengers because challengers can only promise such a trade in the future whereas the incumbent can use public money to back his promise.[2] But because challengers can and do propose different distributions of these particularistic benefits, the system is only weakly biased.

Patronage becomes a strong strategy for bias when the coalition uses the benefit coercively: threatening recipients with losing their jobs if they do not perform political functions, requiring that job holders pay a portion of their salary into party coffers, and/or using political appointees to further bias the political system through practices like vote fraud and intimidation. When workers are assured of economic security if and only if they support the incumbent coalition, they are extremely unlikely to engage in political opposition (Lipset, Trow, and Coleman 1956). The loyalty generated by such uncertainty over maintaining one's job is likely to be even more dramatic when the employee has few options for work in the private sector. In this way, coercive patronage serves as a barrier to entry for challengers and a barrier to exit for voters.

Party-based coalitions in Chicago, Kansas City, New York, New Haven, and Philadelphia employed patronage coercively. In Kansas City nearly all machine leaders and workers held public jobs, some contributing up to 50 percent of their salaries to the party's campaign funds (Larsen and Hulston 1997). In Chicago Mayor Cermak pressured employees to contribute 1 to 2 percent of their salaries (Gottfried 1962). In 1917, when Socialist candidates ran a strong campaign, New York's machine, Tammany Hall, sent police officers to break up the rallies, intimidate supporters and close the public meeting halls. A similar set of events took place during the 2002 election for mayor in Newark, New Jersey, where municipal code enforcement shut down restaurants where the challenger had scheduled meetings and fundraisers (Curry 2003).

In Chicago Boss Richard Daley made certain that his patronage appointees would remain loyal to him by threatening their jobs and controlling which government decisions they made (Royko 1971). To ensure that municipal employees would be beholden to him and not the city council, Daley transferred the authority for budget preparation from the council finance committee to the comptroller and budget director's offices, both controlled by his administration.[3] He also removed the council's authority to issue city contracts and driveway permits, make personnel appointments, and conduct city planning. Each time Daley turned the activity over to a bureaucratic department over which he had control. By using government resources to organize and maintain the coalition, machine organizations successfully biased electoral outcomes in favor of incumbent coalitions.

However, patronage was not sufficient to guarantee long-term dominance for urban coalitions because various factions and opposition parties used the same strategies. Providing jobs, contracts, and other divisible benefits to political supporters may enhance the organizational capacity of the coalition, but it does not equate to unquestionable victory unless the coalition controls all of the available resources. Development of a monopoly using patronage as a biasing mechanism requires that a coalition control *access* to patronage, often through relationships with higher levels of government. Chicago's Mayor Cermak, the first in a long line of Democratic machine builders, artfully positioned a Democrat as governor and secured state jobs to ease the city and his organization through the Great Depression. In the next mayoral election, Democrats won 83 percent of the vote. In Pittsburgh Mayor Lawrence secured over 21,000 county WPA jobs, and in 1937, the Democrats won a landslide victory (Royko 1971). Jersey City's Boss Hague managed to gain control of the entire state WPA allotment, 75,000 positions, by offering President Roosevelt congressmen who would support New Deal programs (Royko

1971). Pennsylvania's Republican leader Matthew Quay used state funds to exert uncontested influence over local politics in Philadelphia at the turn of the twentieth century. He provided and withheld patronage and state appropriations to ensure loyalty in the city (McCaffery 1992).

In Chicago, when Daley rose to power, he built strong alliances in the Democratic Party at county, state, and federal levels. As a result of these ties, the machine faction of the Democratic Party could credibly argue to voters that electing any other organization would translate to a loss of benefits including patronage jobs. As a result election outcomes became biased in favor of the machine. Where organizations had difficulty securing and/or controlling patronage, they did not survive without alternative electoral strategies. For instance, in New York, anti-Tammany governors doled out patronage to various wings of the Democratic Party until the late 1890s. Tammany finally consolidated power only when a new governor supportive of the organization channeled patronage to Tammany leaders after the turn of the century. In Boston divided loyalties at higher levels of government prevented the formation of any city-wide machine (Erie 1988).

Control over the bureaucracy through patronage workers also allowed coalitions in Chicago, Kansas City, New York, New Haven, and Philadelphia to control delivery of municipal benefits and application of city laws. New York's machine made sure that the city's attorney used the power of the office to go after political challengers or their supporters for violations of mundane city ordinances. Near election time "a general raid . . . [was] made on the whole body of store keepers and others in the district, care, of course, being taken not to trouble any who are known to be of the right stripe." Storekeepers were then offered the option of settling their violation in exchange for their vote at the next election. Any fines paid by violators were funneled into the machine's reelection fund (*New York Times* [1857] 1877, 8). Legal and illegal businesses knew that they needed the machine on their side to pass inspections, secure utility extensions, ignore closing laws, sell liquor during the prohibition, run lotteries, and so on (see Erie 1988; Gosnell 1933, 1935; Biles 1995). A 1917 editorial in the *New York Times* explained Tammany's system:

> Bootblacks, pushcart men, fruit vendors, soda water stand and corner grocery keepers, sailmakers, dry goods merchants, and so forth, 'all had
> to contribute to the vast amounts that flowed into station houses, and
> which, after leaving something in the nature of a deposit there, flowed on

higher.' . . . The police was a collecting agency for Tammany Hall every day of the year. (*New York Times* 1917, E2)

Such a system ensured that businesses would organize electoral support for the machine.

To illustrate the power of the political organization over illicit business ventures, Harold Gosnell (1935) recorded a conversation between a precinct worker and district leader in 1933, two years after the Chicago machine won its first election and thirteen years into prohibition. The district leader asks the precinct worker, "What kind of business are you in?" The precinct worker responds, "It's legit' . . . I've got the cops with me. All I do is sell moonshine." To which the district leader responds, "Sell moonshine, why _____ haven't you ever heard of the law?" The precinct worker answers, "You'r' so _____ smart that you oughtta be a lawyer. I don't rob nobody. I don't make the stuff. All I do is sell it. I got cops coming into my saloon all the time. 'Course I suppose you could get to me. That's why I come in here" (118). Two important conclusions can be drawn from this conversation. First, violating prohibition required the support of political leadership. Second, at least one way to achieve such support was to work for the party in power. Incumbent politicians, reliant on their patronage workforce, could use selective application of the law to enhance their probability of reelection.

However, excessive corruption served to undermine a machine's power if it became too offensive to voters or attracted the attention of higher levels of government. Successful machines were careful to use corruption to ensure loyalty, not to aggregate enormous wealth.[4] In the period prior to machine consolidation in both Chicago and New York, corruption was rampant; individual aldermen and bureaucrats negotiated bribes with interested businesses and with each other to ensure the passage and implementation of beneficial legislation (Simpson 2001; Shefter 1976). Such aldermanic rent seeking made it difficult to sustain cooperation, and in both cities the political system remained open to anyone who could marshal a large enough personal following. In other words, too much corruption could make it easier for challengers to emerge and threaten incumbents. But properly controlled, patronage workforces could act as a strong deterrent to opposition, biasing outcomes in favor of incumbents using public funds.

Machines also profited from their skill in employing electoral fraud and repression. Stories abound of politicians throwing uncounted ballots into the river, registering and voting on behalf of the dead or departed, and paying for individual votes at the turn of the century.[5] Kansas City's Boss Pendergast garnered 50,000 phantom voters in the late 1940s (Reitman and Davidson 1972). Between 1930 and 1934 the number of voters in the second ward rose from 8,128 to 15,940 without a significant population increase (Larsen and Hulston 1997).[6] In Richard J. Daley's first election for mayor, the *Chicago Tribune* published photographs of Democratic ward boss, Sidney "Short Pencil" Lewis, erasing votes cast for Daley's Democratic opponent in the primary. Daley's Republican opponent, Robert Merriam, sought to have Daley disqualified because of the fraud. However, the Democratic machine controlled the board of elections, and the commissioner chastised Merriam rather than Lewis or Daley. Merriam estimated that 100,000 ghost voters cast primary ballots. The chief election commissioner charged, "Merriam is following Hitler's tactics which consisted of this—it you tell a lie often enough, people will begin to believe you" (quoted in Gowran 1955, 1). Finegold (1995) reports that an alleged Tammany tactic was to hide a piece of lead under one's fingernail while counting ballots in order to void ballots cast for the opposition.

Yet corruption in elections actually signified the weakness of the machines. Parties rely on fraud when they believe that they cannot win an election fairly and/or lack the institutional power to change the rules to favor their candidates (Kousser 1974). Machines used fraud until they became entrenched because patronage without the coercive elements was an ineffective strategy for ensuring the loyalty of voters, especially after the implementation of the Australian ballot. In the Short Pencil Lewis election, Daley was running against a popular reformist incumbent in the primary, and in the general election he faced the son of a beloved professor and alderman, Charles Merriam. Although Daley had the support of the unions, the committed patronage appointees, and important endorsements from state Democrats, he faced a difficult election. It was not easy to commit vote fraud successfully, and elections would have to have been close for fake ballots to have made a difference in large cities (Argersinger 1985).[7] Additionally, fraudulent voting practices were short lived and labor intense—only one election could be rigged at a time. During years when machine control was strongest, fraud was much less common.

In addition to fixing the votes of people who arrived at the polls, machines preferred for their opponents to stay at home on election day, also enhancing the vote bias of the system. Cox and Kousser (1981) argue that party workers turned from mobilizing supporters with illegal tactics to discouraging opponents with threats when the enactment of the Australian ballot made verifying votes too difficult. Some machines avoided the problem by refusing to oil the voting-machine lever for the opposition candidate. The squeak of an unoiled lever immediately identified opposition supporters to the polling officials (Erie 1988). The Jersey City machine consistently roughed up voters discovered to have cast opposition ballots. While nascent machines engaged in intimidation or chicanery to keep opponents out of the voting booth, in later years, machines supported the passage of laws that legally limited the size of the electorate when it served their needs (Erie 1988).[8] By constructing their ideal electorate through fraud and intimidation, machines biased the system in favor of their incumbent organizations.

Bosses also frequently frustrated their competitors' attempts to organize. Royko (1971) reported that in Chicago Daley constructed an enormous intelligence-gathering wing within the police department so that he had information on anyone who might be working against him. Machines used threats and arrests, denial of meeting or parade permits, and selective enforcement of laws to limit insurgencies against their organizations. They relied on state laws that protected existing parties at the expense of new coalitions. For example, in Chicago, an independent needed 60,000 to 70,000 signatures to get his name on the ballot, compared with the regular party requirements of only 2,000 to 4,000. Next, the independent needed the machine-controlled Chicago Elections Board to approve the entire list of signatures (Royko 1971). In 1931 five minor candidates filed to run for mayor against the machine's founder, Anton Cermak. As president of the county board, Cermak controlled the board of election commissioners, which declared the petitions of all five candidates illegal (Gottfried 1962). These rules worked as barriers to entry for challengers, thus favoring the machine's candidates.

Reformers Shape the Electorate with Institutions

Whereas machines used informal and extralegal tactics like patronage ties, bribery, and threats to shape election outcomes in their favor, politicians in San Jose, Austin, Dallas, and San Antonio relied on legal mechanisms of bias that determined who had the right to cast ballots. Reformers proposed, lobbied for, and supported passage of suffrage restrictions at the state and local levels, including literacy tests, abolition of alien suffrage, registration requirements, poll taxes, obscure polling places, and measures that decreased the visibility or comprehensibility of politics, such as nonconcurrent elections.[9] Reform changes to city electoral and governing institutions had the effect of limiting opportunities for opponents to voice dissent and ensured that those who cast ballots shared reformers' demographics and policy goals.

In Austin only 37 percent of adults over the age of twenty-one had the right to vote in 1933 because of suffrage restrictions including the poll tax and literacy test (Bridges 1997). Phoenix required annual registration renewal four months prior to a primary election, imposed literacy tests, and even as city boundaries expanded, maintained a single site for registration—the county clerk's office downtown. Phoenix also enacted a city charter in 1912 that limited voting to taxpayers.[10] San Antonio required property ownership for bond elections until 1969 and in tax elections until 1975 (Brischetto, Cotrell, and Stevens 1983). California first required voter registration in 1866 with the passage of the California Registry Act sponsored by the Republican wing of the Unionist Party. The act required naturalized citizens to bring their court-sealed documents to the county clerk in order to register and required registration three months prior to elections. Mobile and migrant workers were the focus of increased residency requirements for voters in the 1870s (Keyssar 2000). In 1911 the Progressive legislature established biannual registration.[11] In 1894 California's Republican-controlled state house enacted a literacy requirement that barred from voting anyone who could not write his name and read the Constitution in English.[12] The *Los Angeles Times* applauded the amendment saying "here is one of the greatest reforms of our age . . . for the illiterate herd of voters will no longer haunt the polls on election day . . . and therefore the honest voter will have a chance to carry the election." The article implored, "if you are a true-hearted, patriotic American citizen; if you seek the welfare of your home and native land . . . vote 'Yes' on this question" (Curran 1892, 9). Santa Clara County, where San Jose is located, also had a four-dollar poll tax in the late 1890s (Pitti 2003). A local populist newsletter criticized the tax for its disfranchising effects on "free white men eligible for naturalization," meaning European immigrants and low-income whites. The article made clear it was *not* concerned about "Chinamen or negroes" (quoted in Pitti 2003, 84). Such barriers to registration and voting significantly decreased the size of the electorate and especially impacted participation among poor and working-class residents and communities of color.

By 1900 San Jose and the Santa Clara Valley had already established their position as the agricultural heartland of California. Canneries and orchards employed large numbers of Chinese, then Japanese, and finally

Mexican immigrants throughout the twentieth century. Chinese workers in particular were targeted for restriction from social and political life at the state level. Led by laborers and grangers from San Francisco, California's constitution was amended in 1879 to include a series of anti-Chinese provisions. Chinese were prohibited from voting, owning land, and working in certain occupations, and municipalities were authorized to exclude Chinese from city bounds or to designate specific areas of the city where Chinese residents could live (Keyssar 2000; Yu 1991).

Though the anti-Chinese movement was centered in San Francisco, it also found support in San Jose. San Jose's Chinatown was burned to the ground in 1887 and forced to relocate outside of the city. Community members largely believed the fire was a result of arson tacitly approved by the city council and mayor because the ethnic enclave stood in the way of downtown development. The fire department successfully saved every non-Chinese owned business in the path of the fire, but not a single Chinese-occupied structure (Yu 1991). In a 1902 pamphlet entitled "Sodom of the Coast," leaders of the reform movement targeted gambling operations and graft centered in the Chinese community in an effort to overhaul the city government (Yu 1991). Throughout the first half of the twentieth century, the reform-owned *San Jose Mercury Herald* printed articles in support of excluding Asian immigrants and preventing aliens from owning land, and warning of the "yellow peril" (McEnery interview 2003). Such anti-Chinese and anti-Japanese sentiment suggests that San Jose's leaders would have supported the state-level changes that narrowed the electorate.

In addition to state suffrage restrictions, San Jose reformers were likely aided by the fact that the laboring class worked seasonally and tended to leave the city after harvest. Elections were held when agricultural workers were not living in the city—late winter and early spring.[13] According to one source in 1939, the permanent agricultural workforce in San Jose was 3,000 people. During harvest season this ballooned to 40,000 workers (San Jose Commission 1985). Holding elections when the migrant workforce was not in residence excluded this segment of the community from direct political participation. Pickers and canners earned wages at the bottom of the city's pay scale (Pitti 2003, 82, 222), and given that the working class constituted the most vocal opposition to reform charters, it seems likely that reformers would have been aided by limiting their participation.

Reform incumbents also benefited from institutionalized mechanisms that increased barriers to competition through charter revision and city ordinances. This legally biased the system in favor of certain types of people who were the most likely supporters of the reform agenda. Reformers decreased the pay for city council and other city boards and commissions and increased candidate qualifications through charter revisions. These changes meant that office holders all worked other jobs that had flexible hours or had some independent source of wealth. For example, in Austin council members were required to post $10,000 bonds before taking office in the early 1900s (Bridges 1997, 65). The result was that city councils were increasingly populated by upper-class professionals and small-business owners, the same groups leading the reform movement. As stated in one leader's description of San Jose politics, the city council members would "walk over to city hall, sit down and decide what needed to be done and then go back to their real jobs" (McEnery interview 2003). Between 1944 and 1980, a large proportion of San Jose's leadership community attended Bellarmine College Preparatory, a private Jesuit high school, graduated from Santa Clara University, the local Jesuit college, and lived in one of two wealthy, white neighborhoods.[14] They were part of a "good old boys network" of civic-minded men who "really cared about the city," but who were not representative of the entire community (Hammer interview 2003).

Nonpartisan elections in reform cities also essentially required that candidates have independent sources of wealth for campaign funds. One leader in the Phoenix reform coalition bemoaned "the fact that we're criticized . . . that a little group of people get in a closed room . . . and select a handful of people and put them up. But [we] don't know any better way" (quoted in Bridges 1997, 122). The changes reformers made to government erected barriers to entering the political fray, encouraged certain types of people to become active participants in governance, and actively discouraged others, biasing outcomes in favor of reform candidates.

Machines and Reformers Insulate their Seat Shares

In the final stage of the voting process, the translation of votes to seats, incumbent political coalitions often have immense power in biasing the system because they can insulate coalition members from challenges. In these cities as elsewhere, gerrymandering was used to bolster the chances of incumbent coalitions. During the 1920s, New York's Boss Murphy drew district lines to dilute the votes of Italian neighborhoods (Erie 1988). In Jersey City, Boss Hague also employed gerrymandering, packing the city's Irish into the "Horseshoe District" in order to prevent their votes from influencing elections in other areas (Erie 1988). During the 1960s and 1970s, Daley's machine relied on creative district line drawing to ensure that neighborhoods with black and Latino majorities were dominated by white, machine-loyal representatives (Erie 1988).

Reformers in San Jose, Austin, Dallas, and San Antonio increased incumbents' probability of retaining control through seat bias. They implemented at-large elections, transformed elected seats to appointed ones, and used strategic annexations. By abolishing districts and choosing at-large elections, reform charters ensured that minority preferences, even those of substantial size, remained unrepresented in the city legislature (Gelb 1970; Jones 1976). At-large elections also had the effect of shifting representation toward voters rather than residents. In a ward or district system, regardless of the number of voters in a given area of the city, the area is assured of representation on the council. In an at-large election this is no longer the case. Thus, in reform cities where turnout had already been decreased through suffrage restrictions and registration requirements, it became even less likely that areas would be represented if they had high proportions of people unlikely to vote. Given the nature of the suffrage restrictions, these areas of the city tended to be low income, working class, and communities of color.

In many reform cities, the abolition of districts or wards generated some of the most vocal opposition and contentious argument against the reform charters. Opponents of Austin's 1908 reform charter argued that "under the aldermanic system the citizens are assured direct representation in the affairs of the municipality, and direct control over ward improvements. Ward representation is in line with the democratic doctrine of local self-government." [15] In 1924 Austin's reform charter passed by a tiny margin of twenty votes out of 4,906 ballots cast. Five of the city's seven wards defeated the charter, but the two wealthy areas of town passed it by a three-to-one margin. Because the election was citywide, the supporters won.

San Jose reformers abolished the ward system in 1915 to reduce the "parochial influence" of districts (P. Trounstine and Christensen 1982, 83). The coalition displaced by San Jose's reformers had been able to control city government because it maintained strong support in the city's central wards, the first and fourth, while reformers came to dominate the second and third. One historian described the character of the different wards this way:

The first and fourth wards are the oldest developments and for many years better businesses have been leaving them to move eastward into newer portions of the city. The vote in these declining wards, now containing depreciated residences, cheap hotels and second rate establishments of one sort and another, has generally tended to be machine controlled, pro-labor, morally liberal and antagonistic to municipal reforms. The second ward is of mixed character, while the third has been the traditional stronghold of the better elements, with strict moral views and continued efforts to secure a government which they believe honest and impartial. The state normal is located in this ward and college, business and professional people predominate in its population. (Thorpe 1938, 6)

In revising the charter, San Jose reformers lost in the first and fourth wards but won large numbers of votes in the second and third wards, as well as in newly annexed territory, thereby cinching the citywide victory. According to the political editor of the *San Jose Mercury News*, a movement to return to districts in the late 1970s charged that the at-large system "served the interests of the folks who had established it, not the average person in town . . . [the people who had established at-large elections] didn't want the small, parochial interests of more narrowly based groups to have any influence in politics" (P. Trounstine interview 2003). At-large elections required more campaign funds, more extensive organization and bigger mobilization operations in order to win, and so tended to bias outcomes in favor of reform incumbents.

It is important to note that all of the reform cities studied here implemented at-large elections after suffrage restrictions had been enacted at the state level. This may be both cause and effect. If a political coalition faces opposition of substantial size, creating at-large elections might jeopardize maintaining control. If the opposition won barely more than 50 percent of the vote, they might win 100 percent of the seats. In Austin there is evidence that reform opponent Emma Long was elected because voters pooled all five of their council votes for her in elections. This was known at the time as "single-shotting." In order to combat this tactic, reformers changed the system to a designated-place system where each voter could only cast one vote per at-large seat.[16] It seems likely that reformers would have been wary of enacting at-large elections unless suffrage restrictions had created an electorate amenable to their goals. Further, because charter changes required a majority vote of the city, it also seems unlikely that charter changes abolishing districts would have passed in the absence of suffrage restrictions.

Reformers also benefited from the use of strategic annexation that maintained an electorate that supported their administrations. As they grew, cities like San Jose, San Antonio, Dallas, and Austin selectively expanded their city boundaries and chose not to annex other outlying communities. San Jose's annexations were driven in part by strategies of economic development and city leaders were aggressive in securing state laws facilitating the process (Cavanagh 1953). Its first planned annexation was a one-hundred-foot-wide strip of land leading to the city of Alviso, where San Jose hoped to build a port in 1912. Though the port was never built, San Jose did construct a technologically advanced sewage-treatment plant on the site, which then became the tool by which other communities could be convinced to be annexed to the city (Bogini interview 2003). Given that annexation decisions were made in order to "grow and be able to pay the bill," [17] poorer communities and undevelopable land were not priorities. San Jose reform leaders sought to "capture the cross roads which the administration told us were going to be the shopping centers of the future—where the sales tax would be" (Starbird 1972, 4). Not surprisingly, while San Jose had access to its treatment plant in Alviso, it did not annex the actual city, a poor agricultural community, until the late 1960s. When the annexation did occur it was in response to Alviso's attempt to annex the sewage-treatment plant to its own borders.

Phoenix and Albuquerque annexed and developed communities far from the city center, leapfrogging over poor African American and Latino communities close to downtown. Phoenix annexed its black community in the late 1950s for the 1960 census, while Albuquerque excluded poor Latino communities in the Valley and to the Southwest into the 1960s and 1970s (Bridges 1997). San Jose annexed vast tracts of suburban land, incorporating 1,419 outlying areas by 1969. Yet, as of 2005 there were pockets of county land surrounded on all sides by the city of San Jose. Remaining outside of the official city bounds, these areas have been excluded from participating in local government. In other cities annexation decisions had a more direct and obvious political effect. San Antonio's annexation practices were challenged by the Justice Department under the Voting Rights Act in 1976 because they diluted a growing Mexican American population in the city.[18] Annexations had the effect of creating and maintaining a community and electorate that tended to support reform goals. Had excluded communities become part of the reform cities it is very likely that reform governments would have lost elections. Thus, annexations biased the system in favor of incumbent reformers by determining whose votes translated into seats and whose views would not be counted.

Finally, reformers biased government toward the incumbent regime by transforming many elected positions into appointed offices. Reform charters eliminated popularly elected mayors or turned them into ceremonial heads while investing all executive power in city managers appointed by the council. The purpose of this change was to create a more efficient government. An editorial in the *Dallas News* urged voters to support the new charter by asking, "Why not run Dallas itself on business schedule by business methods under business men? The city manager plan is after all only a business management plan." The article goes on to explain, "[T]he city manager is the executive of a corporation under a board of directors. Dallas is the corporation. It is as simple as that. Vote for it" (quoted in H. Stone, Price, and K. Stone 1940, 286).

The elimination of elected leaders generated extensive controversy. In Phoenix in 1948 city employees and labor organizations opposed the reform charter and the strength of the city manager position because they did not feel that collective bargaining and civil service would be protected. Similarly, in San Jose the reform charter granted the city manager the authority to appoint all of the city's officials without approval from the council and the power to prepare the annual budget. At the same time, the council served on a part-time basis, for very low pay, and was elected at-large in nonpartisan elections. The charter instructed councilors to interact with municipal employees "solely through the city manager" (San Jose City Charter, Section 411). For further clarity, the charter explains: "[N]either the Council nor its members . . . shall give orders to any subordinate officer or employee, either publicly or privately" (San Jose City Charter, section 411). As a result, the manager had an enormous information and resource advantage over the elected legislators. Even if dissenting voices were elected in small numbers to the city council, the control of the city remained tightly bound to the reformist city manager and his administration. In Austin the first council elected following the city manager charter revision was unpopular with the voters because it was not responsive to their needs. One observer noted:

> The council that worked with Manager Johnson was not a representative body at all. . . . It was a super-managerial board. It refused to provide the type of political leadership necessary to keep the administration responsive to public opinion, and to maintain satisfactory public relations. Its members did not acknowledge that their constituents had any claim on their time, and they referred those who inquired about city business to the city manager. . . . The council did eliminate 'politics' in the sordid sense of the

word by ending patronage. . . . it also eliminated politics in the democratic sense of the word. (H. Stone, Price, and K. Stone 1937, 24)

Reformers eliminated the possibility for opposition in their structures of government. Eakins (1976, 3) explains the consequences of this drive to increase the competence of the political system: efficiency "both in theory and in practice meant heeding some citizens and not others . . . [and] the cost of greater efficiency was less democracy." Eliminating politics resulted in an elimination of the pressure and ability to incorporate disaffected and disgruntled constituents. Such strategies of bias effectively insulated incumbent coalitions from shifts in public sentiment and lay the foundation for monopoly control of government.

Conclusions

All political systems are governed by rules. Inevitably, rules advantage some groups and individuals over others. When rules consistently advantage incumbents by limiting information, erecting barriers to entry or exit, or distorting the translation of votes to seats, the system is biased in favor of the ruling group. Throughout the twentieth century, San Jose was governed by a set of rules that limited the opportunity for dissenters to participate in the political arena and minimized the power of minority voices. Regardless of the characteristics of their potential opponents, San Jose's reform incumbents benefited from these rules that shaped who the electorate would be and how their votes would be counted. Likewise in Chicago large numbers of patronage employees loyal to the boss significantly enhanced the power of those politicians who had already won one round of elections. But, however helpful suffrage restrictions and the political use of patronage were to reform and machine leaders, the presence of these institutions did not ensure monopoly control. By the mid-twentieth century, virtually every city in the United States was governed by one or more of the types of rules described in this chapter. What distinguished a biased system from a monopolized system was the presence of organization.

3 Coordinating Monopolies

BY THE TIME Anton Cermak founded the Chicago Democratic machine in 1931, the city boasted large ethnic communities, significant partisan loyalties, well-defined precinct and ward organizations, and a history of trading benefits for votes. The basic map of machine control existed, but party organizations were loose. Parties lacked control over the electorate and elected officials, and alliances with the business community and higher levels of government were fleeting. Chicago's Democratic organization spent nearly sixty years using the ties of patronage to make life difficult for challengers. Not until it became clear that they might lose everything due to their factional struggles did they successfully build the Machine. Cermak achieved this organizational feat by embarking, ironically, on a program of reform. By developing "clearcut standards of performance, whereby party workers advanced or were demoted according to the successes or failures within their own fiefdoms," favoritism was eliminated (Biles 1995, 114–15). In the preceding period factions competed against one another for power and party workers were distrustful of leaders with whom they had no personal ties of loyalty. The new hierarchical party structure helped maintain unity because it bureaucratized the process of winning elections and governing the city. Secure in the knowledge that their political success was predictable, party workers became willing to work for a common goal.

In San Jose, too, the basic components of reform government were in place decades before power was consolidated. Having successfully revised the city charter to implement California's first nonpartisan, at-large, council manager system in 1915, reform leaders were still unable to maintain control of elected offices. Reformers benefited from literacy tests, citizenship restrictions for immigrants, and stringent registration requirements, all of which worked to create low participation. Yet, the city was governed by an informal collection of interests, not dominated by Reform. A series of economic and political calamities convinced San Jose's reform leaders that they must organize or else risk the decline of their influence and, as many believed, the city. However, organization in such an environment was tricky. After having abolished parties, reformers left themselves no institutional mechanism for association. In the early 1940s, reform-minded elites organized San Jose's Progress Committee, a nonpartisan slating group, to recapture the city. The committee represented a trend in reform cities towards coordinated action in pursuit of monopoly.

The implementation of bias through machines' informal tactics and reformers' charters provided a key element in the quest for long-term dominance. But the creation of long-lasting, centralized, powerful monopolies required coordination as well—the mobilization of the electorate, the elimination of divisions within the coalition, and the consolidation of a governing coalition complete with elite support. In addition to bias, the second necessary component for monopoly dominance is the centralization of power. In some cities the implementation of bias and the coordination of the coalition are indistinguishable events. But in most cases, one or the other is achieved first. Monopolizing the local government is an iterative process in these cities. In both Chicago and San Jose, some elements of bias were in place when the coalition became organized, which then went on to bias the system further after winning more power. This chapter seeks to explain the process of centralization and the timing of control.

In order to become organized, machine and reform leaders needed to consolidate their coalitions. This required selecting their core constituency, mobilizing voters, disciplining politicians, and coordinating a governing coalition. For their core constituencies, machines sought the support of white European immigrant communities. They allied with business leaders, who would benefit from centralized and stable political systems. They gained the support of party workers and leaders, religious leaders, organized labor, and state and county governments. Reformers in the Southwest selected white middle- and upper-class homeowners as their core constituents. Reformers did not seek alliances with labor or religious groups, and they benefited from counting business elites as their most prominent leaders. They often won support from middle-class women's clubs and maintained solid ties to state governments. Finally, with their coalitions coordinated and bias in place, machine and reform politicians monopolized political systems.

In order to understand the genesis of organizations that monopolize cities, this chapter addresses two questions. First, why did the coalitions become consolidated at the time that they did, and second, how did they do it? In machine and reform cities, the basic tasks of emergent organizations were similar. However, at the time that these coalitions were consolidated there was no predetermined outcome. In retrospect, we can identify factors that made their emergence more likely and their memberships sensible, but none of this was necessarily inevitable or obvious to contemporary observers.

With the benefit of hindsight, I argue that the organizations consolidated when they faced threats to their desired outcomes. Centralizing power requires overcoming collective-action problems among voters and elites. Although the benefits of organization might outweigh the gains from a loose collection of interests, some entrepreneur must still bear the costs of centralization. This is most likely to happen when the gap between the cost of not organizing and the benefit from collective action becomes larger. Political scientists know from political psychology (Kahneman and Tversky 1979) that the risk of loss motivates action more readily than the possibility of gain. Threats to political power, economic power, and policy goals encouraged leaders in machine and reform cities to organize coalitions to dominate government. Contextual differences dictated varying strategies for machine and reform organizations in winning election to office and taking control of the governing apparatus, and also served to determine the makeup of the organization itself.

Coalitions Built to Win

In both machine and reform cities, the coalition of residents and leaders supportive of the emergent regime can be broken down into various segments: voters needed to win elections every time (the core), voters needed to win elections some of the time (junior partners), powerful figures needed to govern (governing coalition elites), and everyone else (periphery). How a coalition determines which groups shall be its core, the junior partners, and the periphery is dictated by a variety of factors. For instance, Aldrich (1995) characterizes the core membership of a coalition as those groups excluded from the party or group against which the coalition competes. This suggests a sort of path dependence to the makeup of coalitions, assuming that some allegiances are already determined at the time a coalition becomes organized.

Another explanation for the determination of a core constituency is offered by Fenno ([1978] 2003), who describes constituencies as a series of concentric circles. The broadest constituency is defined by the legal boundaries of the community or district; within this geographical constituency is the reelection constituency made up of the voters who will probably vote for the candidate. The reelection constituency can be broken down into two portions, weak supporters and the politician's primary constituency. These circles are similar to the coalition segments described above. The weak supporters are akin to junior partners and the primary constituency is the core constituency; voters not in the re-election constituency but part of the geographical constituency are the periphery. Unlike the junior partners or the periphery, the core can be counted on to support the candidate in all elections, regardless of who the challenger is.

However, Fenno provides few clues for predicting who this constituency is likely to be in any given community. He explains that in homogenous districts the member is likely to have his home style imposed upon him by the community, whereas in heterogeneous districts the member has more flexibility. We might conclude, then, that the more homogenous the community, the more likely the member is to share demographic or socioeconomic traits and policy views with the voters. But it is never clear which comes first, the politician or the constituency; it is a chicken-and-egg problem. It is likely that in some cases the politician is chosen by the electorate, and in others, the core electorate is shaped by the politician through a process of encouraging and discouraging certain groups or individuals to join the politician's team. If we imagine the political arena as a blank slate, a perfectly competitive market, politicians will win if they represent the views or preferences of a majority of the voters. Thus, groups that represent a substantial share of potential voters are one intuitive source of the coalition's core. Groups that share policy concerns with the coalition's leaders represent a second source of core support. We can identify this core, as Fenno and Axelrod (1972) suggest, by understanding which voters consistently back the coalition of interest.

Identifying the characteristics of the governing coalition elites is more straightforward. These are the actors whose cooperation is needed for the political coalition to govern because of these actors' control over resources. Regime theorists like Clarence Stone (1989) and Elkin (1987) have argued that political actors do not have the resources or capacity to make and implement decisions without private support. The institutional and economic structures of the city determine whose participation is needed by the coalition. Because the private sector is responsible for the production of wealth, a community's fundamental health depends on satisfying the demands of these actors. Different communities have different distributions of private resources, which lead to different formulations of the governing coalition. Everywhere the business community is responsible for maintaining jobs, producing revenue for public projects, and generating economic wealth, and so is vital to governance. However, the economic framework determines which businesses are most important. For instance, in older cities, the downtown merchant community controlled the vast majority of resources, while in the Sunbelt, real-estate developers were the central members of the business elite. According to Logan and Molotch (1987), bankers, large property owners, attorneys, retailers, utility and media owners, construction industry leaders, large universities, nonprofit cultural institutions, and organized labor are all important elites in cities. In areas where party organizations are powerful, party leaders and activists represent another set of key elites. Religious leaders can be essential elites, particularly if they are able to influence large numbers of voters. We might summarize this list by saying a given private actor is likely to be important to the governing coalition if he or she controls or affects the production or sale of a significant fraction of the community's goods and services, a significant number of jobs, a significant share of property values, a significant portion of the community's wealth, or a significant proportion of votes.

In addition to private elites, public officials play prominent roles in governing coalitions. This group includes a majority of office holders in the legislative and executive branches of government and officials outside of the city government who control important resources, like county and state officials. The extent of home rule a state grants to its subunits determines how important these outside officials are to the city.[1] No city is completely sovereign in the United States, but cities are constrained to various degrees by state law (and court interpretation of the law) in determining institutional arrangements, incurring debt, raising revenue, owning utilities, regulating development, annexing territory, and providing specific services, among other things. In more constrained cities, municipal control requires having support at the state level in addition to acquiring that of local-level elites. Cooperation from these elites is integral to making and carrying out political activity.

Machine Coalitions

The base of machine coalitions was working class immigrant constituents.[2] Kemp and Lineberry (1982) describe the heavily Irish and eastern European ward Bridgeport in Chicago as the "the basic source of machine strength and predictability" (12). In 1900, when Chicago's Democrats were negotiating among their factions, first- and second-

Table 3.1: Country of origin for Chicago population, 1930

Country of origin	Population (%)
Native stock	35.6
Poland	11.9
Germany	11.2
African American	6.9
Ireland	5.7
Russia	5.0
Italy	5.4
Sweden	4.2
Czechoslovakia	3.6
Other	10.5

Source: United States Census of Population and Housing, 1930

generation immigrants represented 77 percent of the total population. The largest ethnic groups in the city were the Irish (representing 17 percent), Poles (representing 10 percent), and Germans (35 percent). These groups also had high naturalization rates, around 70 percent in 1920 (Allswang 1971, 22). By 1930 the city had become considerably more diverse. Table 3.1 shows the ethnic breakdown of the city by country of origin for immigrants and native-born whites with at least one foreign parent. Native stock includes persons born in the United States to two native-born parents. African American includes all persons listed as "Negro" by the 1930 census. As famous as machines were for catering to the Irish, it was other immigrant groups that solidified Democratic power in Chicago. Given this diversity, machine coalitions could only win elections by building broad electoral bases.

The strongest factions of Chicago's Democratic party prior to machine consolidation were led and supported by the Irish. Other European immigrant groups were important, too, including Poles, Jews, and Czechs (though with naturalization rates between 34 and 45 percent, perhaps less reliable as core-coalition members). When Cermak ascended to power, the dominance of the Irish eroded as he assembled a "house for all peoples" (Allswang 1971). As chairman of the Democratic party, Cermak and his successor, Pat Nash, actively recruited Czechs, Poles, Italians, and Jews into the organization throughout the 1920s, resulting in a sweeping Democratic victory in 1931. In this election Cermak captured nearly 65 percent of the immigrant vote in the city (Zikmund 1982). He courted these groups by offering appointments to municipal posts, improved services paid for with New Deal relief funds, ethnically balanced tickets, and promises to fight Prohibition. Cermak was so successful at wooing this diverse coalition that the original Democratic base in Chicago, the Irish, shifted their votes toward Republican candidates in protest of their diminishing strength within the Democratic party. The Irish were tempted back to the machine by Mayor Edward Kelly and party leader Nash only after Cermak's death.

Allswang's (1971) analysis of party identification and voting behavior in the 1927 and 1931 mayoral elections highlights the machine's coalition. The first column of table 3.2 shows the proportion of each group that voted for the Democratic candidate, William Dever; the second column shows the proportion of each group declared Democratic in the poll books; and the third column shows each group's vote for Cermak.

Regrettably, Allswang does not include Irish ethnics in his analysis, but the allegiances of other groups are instructive. Czechs, Poles, and Lithuanians offered a majority of their votes to Dever, but no other ethnic group did so. Cermak received a majority from every white ethnic group except Italians.

An analysis of Chicago's voting patterns in the mayoral elections of 1935, 1939, and 1947 confirm these relationships for the early period of the machine monopoly. Using a combination of Allswang's ward categorizations, newspaper reports, and census data, I coded wards by their ethnic identity.[3] For each ward in the city, I calculated the "deliverability" of the vote (see Kemp and Lineberry 1982, 9). Because regimes are most interested in having both high levels of support and high levels of

Table 3.2: Ethnic Democratic votes

	% Dever 1927	% Democratic 1931	% Cermak 1931
Czechs	59	69	84
Poles	54	40	70
Lithuanians	57	36	62
Yugoslavs	36	26	64
Italians	42	29	47
Germans	37	29	58
Swedes	38	16	53
Jews	39	50	61
African Americans	7	12	16
Native Americans	55	16	61

Table 3.3: Deliverability of Chicago ethnic wards, 1935, 1939, 1947

	Coefficient	Std. error
Czech	0.12**	0.03
Polish	0.02	0.02
Irish	0.09**	0.03
Jewish	0.11**	0.03
Italian	0.06**	0.03
German	−0.05	0.03
Black	−0.03	0.03
Native White	−0.04	0.03
Year 1935	−0.03**	0.02
Year 1939	−0.03*	0.02
Constant	0.37	0.01
N	150	
R^2	0.29	

OLS regression: $*p < .10$ $**p < .05$

turnout from their core constituents, this measure takes the total number of ballots cast in support of the regime divided by the total number of potential ballots (or eligible voters). Table 3.3 displays the results of regressing deliverability on ethnic neighborhoods.

These results provide support for the claim that immigrants composed the base of the machine. The strongest support for the machine came from Czech, Jewish, and Irish wards. Italian support was also significant. It is clear from this analysis that African Americans were not a strong component of machine control during these elections. Though not statistically significant, German and native-born American wards appeared to offer opposition to the organization. These results add weight to the narrative analysis presented above: the Chicago machine drew support from a white immigrant ethnic base.

In New York the Irish composed Tammany's support base. Controlling for density of the neighborhood and literacy rates, Finegold (1995) estimates rates of support for Tammany candidates in 1913 and 1917. He finds Irish support to be a key component of the machine vote in both elections (57, 64). Lee's New Haven organization also garnered strong Irish support. Kansas City had fewer immigrants than either New York or Chicago, but just as many working-class voters. It was these constituents that served as Tom Pendergast's base.

Not only were machine core coalitions defined by ethnic and class groupings, they were also defined geographically. This was the result of two features of turn-of-the-century society that reinforced each other. To begin with, immigrant groups tended to settle in highly segregated communities in the nation's largest cities. This meant that if a political organization could identify a group of likely supporters in ethnic terms, it would also be very likely to identify entire neighborhoods that would support the coalition. Secondly, city council seats were divided by districts. In response, machines were organized geographically. Ward bosses controlled defined areas that coincided with ethnic and class groupings. The stronghold of the Democratic coalition in Chicago was a set of inner-city wards termed the "automatic eleven" that had high proportions of European immigrant residents and family incomes below the city average (O'Connor 1975, 10; Kemp and Lineberry 1982). Pendergast's base of support also came from the inner-city "river wards," where low income families, immigrants, and African Americans lived (Larsen and Hulston 1997, 93). To some extent, this meant that new residents moving into established machine territories tended to be mobilized along with the core supporters, sometimes as an afterthought but at other times as a deliberate electoral strategy.

While white European ethnic voters provided the foundation of machine organizations, during the early years the coalition actively sought votes from other constituency groups in the city. Throughout the 1930s and 1940s, in order to consolidate control, Chicago's boss Ed Kelly pursued African American votes. He achieved a sizable black following by offering William Dawson, a popular African American Republican alderman, the position of Democratic committeeman. Due to Kelly's efforts, blacks moved into the Democratic party in Chicago earlier than they did at the national level, resulting in the machine winning more than 80 percent of the vote on the South Side in 1935 (Cohen and Taylor 2000).[4] To win the mayor's seat and ensure their power in 1953, Democrats in New Haven sought to reach out to traditionally Republican voters like Italians and the middle class. Dahl (1961) described Lee's first coalition as the following unlikely combination:

> . . . the DiCenzo-Celentano wing of the Republican party; public utility heads, bankers, manufacturers, and retailers who were all Republican, the Yale administration; the liberal Democrats among the Yale faculty, the working-class and lower middle class ethnic groups, particularly Negroes and Italians, and their spokesmen; trade union leaders, educators, small merchants, the League of Women Voters, the Chamber of Commerce; and

enough voters to win elections by a margin so impressive that it guaranteed
not only the continuation of redevelopment but Lee's own long-run political prospects. (129)

In Kansas City, Pendergast worked hard to make inroads into the traditionally Republican black and middle-class votes. Aided by the Depression, he succeeded in doubling the number of voters in the heavily black
second ward between 1930 and 1934, although the population remained
constant (Larsen and Hulston 1997).[5] The machine also gained ground
in the middle class "Country Club District" (93). From these examples,
it is clear that in their rise to power, incipient monopolies courted many
different kinds of voters and built broad coalitions.

A defining feature of machine organizations was that they rarely
excluded large groups of constituents overtly; instead, they selectively
mobilized peripheral voters when it suited their needs. It was not until the machines had achieved monopoly control that it became clear
who received limited benefits. However, some insight can be gained by
understanding which groups voted most consistently for the organization and which deserted for opponents when the opportunity arose. In
New York, Jews actively supported Tammany opponents running on
socialist fusion platforms throughout the early 1900s, while Italians and
native-born whites frequently supported Reform and Republican candidates (Finegold 1995). In New Haven, too, Italians offered strong support to the Republican Party as did the city's middle-class whites. Prior
to Kelly's recruitment, the black vote in Chicago was solidly Republican. Even William Dawson began his career in office as a Republican
alderman. Allswang (1971) found that between 1918 and 1930, Poles,
Czechs, Lithuanians, Yugoslavs, and Italians were more reliably Democratic than Germans, Swedes, Jews, African Americans, or native-born
Americans.

For the most part, machines were built with the support of white
ethnic voters, but the constellation of groups was different in each city.
As they began their ascent to power, machines sought to consolidate a
coalition that could reliably capture a majority of the votes in city contests. This meant that large groups with predictable loyalties became
their base.

Machine Governing Coalition

Perhaps more important than vote coalitions, successful consolidation of the machine required alliances with important elites and the institutionalization of a cohesive governing coalition. Erie (1988) argues

that machines became centralized when local politicians could garner support from state government. There were two reasons for this. On the one hand, most machine cities did not have liberal home rule. This restricted the ability of local leaders to change political institutions to enhance their power and to respond to demands of constituents and crises, and it meant hostile state governments could hinder effective governance. For instance, in 1857, the New York state legislature moved to take control over a number of New York City bureaucracies in order to thwart Tammany's power (Krane, Rigos, and Hill 2001). Only one of the machine cities in the study achieved home rule prior to achieving dominance—Albany, New York, the state capital.

Because they did not achieve home rule until much later in the twentieth century, machine organizations needed support from state government. After Cermak's murder, Chicago's rising machine lobbied the state legislature to allow the city council to select an outsider for the mayoral position so that the machine could handpick the successor and maintain control (Biles 1995). Rakove (1975) argues that the "greatest potential legal danger to the [Chicago] machine [was] the power of the state government in Springfield," but goes on to explain that the state did not often meddle with city affairs because state representatives shared a common interest with city leaders—maintaining power (203–7). Daley made sure that this was true. At one point he secured a Chicago sales tax increase through the state legislature by agreeing to put up only a token challenger to the Republican governor in the next election (Cohen and Taylor 2000). Similarly, Democratic governors in New Jersey gave Boss Hague's fledgling machine in Jersey City the support it needed to consolidate power. With machine-nominated governors in office, Hague gained assurance that the state board of taxes and assessments would allow him to increase taxes on railroad and oil companies to bring in additional city funds (Erie 1988).

The second reason state alliances were useful for machine organizations was that these partnerships allowed them to increase and control the supply of patronage. New York's Tammany faction dominated competitors because it secured support from the state Democratic Party during the 1870s and 1880s. When Republicans were in control of the state house, Tammany lost its edge. Similarly, in Kansas City, as an attempt to gain power over a rival Democratic faction, Boss Tom Pendergast helped elect Republican George Edwards governor. Edwards, forever grateful, rewarded Pendergast with patronage and independence.

Machine politicians, relying on party connections, also built ties with county governments and political organizations. Daley's first elected position to the Cook County Clerk's Office allowed him the opportunity to form strong alliances, which he relied on once he took over the city government. For Chicago's machine, having a friendly politician elected to county office conferred control over the location of deposits of county funds, name placement on ballots, the selection of polling places, the enforcement of election laws, and the assessment of real estate (Rakove 1975). It was Pendergast's capture of the county government that gave him the power to eliminate his rival Democratic faction (Dorsett 1968). Boss Hague's good relationship with the local civil service board in Jersey City allowed him to hire and fire city employees for political purposes (Erie 1988).

Not only were relationships with state and county officials important, machines needed to secure support from other local political actors. In Kansas City Tom Pendergast rose to power, as many machine leaders did, by organizing the support of influential ward bosses within the party. In many cases party workers supported centralization of the party because it could minimize political corruption and ensure that they retained power. The consolidation of Tammany Hall under "Honest" John Kelly promised to deliver such a collective good (Shefter 1976). Similarly, Daley won election to mayor against an established incumbent in part because he garnered a dedicated following among the party regulars—precinct captains and ward leaders. But because autonomous ward bosses could damage monopoly control, after winning the mayoralty Daley took steps to reduce the power of ward bosses, eliminating potential competitors who could organize their own followings. In all machine cities, an enterprising organization needed to have support from powerful party members and workers at the city, county, and state levels in order to take control (Rakove 1975); without it, monopolies failed to emerge or lost power.

A lack of centralization among elected office holders or powerful bureaucracies also stymied monopoly building. One of the main reasons that Tammany did not achieve a monopoly over New York's city government at the turn of the twentieth century was the organization's lack of control over the mayoralty and large segments of the city council (Shefter 1976, 1978; Finegold 1995). In later years, the untouchable power and independence of Robert Moses prevented machine rebuilding (Caro 1975). Unionization of municipal employees also had the potential to disrupt machine control over city government. In 1902, New York sanitation workers organized under the street-cleaning commissioner in order to allow workers to "present their problems through elected representatives rather than to a ward boss who exacted a price" (O'Neill

1970, 2). Almost as soon as the fledgling union was born, party leaders ensured its destruction. Such organizations were threatening to the machine for a number of reasons. First, they made it difficult for the machine to use patronage for political purposes. They also offered residents an important source of alternative ideas, leadership training, and education in political skills that could foster challengers and encourage an opposition base.

While machine leaders worked hard to maintain good relationships with public officials, they also sought to secure support from elites outside of the government, like the business community, labor unions, and religious and educational organizations. Shefter (1978) has argued that the primary determinant of a successful political machine was its alliances with the local business community. Unlike reform coalitions, political machines did not naturally have the support of the business elite. Many party politicians had grown up in poor and working-class families and so were not socially or economically connected to traditional city elites (Zink 1930). In fact, in some cities, the business community represented a powerful source of opposition to rising machines. In other cases, the machine boss was defined by his ability to create an informal power structure connecting business and politics. In neither case were the machine politicians and the business elite wholly the same community.

When the Chicago machine was first elected to office during the Great Depression it did not enjoy the reliable support of the business community, which was loyal to the Republican Party. During the late 1930s, Democrat Mayor Kelly won business support by providing services for the downtown area, keeping the city solvent, and opposing personal property and income taxes. He ensured that downtown had good street lighting, snow removal, street cleaning, police protection, parking facilities and efficient public transportation (Rakove 1975). These services resulted from negotiations that evolved over the life of the monopoly. Later, Daley won support from developers, downtown merchants, and financiers with a pro-growth regime focused on redevelopment (Cohen and Taylor 2000). In New Haven, Richard Lee also won the allegiance of the business community with a redevelopment platform. In 1953, the first year of monopoly control, the chamber of commerce organized $1 billion in loans and $500 million in capital grants for the city. Lee's predecessor, Celentano, never won the loyalty of the business community, which ultimately undermined his political success (Rae 2003). Lee was able to secure support from the city's major educational institution, Yale, because of ties he had made working at the university early in his career.

In both Chicago and New Haven, the support of labor unions was important. Machine organizations had long been allies of labor, given their working-class constituency, but maintaining a good relationship with labor *leaders* was vital to the success of machine coalitions because of the influence unions had over voters' decisions. They guaranteed this by using only high-wage union labor for city projects and embarking on massive public works to generate new jobs. Many bosses also arranged for the union label to be printed on city supplies (Dorsett 1968). In some cities, like Chicago, the machine also promised a living wage for union work or comparable jobs for city employees. Rae (2003) explains that the union movement peaked during the 1950s and 1960s in New Haven, which made securing the support of labor leaders vital to constructing Lee's political machine in 1953.

Catholic parishes were another source of support for the machine in New Haven and Chicago. The church, one of the most stable civic organizations in the community, can mobilize voters, offer a network for politicians, and encourage congregants to contribute resources to the organization. Gosnell (1933) explains:

> The religious tie has bound together many of the Tammany chieftains and ward heelers. The Brennan-Cermak Democratic machine in Chicago has also relied heavily on the Catholic elements found in the sections of the city where the foreign-born groups predominated. On the other hand, the notorious Stephenson machine in Indiana had the active support of many Protestant churches and the Mayor Thompson machine in Chicago was aided by white and colored Protestant ministers. Ministers can make speeches, advise their congregations as to how to vote, and help to distribute the party funds. (22)

Rakove (1975) underscores the power of the church, saying, "it is with good reason that the state of Illinois annually awarded license plate number one, not to the governor, but to the Roman Catholic cardinal of Chicago" (32). It was support from unions, business, religious institutions, party leadership, and county and state governments that ensured machines a platform from which to launch their monopoly control.

Reform Coalitions

The communities of the Southwest in which reformers dominated were less diverse than the homes of their machine counterparts, which meant that the core of reform coalitions was likely to look very different from that of the machines. When San Jose reformers won their first victory in 1915 with a city manager charter, the city's population was about 3 percent nonwhite (Asian and African American) and about 54 percent first- and second-generation immigrants. In 1944, when reformers centralized power, the nonwhite proportion had declined to about 2 percent and the foreign-stock population to 40 percent. Reform cities in Texas, like Austin and Dallas, had substantial African American communities (15 to 25 percent during the pre-monopoly period), but smaller foreign-stock populations. There was economic diversity in these cities, but in most places not great extremes of wealth. The fact that these communities were less demographically diverse did *not* mean that everyone agreed on policy goals and political structure, but it did mean that determining a core reform constituency was more straightforward.

While machines spent a great deal of effort consolidating a broad coalition, reformers adopted a different strategy. They identified core supporters and legally excluded or minimized the influence of those portions of the electorate that might oppose them. Reform in the South and West was popular with a new, young elite determined to refashion city government, enabling their engagement in the rapidly developing economy. Opposition for these government programs came from labor groups, the working class, and persons of color (Bridges 1997). Municipal reformers, advantaged by state governments that narrowed electorates with suffrage restrictions, further minimized the threat of potential opponents through requirements like onerous registration, property qualifications, and at-large elections. As a result the political communities in the South and West were predominately white and middle class. It was this group of voters that shared reform goals and became the core of reform coalitions.

Reform charter changes and nonpartisan slating groups throughout the South and West drew the vast majority of their votes from affluent Anglo voters. The passage of San Jose's reform charter in 1914 was driven by two of the city's four wards, the second and third, along with the newly annexed areas, which were populated with white, middle-class, and upper-class professionals (Thorpe 1938). When San Jose expanded in the following decades, these old wards were deserted by white homeowners for greener pastures to the west and the south of the city. As reformers' core constituents moved out, the patterns of support in the city changed too. By the time San Jose reformers consolidated power in 1944, the old wards of the city were indifferent to the rising regime; the core areas of support had become the newer, richer neighborhoods away from the city center. The primary opposition to reform came from poor and working-class neighborhoods.

In order to clarify the coalition supportive of San Jose's reformers, I coded election precincts into seven neighborhoods—each of the four old wards; two middle-class, white home-owner areas (Willow Glen and Hester Hanchett); and the working-class, Latino community of East San Jose. The boundaries of these neighborhoods were defined using GIS mapping and then precincts were labeled by polling-site address. Four elections were selected to represent time periods before the consolidation of power (1938), just after consolidation (1946), and at the highpoint of monopoly control (1958 and 1962).

To understand reform support, the following analysis compares the mean reform "deliverability" of different areas of the city. The results in table 3.4 substantiate the conclusion that middle-class areas supported the reform candidates at higher levels than the rest of the city. The cells show the average percentage of registered voters in the neighborhoods that supported reform candidates and platforms, with standard errors in parentheses.

Table 3.4: Deliverability of San Jose neighborhoods, 1938–62

	Middle class	Old wards	Working class
	0.209	0.181	0.169
	(0.004)	(0.003)	(0.007)

Although the differences are not enormous, they are statistically significant. It was the middle-class areas that provided enough votes for the reformers to win both charter changes and later elections to city council.

Similarly, in Austin, where the change to a city manager charter won by a mere twenty votes in 1924, only two of the city's seven wards approved the charter changes. The overwhelming margin of approval offered by the city's "two most wealthy residential wards" carried the reformers to victory in the citywide election (H. Stone, Price, and K. Stone 1937, 427–28). Austin voters were rewarded throughout the 1930s with a new sewage-treatment plant, a city traffic engineer, hundreds of blocks of newly paved streets, and an improved police dispatch system (H. Stone, Price, and K. Stone 1937). In Dallas the city manager charter was passed in 1931 by overwhelming margins in the "fashionable residential areas." The precincts in which a majority opposed the changes were the industrial areas, home to working-class and African American residents. Dallas was known as a "leading open-shop city," and the chamber of commerce, backers of the new charter, had "long worked closely with the Dallas Open Shop Association to prevent the organization of labor" (H. Stone, Price, and K. Stone 1940, 265).

Dallas's first organized opposition to the reform of city government came from former employees of city government (fired by the new city manager), who founded the Home Government Association (HGA). The HGA slate developed a strong following among the city's working class and argued that the reformers had "neglected the interests of the forgotten man while safeguarding vested interests."[6] They were succeeded by the Forward Dallas Association, which ran on a platform that promised to hire black policemen and improve black schools. This platform earned Forward Dallas the support of the black Progressive Voters League as well as the white working class.

Bridges (1997) argues that at the apogee of big city reform, 1960, in Austin, Phoenix, and Albuquerque, support for the reform candidates and turnout were directly related to the wealth and whiteness of a neighborhood. Table 3.5 shows the results of her analysis.

Table 3.5: Reform support by neighborhoods

	% white	% turnout	% vote for winner
Austin			
Affluent	91.7	26.8	70
Middle income	87.6	18.3	47
Low income	76.5	9.8	52
Poor	21.4	12.3	23
Phoenix			
Affluent	98.2	20.7	83
Middle income	97.2	18.5	71
Low income	83.1	10.1	58
Poor	40.0	10.0	50
Albuquerque			
Affluent	93.7	25.9	60
Upper-middle income	91.2	30.1	53
Middle income	80.8	15.4	43
Low income	57.3	19.4	33
Poor	29.7	19.3	41

In sum, reformers consolidated power with a dedicated following of affluent, white homeowners supportive of the business agenda promoted by the new governments while poor and working-class voters remained peripheral. Whereas machines were forced to compete by increasing the size of the electorate, reformers worked to keep the electorate small and homogenous. In San Jose, as in other reform cities, the demographics of the dissenting community changed over time. At the turn of the twentieth century it was laborers, Asian immigrants, and the illiterate that were excluded from participation. By the end of the twentieth century, those peripheral to the process were Mexican Americans, residents of small neighborhoods, and environmental activists. Throughout, the core of the coalition remained stable.

Nativism was one of the defining features of the Progressive movement in California, and a leading San Jose reformer became one of its loudest voices. In 1905 Everis Anson "Red" Hayes, San Jose's congressional representative and co-owner of the *San Jose Mercury Herald,* made the first ever anti-Japanese speech before the United States House of Representatives. He argued that "if the Japanese are a menace to the peace and progress of the Pacific Coast in a competitive sense. . . . as a menace they should be very much more feared in a racial sense. . . . there is no common association nor can there be between the yellow and white races" (quoted in Lukes and Okihiro 1985, 46). In 1916, a *Los Angeles Times* article reported that Hayes "brings up this question [a Japanese exclusion act] nearly every session" (*Los Angeles Times* 1916, 16). In 1920, both Hayes and his newspaper urged the adoption of California's Alien Land Law. A *Mercury Herald* editorial explained, "[I]n a very short term the state may be overrun by the peoples of the yellow races; and as in the case in the Hawaiian Islands, the white population will be in the humiliating position of having a limited authority both in the direction of industries and agricultural matters" (quoted in Lukes and Okihiro 1985, 58). Nonetheless, Japanese immigrants became an established part of the agricultural community in San Jose, and many returned to the area after being released from World War II internment. According to the 1940 census, San Jose had 165 Japanese farm operators and 4,049 Japanese residents, 6 percent of the total San Jose population (Matthews 2003; Lukes and Okihiro 1985).

In the California statehouse, Progressives openly attacked Mexican and Chinese immigrants, calling for restrictive immigration quotas and new election laws to prevent their participation. San Jose's reform newspapers published inflammatory articles about the "hordes" of "Japs" "crawling" through the city, and organized a rally to encourage drastic reductions in the number of Chinese immigrants allowed to enter the country (San Jose Commission 1985). In addition to the legal restrictions on immigrant participation, San Jose's leaders took informal steps to exclude the predominately immigrant agricultural workers from city life. As migrant workers, Mexican, Chinese, and Japanese laborers were the targets of changes to the timing of elections, newly scheduled for just prior to the start of the picking season.

World War II brought thousands of Mexican American workers to San Jose. They settled in working-class neighborhoods close to the canneries and orchards. By 1940 the city directory listed 5,337 people with Spanish surnames, about 8 percent of the city population. By 1950 the community had grown to 16,874, nearly 18 percent of the total population (Matthews 2003).[7] The Latino community and other minorities played virtually no role in political life. One member of the reform coalition in San Jose bluntly explained in an off-the-record interview that minorities would never be part of the governing coalition:

> If you're gonna choose up sides, the minorities always are gonna lose. It takes the white middle class to have the time and the money and the talent to solve problems. And what's San Jose if it isn't white, middle class to the core—semi-redneck, conservative, non-integrated—educated yes—that's the most dangerous kind.

In Austin, reform leaders tended to "leave [Mexicans] alone" (H. Stone, Price, and K. Stone 1937, 18) since their vote was negligible. African Americans constituted a much larger portion of the population, but reformers felt "it was not worth while to campaign in the Negro neighborhoods" because "it was too hard to explain the theory of city manager government to them" (H. Stone, Price, and K. Stone 1937, 19). Reform opponents in Austin, on the other hand, invested a great deal of time and energy into mobilizing the African American vote (albeit without relinquishing their racist views). One leader explained, "We get the nigger votes by going down there and talking nigger talk. By that I don't mean talking down to them, I mean talking up to them" (quoted in H. Stone, Price, and K. Stone 1937, 19). Similarly, in Dallas reform opponents courted the African American vote and won elections in 1935 and 1937 before reformers organized their nonpartisan slating committee.

There was also a class slant to reform coalitions. San Jose reformers sought to minimize the influence of laborers in city politics by closing charter reform meetings to labor representatives and abolishing district elections. The weak machine that existed in San Jose prior to the ascent of reform was backed by labor and the "nationality vote, especially Italian" (Thorpe 1938, 9). It maintained control through its heavy support from the first and fourth wards, home of dilapidated business areas, immigrant communities, and poorer residential sections. Reformers sought to eliminate the influence of these wards by promoting a change to citywide elections. They succeeded by campaigning loudly against the machine's association with "illegal Chinese lotteries, unlicensed liquor houses, a capricious policy of street improvement and political discrimination in the supervision of business affected with the public interest" (Thorpe 1938, 9). In Austin the working class supported reform opponents throughout the 1920s and 1930s. The politicians they elected to office "were considered distinct political liabilities to the city by those who established city manager government" (H. Stone, Price, and K. Stone 1937, 17). Through this process of courting the votes of white middle- and upper-class city residents and demobilizing poor and minority populations, reformers built solid core coalitions.

Reform Governing Coalitions

To organize successful governing coalitions, machine politicians focused on winning support from party workers and factional leaders, from business elites, labor unions, religious leaders, and county and state governments. Reformers faced different hurdles. They did not need the support of ward bosses, labor leaders, or religious organizations, and they already had the support of business elites. With the implementation of council manager charters they also gained a highly centralized bureaucracy. As one observer explained, "nobody had more power than an old San Jose city manager," (McEnery interview 2003). What they needed was support from state government and organization of their members. Relative to machine coalitions, reformers had a more difficult time mobilizing voters and disciplining politicians who presented challenges to building a governing coalition.

In many reform cities, securing the support of all party leaders became unnecessary with the passage of nonpartisan elections. Both of the times San Jose reform leaders organized (first to change the city charter and then to win control over the city council) the coalitions were bipartisan, made up of Progressive Republicans and Democrats (Arbuckle 1985; McEnery interview 2003). Reformers frequently benefited from the support of women's groups like the Women's Civic Study League in San Jose, whose support was useful because women had been granted the right to vote by a 1911 amendment to the California constitution. Women's clubs were also "extremely influential" in the passage of Dallas's city manager charter (H. Stone, Price, and K. Stone 1940, 286).

Reformers did not choose alliances with labor in municipal politics.[8] In 1908 the Union Labor Party, led by Walter Mathewson, managed to win a majority of San Jose's city council seats (Matthews 2003). This loss convinced reformers to pursue a new city charter, and prompted the movement for the abolition of the ward system. Unsurprisingly, the primary opposition to the charter changes came from labor, led again by Mathewson. He lobbied to have labor candidates included on the board of freeholders, responsible for drafting the new charter. The *San Jose Mercury Herald,* owned by reform leaders, argued that although Mathewson's candidates were "representative citizens," they were not fit to serve as freeholders because there was "evidence that they have not waked up to the fact that business methods can be applied to city government" (quoted in Ellsworth and Garbely 1976, 16). Similarly, the Dallas Citizens Council prohibited labor leaders from joining its ranks (Hanson 2003). By midcentury, when reformers regrouped, unions had become more threatening to the program of reform. In Austin, reformers' most formidable opponents, Emma Long and Ben White, actively supported labor issues. For instance, Long vociferously opposed the city council choice to award a building contract to an open-shop company for improving the city's power plant (Orum 1987). In response, Austin's reformers campaigned against Long at every election (Orum 1987; Bridges 1997).

Reformers also did not actively seek alliances with religious leaders in their cities. Where the mayor of Chicago would have been present at any significant religious convocation, this was not a role that San Jose's reform leaders appeared to play. This may have been a question of numbers. Between 1890 and 1936 the United States Census of Religious Bodies collected information on the membership of religious organizations at the county level. About 36 percent of Santa Clara County residents (where San Jose is located) were affiliated with a religious organization in 1936. In Cook County, Illinois (where Chicago is located), approximately 51 percent of the population was affiliated with a religious organization in the same year. Another possibility is that reformers had the support of religious organizations without having to make official overtures. In some cities, like Dallas, churches supported charter reform because "they wanted stricter enforcement of moral regulations than the police under commission government were providing" (H. Stone, Price, and K. Stone 1940, 286). In any event, evidence on the relationship between religious leaders and reformers is virtually nonexistent.

Reformers had a distinct advantage in organizing governing coalitions with economic elites. The leaders of municipal reform movements *were* the economic elite of their cities, which meant the hurdle was coordinating, not winning support. San Jose's reform organizations at the turn and middle of the century were populated with merchants, attorneys, industrialists, and property owners. The most influential leaders in the early reform movement were brothers Everis Anson and Jay Orley Hayes, wealthy lawyers turned orchardists, who purchased two of the city's three newspapers. They also owned and operated several gold mines and were active in social organizations like the Independent Order of the Odd Fellows. J. O. "Black" Hayes helped to organize the California Prune and Apricot Growers Association. Another prominent reformer, Elmer Chase, led the California Canners' League for twenty years. In Austin a caucus composed of members of the chamber of commerce, downtown retailers, construction interests, and developers organized to promote the reform agenda.

Reform coalitions everywhere counted the city newspaper owners as members and fervent supporters. When reform officials lost the support of this important group, as Dallas's Charter Association did in 1933 and 1935, they lost control of the city council. Following these elections Dallas reformers regrouped under the leadership of R. L. Thornton, who convened a "collection of dollars represented by men"—the heads of every major firm doing business in Dallas (Warren Leslie quoted in Hanson 2003 p53). Thornton excluded "lawyers, accountants, physicians, ministers, public officials, and labor leaders" by requiring an invitation for membership to the organization (Hanson 2003, 53). The founder of San Antonio's reform organization, the Good Government League, was also the president of the chamber of commerce.

Like their machine counterparts, reform leaders also needed the state government to grant approval of their programs. It is significant that all of the reform cities in this study are located in states that broadly granted the option for home rule charters early in their history. A number of the cities took advantage of the option as soon as it was offered. No doubt, many of the state constitutions were amended as a consequence of lobbying by municipal reform leaders. San Jose reform leader J. O. Hayes was elected to the state legislature and served as a member of the State Republican Central Committee. Hayes strongly supported Progressive changes to the state law that liberalized municipal control in the

Table 3.6: Reform monopoly success

City	Broad charter authority option	Reformers' first success at charter change	Reformers' second success at charter change	Organization	Monopoly begins
Austin	1913	1909	1924 (1953)	1953	1954
Dallas	1913	1907	1931	1941	1942
San Antonio	1913	1914	1951	1954	1955
San Jose	1892	1915	1940	1944	1945
Phoenix	1910	1913	1949	1949	1949

first decades of the twentieth century. In Hayes's 1918 campaign for governor, his platform argued that "the advances made during the past eight years should be preserved and perfected" (*Los Angeles Times* 1918, 12).

Table 3.6 displays the dates that home rule was granted by each state governing the reform cities, early reform victories through commission or manager governments, refinement of reform charters, and the date at which elites became organized. Having the freedom to change electoral rules and governmental structure aided the reformers in pursuit of their goals. Through changes in state law they also won the freedom to annex outlying territory and raise and spend money as they saw fit. In contrast, machine cities remained heavily constrained by state law throughout the twentieth century.[9]

Machines Organized in Response to Political Threats

In both machine and reform cities, a series of political and policy calamities crystallized the need for cohesion. Some scholars argue that the rise of cohesive machine organizations can be explained by the emergence of a professional class of politicians seeking careers in public life. For example, Shefter (1976) argues that the man who consolidated Tammany Hall, John Kelly, had fundamentally different goals than his predecessor, William Marcy Tweed. Where Tweed's quest for personal wealth and power epitomized a period of "rapacious individualism" (21), Kelly sought to build a centralized political party which he intended to lead. Scholars attribute a similarly ambitious program to Chicago's Anton Cermak. A first generation Czech immigrant with three years of formal education and a childhood marked by desperate poverty, Cermak is described by his biographer as "aggressive" and "ambitious" (Gottfried 1955, 235). He began his career in his early teens as a leader of neighborhood gangs of boys. According to Gottfried (1962), "[Cermak's] entire life effort was dedicated to his career. He appears to have had no other powerful needs or desires outside of . . . expanding his political power and prestige" (336). Cermak rose through the ranks of the Democratic Party incrementally, at each stage capturing the loyalty of a new set of followers until he had assembled the pieces for a powerful ethnic base. He was known as a detail-oriented workaholic with no tolerance for dissent (Green 1995a). His tenacity and focus are compared with that of his predecessors, bosses Roger Sullivan and George Brennan, who "were more interested in maintaining their own control over the party than they were in victory" (Allswang 1971, 152). Daley, too, was supposedly "motivated first and foremost by a drive to accumulate and retain power" (Cohen and Taylor 2000, 8).

However, explanations of party building that rely on the extraordinary leadership qualities or desire for power of individual men are incomplete. They fail to account for the emergence of such leaders and so offer no predictive power. While personalities are an integral component of understanding coalition organization, each of these men came to power in a larger context in which collective action offered elites and voters the opportunity to avoid loss of power and resist threats to policy goals.

In the period leading up the founding of the Chicago Democratic political machine, both parties were beset by internecine factional struggles. Between the 1890s and 1920s, powerful factions prevented Democratic unity. One faction allied famous aldermen "Bathhouse" John Coughlin and "Hinky Dink" Mike Kenna with mayors Carter Harrison I and II. A different faction, the Hopkins-Sullivan gas crowd, was an alliance between the private sector and other powerful aldermen. Legislators created personal followings held together through corruption. This engendered factious, divided councils that operated through logrolling. There was no real center of power, and the floor vote tended to follow the recommendation of committees and factional leaders (Simpson 2001). Factions were dominated by the "Gray Wolves" named by Lincoln Steffens for the "color of their hair and the rapacious cunning and greed of their natures" (Steffens [1904] 1957, 165). These "petty feudal chieftains" sought individual power and wealth, not success for the party (Charles Merriam quoted in Simpson 2001, 74). This rent-seeking behavior prevented the organization of a citywide coalition because factions could not be trusted to adhere to negotiated settlements; under-the-table deals with opponents were common. Similarly, in New

York the corruption during Tweed's reign stifled the organization of the Democratic Party because political alliances could be undermined by bribery (Shefter 1976).

Party factions were generally able to focus their energies on nominating a single mayoral candidate, but there were exceptions; throughout this period control over city government vacillated among factions and between parties. Chicago operated under plurality rule, and third-party contenders often appeared on the ballot. The average winner's vote share in mayoral elections between 1905 and 1927 was 49 percent of the total ballots cast. Mayoral incumbents (candidates and parties) averaged only 42 percent of the vote during this period.

In Chicago, as in other machine cities, struggles between the factions of the Democratic Party were played out in primary elections. When the fighting spilled into the general election, the Republicans won. Chicago Democrats controlled the mayoralty from the turn of the century through 1911, but lost the office to Republican "Big Bill" Thompson in 1915, 1919, and 1927 because of factional divisions. Those Democratic wings losing the nomination frequently supported Thompson (or abstained) in the general election (Gottfried 1962; Allswang 1971). The party was reunited in 1931 only after it was clear that no one faction could win alone. Bosses Kelly and Nash made keeping the peace among different factions of the party a high priority. They created a new "inner circle" with representatives from each wing to make decisions for the party (Green 1995a; Gosnell 1937). Similarly, after finally winning the mayoralty in 1908 Kansas City Democrats lost the seat and a number of other key patronage positions in 1910 because the Goat and Rabbit factions could not agree to work for the same candidates. This loss led to a negotiated settlement between the two factions. They agreed to unite in elections and share patronage equally once victory was achieved (Dorsett 1968). In every machine city included in this analysis, the election immediately preceding organization of the coalition was marked by a loss of power for the party.[10] Such losses spurred budding machine leaders to develop new tactics to ensure cooperation in pursuit of long-term dominance.

Centralization was also supported by emerging economic elites who stood to gain from stability in political and economic markets and limited political corruption. Coalition building in machine cities suppressed systems of "boodle" common in the preceding periods because emergent bosses kept a tight lid on fraud and bribery in order to protect the organization.[11] Shefter (1976) explains that in New York, Kelly's coordination efforts were promoted by specific sectors of the business community: lawyers, entrepreneurs who managed and owned firms, and merchants who dealt in markets that "depended upon the assumption of good faith among the parties" to function (29). These business sectors did not seek public contracts or franchises as their main source of income and so had little to gain from corrupt government. They needed stability in both political and economic markets in order to achieve fiscal success. These "swallowtails" were willing to absorb the costs of collective action because they sought to control government in pursuit of their goals (27). McCaffery (1992, 1993) makes a similar argument about Philadelphia's Republican organization. Utility interests preferred to deal with a centralized machine because it reduced the time and energy they spent securing favorable policies while increasing their certainty about the outcomes.

In Chicago, Cermak's organizing urge was also supported by stability-seeking business sectors. He was endorsed by the Chicago Association of Commerce, merchants, lawyers, bankers, and railroad interests, who worked together through the Businessmen's Committee for Cermak, which sponsored radio and print advertisements, contributed funds, and organized meetings and speakers (Gottfried 1962). However, unlike New York's economic elites, this group of business leaders did not initiate the centralization of the party. Throughout the period leading up to Cermak's mayoralty, divisions among the business elite meant that they "seldom . . . chose to act . . . in concert" to influence political outcomes (Bradley and Zald 1965, 162). This factionalization among the business elites contributed to divisions in the political arena. In Chicago, pressure for centralization came from below.

Among Chicago's immigrant populace, there *was* unity—against prohibition. The wet/dry debate animated city politics throughout the 1910s and 1920s. The state of Illinois began to enforce restrictions on drinking establishments in Chicago in 1906, which spawned angry protests among ethnic immigrants who saw it as a personal attack (Gottfried 1962). Within months these groups organized as the United Societies for Local Self Government to endorse political candidates and lobby city and state governments to protect the free sale and consumption of liquor. The spokesman for the organization was none other than Anton Cermak. His leadership role in this powerful pan-ethnic group gave him the political resources to become the leader of the Chicago Democratic organization. In 1922, following on the heels of the Eighteenth Amendment, Cermak's leadership of the wets and his strong immigrant support

vaulted him into the presidency of the Cook County Board of Commissioners—a position that offered him the patronage to consolidate the
Democratic coalition.

These diverse immigrant groups as well as the ward leaders and elected officials representing them stood to gain increased municipal benefits
by organizing. During the decades preceding the Depression, the Irish
had tightly controlled all of the party's best patronage positions and the
most important elected positions while their population numbers were
dwindling (Gottfried 1962). Population shifts in many machine cities
urged cooperation either to prevent a dominant group from losing power,
or, for underrepresented groups, to take advantage of growing numerical
strength. Not only had the European ethnic immigration pattern shifted
in Chicago, but also the increasing size of the African American population encouraged Democratic factions to bury their hatchets. It was
well known that Republicans had maintained a hold on the mayoralty
due to strong support in the black community, and throughout his reign
Thompson's administration was hostile to immigrant priorities. In his
1931 campaign for mayor, Thompson spewed a virulent anti-immigrant
message, famous for the taunt "Tony, Tony, where's you're pushcart at?
Can you imagine a World's Fair Mayor with a name like that?" (*New
York Times* 1931, 18). If they could unite, ethnic immigrants could put
municipal government to work for their communities.

The organization and triumph of Chicago's Democrats was aided by
the widespread belief that Thompson needed to be replaced. Thompson
had governed over perhaps the most corrupt, lawless, and extravagant
period in the city's history. An editorial in the *Chicago Tribune* argued:

> For Chicago Thompson has meant filth, corruption, obscenity, idiocy and
> bankruptcy. He has given the city an international reputation for moronic
> buffoonery, barbaric crime, triumphant hoodlumism, unchecked graft
> and a dejected citizenship. He nearly ruined the property and completely
> destroyed the pride of the city. He made Chicago a byword for the collapse
> of American civilization. In his attempt to continue this he excelled himself
> as a liar and defamer of character. (*Chicago Tribune* 1931, 14)

To make matters worse, the Depression dealt a strong blow to the city
of Chicago. In order to finance the government, city leaders borrowed
against future revenue that never arrived. In 1930 banks refused to lend
the government more money, and the city was unable to pay the salaries of its employees. An impromptu citizens committee arranged for the
workers' pay to be financed by subscription, and the state issued bonds

to cover the deficit (Reed 1931). Meanwhile, Cermak had convinced bankers to lend money to the county government to cover operating expenses. Cermak's economy-minded governance style made him an obvious favorite for a business community seeking responsible budgeting, and they actively supported his centralizing force.

Reformers Organized in Pursuit of Growth

If machines organized in response to political losses, changing demographics, and economic structures, reformers organized in pursuit of economic development; the threat they faced was to their policy goals. Reformers in the South and West inhabited a very different political context from their machine counterparts. In contrast to machine organizations that came to power in highly institutionalized, competitive political structures, reform organizations built the political system from a virtually clean slate with less vigorous opposition. In the Southwest the impetus for reform organization was a desire to elect office holders who would be more attentive to the goals of a certain segment of the cities' business classes. Due to the precarious economic position of their cities, municipal reformers in the Southwest sought to institutionalize new systems of governance that promoted growth and development. They argued that political structures that allowed for informal exchanges of benefits and corruption were too costly for their struggling cities. According to one observer, "the concerns of San Jose reformers . . . were centered, again and again, on the failure to attract new commerce; on the growth-inhibiting tax levels; on the failure to encourage new construction; on the lack of roads and efficient rail service; on the stultifying cost of corruption and inefficiency in every basic municipal service" (Eakins, 1976, 3).

Thus, municipal reformers began their ascent by seeking to implement commission and then council manager governments, civil service reform, and the elimination of districts and parties at the local level.[12] Not only did reformers argue that such changes would prevent corruption in politics but that they would have the further benefit of creating an efficient city government in the service of growth and development. However, because politics were not nearly so well organized in the South and West as they were in the East, reformers first had to create order in their systems.

Reformers in San Jose, Austin, and Phoenix organized in two distinct phases, first around the passage of new city charters and then to take control of city government. In these cities reformers imagined that institutional changes would be enough to serve their interests without continued activity in politics. According to a Social Science Research Council report on Austin, "business men [*sic*] felt that city manager government, even under a political council, would not be as dangerous to their interests as a less efficient type of administration . . . They are more than glad to have politicians assume the burden of service as long as their interests are not at stake" (H. Stone, Price, and K. Stone 1937, 15). When it became clear that this was not the case, that their interests were not going to be protected, reformers organized again to ensure officials would be elected who were more dependable. In other cities, like Dallas and San Antonio, organization happened once, with a group of city leaders coalescing to lobby for a new charter while promoting slates of office holders immediately or soon after.

In San Jose, a political coalition—"the gas-house ring," made up of utility interests, streetcar operators, and canneries, and backed by Southern Pacific's state organization—dominated local politics during the 1880s and 1890s (Thorpe 1938, 2). The primary focus of the gang's city government was protecting railroad and utility interests, not promoting community development. As a result the city had a large public debt and poor municipal services. At one point half of the city's streetlights were shut off to cut back on costs (Thorpe 1938). San Jose's expanding merchant class sought to redirect the city's energies toward economic progress. They wanted the growing city to have paved and lighted streets, improved transportation and sewer systems, and an efficient, modern government. In 1881 the owner and publisher of the *San Jose Daily Mercury* led a group of enterprising city leaders to electrify San Jose's streets. An enormous tower, 237 feet high and the only one of its kind in the world, was erected in the center of downtown. This, it was hoped, would eliminate the need for gas street lamps and put San Jose on the cutting edge of technological innovation. Needless to say, the gas merchants were not pleased by this development. But San Joseans glowed with pride at their new structure. The *San Jose Daily Herald* boasted, "This is a monument to progress and the diffusion of light in our midst" (December 13, 1881). Cities throughout California were envious. The *Los Angeles Times* (1882, O3) noted, "[T]he success of the project is heralded with unfeigned delight by all." Unfortunately, given the physics of the tower, light was only cast in an arc directly below the structure, insufficient to brighten even the downtown block. San Jose's leaders understood that development of the city required broader and more intense efforts at reform.

In 1896 San Jose merchant and professional leaders, including businessmen, orchardists, doctors, lawyers, and judges, organized the bipartisan Good Government League, garnered the support of dissident gashouse gang leaders, and successfully passed a revised charter weakening the power of the mayor and strengthening the bureaucracy (P. Trounstine and Christensen 1982; Herberich and Cannon 1976). But following the charter revision, the Good Government League disbanded, reform-minded candidates did not win elections regularly, and the council refused to cooperate with reform goals. In 1901 a series of bonds intended for municipal improvements failed to win enough votes to pass. Then, in 1908 a labor slate swept municipal offices, and the newly elected council announced its intention to employ union labor for all city projects (Matthews 2003). In 1912 the reformers regrouped and successfully garnered signatures of the requisite 15 percent of the electorate to force a vote on a new charter.[13] But when it finally came to the election, one observer notes, "[T]here was no effective citizens group active on behalf of the proposal and the balloting, devoid of the interest lent by a contest of personalities, brought only 35 percent turnout. The charter lost by 269 votes" (Thorpe 1938, 10). Clearly, implementing reform would require better organization and a more convincing charter.

A number of state-level changes led by Progressive governor Hiram Johnson, including the implementation of nonpartisan local elections, aided local reformers. A Progressive slate won control of San Jose city government in 1914 and proceeded to hire Berkeley professor of political economy and well-known Progressive, Thomas H. Reed, to draft a new charter.[14] For the 1915 election, reformers broadened their support base and passed a new charter, abolishing the office of the mayor, eliminating district elections, and institutionalizing power in the hands of the new city manager (Thorpe 1938).

Reformers' success was short lived, however. Following the 1916 election, the Charter Club, which had backed Reed's 1915 reforms, disbanded. Then, after the city manager began cleaning up the city in earnest, the newspapers, civic organizations, businessmen, and merchants, who had supported the reforms, began to voice new opposition to the changes. They complained about too much efficiency and lack of popular control in the new government. Worse, they felt that the manager was independent of their wishes. Both sides of the reform debate fell into disarray.

By 1920 those who had opposed the charter regained power. Charter supporters began a petition to recall two of the newly elected councilors, but dropped their petition when the council agreed to a compromise candidate for the new city manager. As the middle ground between reform and antireform forces, the new manager was not above making room for San Jose's small-time political bosses to run the show, machine-style, behind the scenes while still making sure most reform needs were being met. This negotiated agreement among city leaders continued for more than twenty years. Reformers did not come back to power until their goals were threatened.

In Austin reform forces organized in the mid-1920s to implement city manager government after it became clear that the commission form that had been in place since 1909 was inefficient and unresponsive to the demands of a growing city. They were successful in 1924, and after a lengthy court battle, the new charter became operational in 1926. But, similar to San Jose's experience, reform forces ceded control to more organized machine-style candidacies by 1933. The businessmen most supportive of reform found that political activity had the unpleasant consequence of "offending . . . patrons" and disqualified them from seeking city contracts (H. Stone, Price, and K. Stone 1937, 15). They also felt that while "politicians" should be "prevented from giving special favors to their henchmen," they did not want "impersonal or honest government as much as favors for themselves" (H. Stone, Price, and K. Stone 1937, 15). This led to a lack of interest in organizing against the politicians who maintained control throughout the 1930s and 1940s.

In Phoenix reformers organized and successfully passed a commission government with a city manager in 1913. Following this victory the city's manager colluded with politicians to award contracts, manage gambling and prostitution businesses, and control the police department. The 1915 *American Political Science Review* reported that the city manager "has been tried and found guilty of incompetence, extravagance and inefficiency" (Holden 1915, 562). In Dallas reformers organized to rid the city of dominance by the lawless Ku Klux Klan (Hanson 2003) and the ineffective commission-style government that governed the city between 1907 and 1931 (H. Stone, Price, and K. Stone 1940). Throughout this period business leaders of the community did not attempt to promote their agenda by nominating commissioners for office, but "[i]nstead . . . [they] persuaded whatever commissioners were in office to adopt their ideas" (H. Stone, Price, and K. Stone 1940, 272). Of course, this only worked as long as the commissioners could be convinced to support the leaders' plans, which was not easy, given the propensity for commissioners to work for their own reelection rather than for collective governance of the city.

Dallas reform leaders, dissatisfied with their part-time influence over municipal affairs, organized the Citizens Charter Association to ensure adoption of the city manager system. But their theory of governance dictated that reformers avoid the political fray and refrain from promoting candidates or issues to voters (H. Stone, Price, and K. Stone 1940). So, unsurprisingly, after their first victories, reformers lost to slates backed by former municipal employees, the white working class, and African Americans. Similar to the experience in Dallas, throughout the 1930s reformers in San Antonio organized informal committees to challenge machine candidates in local legislative races when the "commission ring" failed to deliver basic city services and the economy stagnated. The most prominent of these, the Wednesday Club, collapsed after a popular mayor nominated by the organization deserted the mission to reform city government (Johnson, Booth, and Harris 1983, 18).

Reformers Organize (Again) in Response to Political Threats

As in the machine cities, during the period prior to coalition consolidation, unity remained elusive for reformers. Factionalism, the overriding feature of these early governments, resulted primarily from the abolition of mayors and parties and the lack of organized political institutions. Divisions among economic elites also contributed to disunity. In San Jose throughout the 1930s fruit processors (cannery owners) and growers battled vigorously over the price of fruit, and both segments of the industry were prominent in the reform movement. This was no small problem for unity. Orchardists sought high prices for their products while packers wanted to purchase fruit as cheaply as possible. Meanwhile, a new group of leaders saw the city's reliance on agriculture as a severe constraint on economic vitality and growth. During economic downturns fruit could be eliminated from consumers' diets, making the city's economy heavily reliant on external economic factors. These emerging elites sought diversification in the economic base, expansion of the population, and attraction of new industry. As a result of these elite divisions, throughout the 1930s San Jose's officially nonpartisan government was dominated by loose factions of the Republican Party vying for power (San Jose Commission 1985; Hopper 1975).

In each of the reform cities, a series of setbacks to political and policy goals led to the coordination of coalitions that would dominate city government for multiple decades. Everywhere, reformers were worried about growth. From the turn of the century until the early 1920s, growth in Southwestern cities was sporadic, and cities frequently suffered decline. This began to change for some cities during the 1920s, but growth nearly stopped following the Great Depression. During and after the Second World War, some cities, like Austin and San Antonio, saw veritable explosions of population due to advantages like the presence of universities, federal investment, and open-shop laws. On the one hand, city leaders felt that continued economic health and political prowess depended on increasing populations. According to the leader of the businessmen's group in Austin, growth meant "[M]ore people, more money in circulation, more business" (quoted in H. Stone, Price and K. Stone 1937, 4). On the other hand, leaders worried that city governments with outdated charters and parochial governments would not be able to contend with rapid increases in the size of the community. Dips and spikes in the growth rate were part of the impetus for collective action in Dallas, San Jose, Austin, and San Antonio.

More worrisome than growth rates were the other social and economic forces wrought by the Depression and the war. In the decades immediately prior to the development of strong reform coalitions in San Jose and Austin, organized labor came to play an increasingly important role in the politics and economics of these cities. During the 1910s and 1920s, San Jose was not known as a particularly friendly place for labor, and reports of strikes were few and far between. In 1927 the *Mercury Herald* newspaper was boycotted by local labor for hiring nonunion construction labor, and the *Los Angeles Times* reported, "[R]ather than causing concern the action tends to establish more firmly the principles of the American plan [open-shop system of employment] in San Jose" (*Los Angeles Times* 1927, 5). During this period San Jose's economy was dominated by agriculture, both growing and canning. Until 1935 both types of work were excluded from worker protections and collective bargaining. As canning became more mechanized it was reclassified as industrial work and covered by the 1935 National Labor Relations Act. Organization of workers and confrontations escalated throughout the 1930s, which, no doubt, was cause for concern in San Jose's business community.

Mexican and Filipino pea, pear, and cherry pickers went on strike in the early 1930s (San Jose Commission 1985). Cannery workers struck during the summer of 1931 and then marched on city hall demanding release of those arrested in connection. Following these events the cannery workers were organized into the Cannery and Agricultural Workers Industrial Union. In 1934, 300 of San Jose's leading citizens formed the Growers' and Allied Industries Association to "protect growers, workers, and canneries" from "strikes instigated by Communist and radical agitators." Days after the first meeting, vigilantes raided Communist "hot spots" and beat a number of radicals (*Los Angeles Times* 1934, 15; Matthews 2003, 62). In 1936 San Jose's laundries were closed by striking workers.

In 1933 San Jose became the focus of national news as another wave of violence swept the city. Two (white) men kidnapped and brutally murdered Brooke Hart, son of a local department-store owner. Following the arrest of the two criminals, a vigilante mob battered down the doors of the jail with iron pipes, yanked the murderers from their cells, dragged them to the city's central park, and lynched them. In the days leading up to the violence, the Santa Clara County sheriff repeatedly asked the state government and San Jose leaders for reinforcements; both refused. Only two San Jose policemen were dispatched to the scene. No one has been able to certify who gave the order to the San Jose police and fire brigades to hold back; one historian reports that neither the fire chief nor the city manager could be located on the night the mob stormed the jail (Farrell 1992). However, it was clear that San Jose's unofficial political boss, Charles Oneal, was intimately involved. Eventually, the sheriff convinced the police chief from Oakland to send officers. At the last minute, "deputy sheriffs, police, and hastily sworn in peace officers threw up barricades and prepared to use machine guns, sawed-off shotguns and tear gas bombs" to stop the crowd, but were unsuccessful (*Los Angeles Times* 1933a, 1).

In response to the violence, California governor James Rolph proclaimed that the lynching was "the best lesson that California has ever given the country" (quoted in the *Los Angeles Times* 1933b, A4). Newspapers across the country condemned the violence and the governor's stance. While there is no direct evidence to indicate that this is the case, it is not farfetched to believe that city leaders would have been alarmed at the lack of law-enforcement control and embarrassed by the negative publicity wrought by these events. Throughout the process, the *San Jose Mercury Herald* (owned by reform leaders) had been "San Jose's foremost voice for moderation" (Farrell 1992, 186).

During the late 1930s, San Jose's cannery unions became more vocal and politically active, registering an increasing number of voters and making demands on city hall (Matthews 2003). At about this same time the demographic makeup of the cannery workforce began to shift from predominately Italian and Portuguese to Mexican American and Mexican immigrants, as ethnic Anglo workers found new job opportunities made available by the war economy (San Jose Commission 1985; Pitti

2003). According to one historian of San Jose's Latino community, the city "soon became a startling hotbed of white and Mexican coalitional politics" (Pitti 2003, 111). During the late 1930s and early 1940s, the union representing these workers began to lobby city hall to improve conditions in the East Side barrio, home to Santa Clara County's largest population of Latinos. They sought paved streets, increased police and fire protection, and a community park (Pitti 2003). Given the informal political arrangements that governed the city at the time, it seems likely that these demands might have been supported by city hall. In 1936 the city council used WPA funds to build a recreation center for Mexican and Puerto Rican children in East San Jose. Further cause for worry arose in 1938, when San Jose's municipal employees unionized (*Christian Science Monitor* 1938, 4). Democratic registration went from 18 percent in 1930 to 53 percent in 1940 in Santa Clara County, where San Jose was the largest municipality (Matthews 2003, 79). In 1941 a massive strike in the canneries brought production to a halt. All of these changes were likely seen as threatening to reform goals.

While clearly giving rise to a more unified labor voice, the Depression also increased unity among San Jose's economic elites. The argument for diversification of the economy had been won, and by the early 1940s, growers began to uproot their own trees (Matthews 2003). The Depression had increased California's reliance on property taxes for revenue (the state had no income tax). For many growers the increased burden meant foreclosure. Canneries in the area also reported heavy losses during the early 1930s. In 1932 nearly 20 percent of the city was unemployed. With all of the upheaval throughout the late 1930s and early 1940s and the increasingly similar objectives in the business community, the coordination of San Jose's civic elite in 1944 makes perfect sense. Once organized, they swept elections to the city council.

Elsewhere in the Southwest, similar unrest and political setbacks led to the organization of reform coalitions. In 1933 a review of the city manager system in Austin reported that "organized labor . . . is an insignificant force" (H. Stone, Price, and K. Stone 1937, 20). This changed following the end of the Depression. In 1948, a wing of the Democratic Party, sympathetic with labor and the New Deal, elected Emma Long to the city council by establishing precinct organizations and mobilizing voters. In 1949 and 1951, African American candidates ran for office. Neither won a seat, but the 1951 candidate polled nearly 25 percent of the vote. A second labor-friendly candidate, Ben White, was elected to the council in 1951. In this same year, a professor of government from one of Austin's black colleges began a fight against Jim Crow by demanding that the city's main library be integrated. He won by securing the votes of Long, White, and a third councilor, Stuart McCorkle, and went on to fight for integration of the fire department and the city's public pool. The inability of the anti-integrationist reform coalition to prevent this vote signaled that they did not have control over government decision making. Not intending to take these developments lightly, in 1952 the chamber of commerce and other business elites established the Good Government League of Austin, which worked to change the council electoral system,[15] and began coordinating slates of candidates.

Machine Strategies for Winning Offices

Once the environment in machine and reform cities provided the right mix of opportunity and threat, leaders organized for political action. They succeeded by mobilizing voters, defeating the opposition, disciplining politicians, and coordinating governing coalitions. However, machine and reform leaders achieved organization using different strategies, given their different political environments. The ascendancy of powerful, dominant coalitions in machine cities occurred in the midst of institutionalized fighting for control over city government among multiple factions and parties. Those who succeeded in this milieu were masters of inclusive coalition politics. Machines, reliant on preexisting ward organizations, which generated loyal electorates, focused on winning nominations, creating hierarchy, and turning out voters in support of their candidates. Reformers, reliant on suffrage restrictions, which narrowed the electorate, focused on nominating candidates for office, encouraging voters to cast ballots in support of them, and institutionalizing their gains through charter changes.

For machine politicians, mobilizing voters was a component of the party system that existed when they came to power. The spoils system, developed during the Jacksonian period, predated the rise of most of the urban machines in this analysis. By the time consolidation became an option, political parties and ward organizations already possessed a strong presence. High turnout was guaranteed through a combination of face-to-face canvassing, the maintenance of relationships with voters in between elections, and the incentive structure of the parties. Chicago machine politician Jacob Arvey was once quoted as saying, "[P]eople wonder why we won. It was because we were active almost every day of the year" (Simpson 2001, 98). In the years preceding consolidation, machine leaders focused on increasing their vote totals to win elections.

Competing against factions and other parties, local Democratic Party organizations set records in increasing the size of the electorate with naturalization and registration mills. From 1901 to 1909, the total number of ballots cast in New York's mayoralty race increased only 4 percent. During the following decade, from 1909 to 1921, the vote increased 100 percent. A look at census figures suggests that the rate at which foreign-born men became citizens significantly increased during this period. Between 1900 and 1910, the population of foreign-born men over the age of twenty-one increased about 54 percent. During this same period, the population of naturalized white males over the age of twenty-one declined by about 18 percent. Between 1910 and 1920, this dramatically reversed; the foreign-born male population increased by about 12 percent, while the number of naturalized white males increased by 88 percent.[16] In Chicago, newly arriving southern and eastern European immigrants were wooed by both parties throughout the first decades of the twentieth century. The number of voters in Chicago rose from 328,188 in 1905 to 1,148,111 in 1931, a 250 percent increase.[17] In 1931 the parties managed to bring 82 percent of registered voters to the polls.

Pittsburgh's electorate grew by nearly 120 percent between 1924 and 1936. Between 1930 and 1936, Democratic voter registration jumped from 5 percent to 56 percent of total registered voters, tipping the city from heavily Republican to marginally Democratic. The 1914 election in Kansas City, the moment before Boss Pendergast consolidated power, saw a 74 percent turnout of registered voters. Dorsett (1968) explains that the impressive showing was the result of an unprecedented get-out-the-vote drive by the city's influential politicians. Politicians were similarly active in New Haven. According to a citywide survey, 60 percent of all respondents had been contacted by local political campaigns prior to the 1955 city election, compared to only 10 percent contacted prior to the 1956 presidential election (Wolfinger 1974). In every machine city, political workers provided services to make voting easier, such as offering transportation to the polls, babysitting, and providing chairs for waiting in the long election lines.[18]

As explained above, the population in these cities was diverse. In Chicago's 1923 mayoral election, Allswang (1971) calculated that 25 percent of the electorate was native born to native parents, 6 percent was African American, 39 percent was native white born to foreign parents, and 30 percent was naturalized foreign-born citizens. In 1930 approximately 65 percent of the population was a first- or second-generation immigrant. With no single group representing more than 12 percent of the total, many different constellations were possible. Cermak drew on this diversity to undermine the power of the Irish bosses, who had prevented unity throughout the 1920s. Similarly, Shefter (1976) reports that in New York, the period preceding machine consolidation, from the mid-nineteenth century through the Progressive Era, was one in which a number of different winning coalitions were possible. Ethnic loyalties were highly sought after in many machine cities and the "ethnically balanced ticket" was one strategy enterprising politicians used to secure them (Erie 1988, 102). For example, in Chicago's 1912 Democratic primary, the one faction slated "two Germans (one Jewish), two Bohemians, one Pole, an Englishman, and three Irish" for the nine major county offices (Erie 1988, 102). Furthermore, Shefter (1976) argues that Tammany generated ethnic loyalty through a network of neighborhood organizations that brought voters into the machine and helped to suppress divisions of economic class. Machine politicians also championed immigrant issues in elections. For example, Cermak, Chicago's first and only immigrant mayor, won notoriety and a strong ethnic base by fighting prohibition at all levels of government.

With such large electorates, the only way to consolidate power in machine environments was to organize the factions into a single structure. Leaders accomplished this by creating rigid hierarchies within their parties and disciplining politicians with their control over the electorate. Machine parties were organized in a pyramid with hundreds of precinct workers at the bottom and one or a few party leaders at the top. Lower-level party workers were rewarded with material benefits for themselves and their voters, and promotion within the party was based on the size of the vote achieved. In order to calm tensions among the diverse ethnic groups included in the Democratic coalition of the 1920s, Cermak institutionalized civil service. He intended to depersonalize and depoliticize government operations and to open decision making to more voices (Green 1995a). This encouraged groups that rarely trusted each other to work together. Following in Cermak's footsteps, machine leaders Edward Kelly and Patrick Nash perfected the Democratic organization in Chicago by establishing well-defined procedures for advancement and demotion. This offered each party member the opportunity to rise through the ranks, and it further encouraged cooperation. Party functionaries were required to give estimates of their vote totals prior to an election, and their performance was judged by this guess. A worker had to be careful not to estimate too high a turnout because he might lose valuable patronage or other benefits, or possibly face demotion. If his estimate was too low, the worker might be judged out-of-touch with his precinct and fired just the same. In every machine city, block captains reported to precinct captains who reported to ward bosses who reported to party leaders (Biles 1995). This bureaucratized structure centralized decision making, prevented the appearance of favoritism, and encouraged diverse groups to work for common goals.

Though machines operated with clear lines of authority, power was delegated almost completely, so that within his ward, the ward boss was given absolute authority to dispense patronage and select party workers at lower levels. William Dawson, Chicago's black submachine boss, was said to have controlled nearly a quarter of a million votes when Daley was first elected to office. These submachines were another mechanism to accommodate diverse interests within the party. In Kansas City sixteen ward leaders within the city and eight township leaders in the outlying county functioned as sub-bosses. A large percentage of these leaders and the precinct captains who reported to them were actually part of a rival faction within the Democratic Party. Pendergast allowed the "Rabbits" to operate within the confines of the larger organization because without their cooperation, the local Republican Party dominated elections. In return for such autonomy, parties demanded unflinching support for their chosen candidates from subleaders (see Rakove 1975 for examples from Chicago).

Not all power was delegated in machines though. Nominations for office were tightly controlled at the top of the hierarchy. Bosses controlled party caucuses and conventions, and when they had to, they controlled direct primaries with patronage votes in order to guarantee that the nominee for office was of their choosing. In Philadelphia, Boss Israel W. Durham governed over changes in the party rules that allowed him to centralize power, dictating who sat on the nominating committees (McCaffery 1992). In Chicago, Daley's dedication to reviewing *every* new city hire testifies to his caution in "making" someone who could "unmake" him (Green 1995b, 155). He reportedly controlled about 35,000 patronage positions (*Newsweek*, April 5, 1971, 82). And Daley's decision to continue as party chair after he was elected mayor allowed him to control the ascent of potential competitors. By the 1960s the central Democratic Party organization could decide on the slate of candidates and force precinct captains to go along (Simpson 2001). In 1975, when Daley faced primary competition, the Democratic Party supported only his candidacy.

In the period prior to consolidation in machine cities, maverick politicians could run for office and win with a large personal following. New

York's Democrats were particularly beset by this problem. Until Tammany's nomination was both necessary and sufficient for election, the party remained divided. Shefter (1976) attributes Tammany's increased control over politicians to its increased control over the electorate after developing a network of political clubs that brought voters into the machine. In New Haven, leaders Richard Lee and John Golden won a series of primary elections against a rival faction, stripped the rivals of patronage, and consolidated the machine (Wolfinger 1974). In Chicago, Cermak's overthrow of the Brennan faction was made possible because he appealed to so many voters. When one faction could clearly command a majority of the votes, it won control of the party.

Centralization also required leaders to be ruthless about expulsion for failure to conform to the machine's will. Shefter (1976) explains that New York's John Kelly chose this path for the organization. Members were barred and party committees reorganized when ward leaders did not work for Kelly's chosen candidates. All decisions of the machine's subunits became subjected to review by the central leadership. After Kelly's death, Richard Croker continued the unification of the party, including centralizing the system of graft so that public and private officials answered to only the top leaders. Similarly, in Chicago both Cermak and Daley were well known for their tendency to punish dissidents within their organizations. During Daley's first years as mayor, he played the role of a broker. He cooperated with the council and took an active, hands-on role in governance. As his power and control mounted, Daley became more intolerant of dissent and disagreement. He shouted down opposition on the council and, when all else failed, turned off the offending alderman's microphone (Royko 1971).

In some machine cities politicians were disciplined through negotiated agreements. In Kansas City, once it became clear that a divided Democratic Party would continue to lose elections, the two factional leaders compromised. The wings would agree on a candidate, and the winner would divide the spoils of office equally. This became known as the Fifty-Fifty Accord (Larsen and Hulston 1997). Cermak was also known to share powerful positions with both Republican opponents and losing wings of his own party. According to Green (1995a) this "signaled an end to alternative routes of political power within the local Democratic party structure" (102).

These institutional features—a well-oiled party organization, powerful hierarchies, and a system of incentives—allowed politicians in machine cities to win election to office by turning out massive numbers of voters while maintaining control over precisely who won elections.

Building their organizations and utilizing strategies for unity were key components of monopoly control.

Reform Strategies for Winning Offices

By the time reformers consolidated their organizations, states in the South and West had enacted suffrage restrictions. This made the electorate much more manageable than it was in machine cities, and reduced the possible constellations of winning coalitions. However, organizing in such an environment was not easy. Reform charters and Progressive action at the state level made local elections nonpartisan, and in some cities experience with commission governments left political arenas factionalized. Reformers had no obvious mechanism for coordination, but in order to monopolize government they needed to mobilize voters and unify action among elected officials. To do this, municipal reformers organized groups of concerned citizens into party-like coalitions that slated candidates. These organizations were much less structured than the hierarchical coalitions in machine cities, but they served a similar purpose.

By the start of World War II, nearly thirty years had passed since the passage of San Jose's final reform charter in 1915. During this period elites were relatively satisfied with the status quo in which different interests in the city were accommodated by the city manager. In response to the unrest of the 1920s and 1930s, this began to change. Literally, the sons and grandsons of the earlier reform movement constituted a new generation of elites that emerged to take power and pursue development on a much grander scale. In the early 1940s, Harvey Claude Miller (son of Albert Harvey Miller, who had been the barber of the Hayes brothers)[19] organized a group of elites into the San Jose Progress Committee in order to recapture the city for the forces of reform (Lundstrom 1993). The committee that Miller organized was a bipartisan group that benefited from the added support of the old machine-style boss Louis Oneal. The first step the committee took was to oust the city manager, Charles Goodwin, from office.

Because they could not get enough support on the city council to fire the manager, the Progress Committee brought forward an initiative to amend the charter to require the manager to stand for biennial approval from the voters.[20] Although the amendment was opposed by two incumbent council members, it passed by a narrow margin of 11,009 votes to 10,415, with a turnout of 52 percent. In a further attempt to weaken the hold of the officials in power, a second initiative in the same election reduced the council's terms from six years to four years.[21] City manager Goodwin stood for his first voter approval in 1942 and won by a mere 500 votes out of nearly 19,000 ballots cast. Goodwin survived the political storm and remained in office until public outrage erupted over the inadequate use of personnel and equipment in fighting a fire at a local business. Goodwin resigned, and the council appointed John Lynch, who had served as the city clerk for Goodwin's entire time in office and was clearly not the choice of the reform faction trying to oust incumbents. In 1944 six of seven city council seats became vacant on the city council from a combination of the usual terms ending and a number of members leaving for military service in the war (Lundstrom and Zapler 2003). This time the Progress Committee left nothing to chance, carefully selecting a slate of dedicated reform candidates and campaigning hard for their election. Miller, still the head of the Progress Committee, convinced Al Ruffo, Ernie Renzel, Ben Carter, Fred Watson, Jim Lively, and Roy Rundle to run as reform nominees (Lundstrom and Zapler 2003). Although the reform slate was swept into office, the antireform manager Lynch won his vote of confidence by the people. In 1946 the new reform council and the Progress Committee campaigned for Lynch's removal, and won. The council appointed an interim manager in 1948 and then, in 1950, in a close four-to-three vote, they installed Anthony "Dutch" Hamann to the crucial post (P. Trounstine and Christensen 1982).[22]

Once the reformers organized effectively, they became unstoppable. Even when temporary opposition cropped up on the council, the reform majority held firm. The council and the media downplayed disputes and rarely reported on debate or discussion in the council. San Jose's Progress Committee represented a new movement in reform cities toward more organized competition for office and policy in which elites would nominate slates for council elections, hold meetings to determine the course of the city, and mobilize voters when needed.

Nonpartisan slating groups (NPSGs), like San Jose's Progress Committee, were small, private organizations that eschewed candidates who put themselves forward, nominating instead local civic leaders and businessmen. They were the vehicle by which reformers could take advantage of the institutional setting that their reform charters provided. NPSGs campaigned for slates and tickets, not individuals, and ran on platforms offering to "serve the interests of the community as a whole," (Ellsworth and Garbely 1976, 12). They promised efficiency and lower taxes, government by businessmen rather than politicians, bureaucratic authority, and an end to politics.

In many cities, the NPSG was institutionalized after reformers or their charters did poorly at the polls. Dallas's Citizen's Charter Association, founded by businessman Robert Thorpe, began fielding candidates and rallying the electorate after the reformers lost elections in 1935 and 1937. Dallas's NPSG was maintained in order to ensure that the "right type of men" were nominated and elected (Fairbanks 1990, 127). The Charter Association had a campaign manager and "lieutenants" in fifty-nine precincts throughout the city that made phone calls and held meetings in support of the organization. According to a report on the Dallas city manager system, the Charter Association organized "a 'flying squadron' of speakers . . . to make brief addresses at industrial plants and firms." The association asked these businesses to call workers together on company time, "and not a single one refused." The report explains that "the plants did not extend the same privilege to the opponents of the charter" (H. Stone, Price, and K. Stone 1940, 286).

In Austin the work of educating the electorate about the benefits of charter reform was begun by the city chamber of commerce, which later went on to form the Council Manager's Club to guide the new charter's passage. The Council Manager's Club was governed by a chairman (the secretary of the chamber of commerce), an executive committee of thirty-five, and a finance committee to raise funds for the campaign. Neighborhood meetings and rallies were held, and block and precinct organizations were formed to mobilize voters (H. Stone, Price, and K. Stone 1937). Following the passage of the charter, this organization disbanded, but was reorganized in 1953 to regain control over the city after labor candidates won two seats on the council (Orum 1987).

San Antonio's Citizen's Committee lost its first attempt at charter reform and, on its second try, avidly pursued votes in a "highly targeted and personalized strategy aimed at motivating and turning out a known electorate" (Sanders 1991 quoted in Bridges 1997, 118). Their plan worked, tripling turnout in important precincts. Following the adoption of the new charter, the Citizen's Committee disbanded, soon to be replaced by the Good Government League when reformers realized that maintaining control over the city council was just as important as the passage of the charter itself. Some NPSGs took a page out of the book of machine organizations. In Albuquerque, reformers developed an effective precinct organization for turning out votes in support of the right candidates, hierarchically organized as a "nonpartisan political party."[23]

So, while reformers everywhere railed against the evils of the party system, they quietly but unabashedly formed nonpartisan slating groups to carry out critical party tasks: controling nominations, mobilizing the electorate, increasing name recognition, and offering cues to voters. Through NPSGs municipal reformers succeeded in implementing charters that reorganized city government in pursuit of progress, and then elected candidates who shared these goals. By the 1960s, in San Jose and other cities in the Southwest, political and economic elites, the majority of the electorate, and those elected and appointed to office all agreed on the priorities for the city; reformers were poised to take advantage of their monopoly.

Conclusion

Organization of coalitions was the final step in establishing political monopolies. In machine and reform cities alike this task posed a formidable challenge. The vote base of each monopoly coalition was determined to a large extent by the composition of the potential electorate. In machine cities the support of white, foreign-stock, working-class residents was necessary to win elections during the machine's rise to power. Sensible politicians invested significant time and energy mobilizing these voters. In reform cities the coalition base tended to be white, middle-class residents who shared the developmental focus of reform regimes. In both types of cities, elites who held resources by virtue of their elected offices, economic power, or social influence were also key components of the coalition. Both machines and reform coalitions consolidated when groups of politicians faced threats to political or policy goals. Machines built hierarchical parties, and reformers established NPSGs to organize voters and elites into coalitions that could dominate government.

The different paths to coordination taken by machine and reform organizations are indicative of the many possibilities available for achieving cooperation. Reformers' unity was driven by similar ideological approaches to governance among elites and institutional structures that limited the size and composition of the electorate, while machines relied on strict party control and penetrating neighborhood organizations. But there are other possible paths to coordination that fit neither the machine nor the reform model—like the dominance of a coalition in a company town (as Anaconda Copper in Butte, Montana) or the cohesiveness of classic suburban politics driven by likeminded voters and elites (as in Banfield and Wilson's [1963] understanding of Winnetka, Illinois). When these alternative approaches to organization are marked by strategies of bias, they represent additional subtypes of monopolies. But a well-organized, dominant government might be an example of a responsive regime if its hold on city government is a result of attending to the preferences of voters.

Aside from different approaches to coordination, coalitions vary in the degree to which they achieve cooperation. The coalitions analyzed here all represent relatively high levels of coordination, though there is variation among these cities. Machines, on the whole, had more structured organizations both to connect with voters and to link politicians, while reform coalitions tended to be looser and more fluid. Yet even within the machine and reform categories some coalitions had higher degrees of coordination than others. In San Jose, the reform coalition secured cooperation from all but a handful of councilors during the dominance period, but in Austin reform opponents frequently captured between 20 and 40 percent of the council seats. In all of the examples here, the coalition under examination achieved the cooperation of at least a majority of elected officials and a sufficient number of private elites to be able to make and carry out city policy, setting the stage for monopoly control. But down the road the differences in organizational choices and strength affected the stability of these coalitions.

Establishing Political Monopolies

FOR FORTY-FOUR YEARS Richard Daley's faction of the Democratic Party governed Chicago with virtually no viable opposition. He regularly raked in more than three quarters of the total mayoral ballots in general elections. Likewise, between 1944 and 1978, Dutch Hamann's growth coalition dominated San Jose municipal government and policy-making process without challenge. At the height of the monopoly's power, council candidates commonly received 70 to 90 percent of the vote. During this period, only a handful of councilors were elected outside of the ruling group.

Though similar in their effects, the San Jose and Chicago monopolies achieved these outcomes using different strategies. At the turn of the century, San Jose's reform leaders had implemented a city manager charter with nonpartisan, at-large elections; by midcentury the electorate had shrunk to a small proportion of the city's population. But elites were plagued by disorganization until economic downturns, a slowing of the population boom, a large influx of Mexican American workers, and increased union activity inspired them to organize. In Chicago a patronage-based political system had regularized competition for elected offices after the turn of the century. Parties competed for the votes of the thousands of immigrants making Chicago their new home. During the 1920s, the city was rife with corruption as politicians became the protectors of the underworld. But the would-be Democratic machine remained factionalized until the opportunity to unite behind an anti-Prohibition candidate emerged. After having lost the mayoralty to an eccentric, charismatic leader, and with the Irish share of the population dwindling, Democrats understood that to dominate the city they would need to build a strong, diverse organization.

Should these histories be categorized as isolated vignettes or as indications of monopoly patterns elsewhere? By looking carefully at the claims presented in chapter 1, this chapter provides evidence that they should be viewed as the latter. My argument begins with the assertion that incumbents have incentives to increase their probability of maintaining power by biasing the system in their favor. I propose that if a coalition can effectively coordinate voters and elites in a biased system, the incumbent group can dominate governance for an extended period of time. This chapter asks whether or not the combination of bias and organization is actually sufficient to guarantee dominance, and under what conditions the combination is most likely to occur. In other words, do bias and organization work to increase the coalition's chances at reelection? When are monopolies most likely to arise, and what strategies are they likely to use?

Using a new collection of city electoral returns, I show first that implementing biasing mechanisms and coordinating a coalition reduces competition for office and increases the likelihood of victory for incumbents. Then I use census data to investigate the ways in which political context dictates the type of monopoly that emerges. Machine and reform cities were characterized by different political environments and demographics. I demonstrate that where machines came to dominate by relying on patronage, the cities were characterized by weak institutional control and large poor populations. In contrast, cities dominated by reformers using suffrage restrictions and vote dilution were characterized by a high degree of institutional control and more homogenous populations. Finally, I analyze the environmental factors that increase the likelihood that a coalition will establish a monopoly. I find that changes in political context that threaten coalitions' electoral prospects or policy goals instigate the development of monopolies. In sum, the quantitative data offer evidence that mirrors the qualitative narratives presented in chapters 1 through 3.

Literature on Urban Elections

There is relatively little work on the factors that contribute to reelection and margin of victory in urban elections across both time and place, but some literature has explored the factors that affect candidate success in specific local elections. In studies of a number of different cities, scholars have determined that incumbency plays a strong role in electoral success (Krebs 1998; Prewitt 1970; Lieske 1989). Krebs (1998) and Lieske (1989) also find that support from the incumbent party significantly increased candidates' vote share in Chicago and Cincinnati council elections. Davidson and Fraga (1988) analyze the effect of nonpartisan slating groups in four reformed Texas cities, and find that candidates nearly always won when they were slated by the organization.

Candidate experience (Krebs 2001; Merritt 1977) and the possession of certain occupational/educational credentials (Lieske 1989) can increase candidate success as well. Scholars have argued that this is likely to be especially true in a nonpartisan setting. A number of early studies found that nonpartisan elections resulted in a Republican "bias" on the city council (Hawley 1973; Lee 1960; O. Williams and Adrian 1959) and enhanced the election prospects of high-socioeconomic-status candidates (Welch and Bledsoe 1988), which may indicate an incumbency advantage. Work by Schaffner, Streb, and Wright (2001) tests this connection directly and finds that nonpartisan elections enhance incumbent reelection chances. Additionally, Lieske (1989) finds that a candidate's previous vote total is a significant predictor of a candidate's total vote in nonpartisan, at-large council elections in Cincinnati.

Scholars have also determined that campaign spending is positively correlated with reelection (Krebs 1998; Lieske 1989; J. Lewis, Gierzynski, and Kleppner 1995), as are endorsements from local media (Krebs 1998; Stein and Fleischman 1987; Gierzynski and Breaux 1993).[1] Lascher (2005) finds that incumbents are more likely to be reelected and win by larger margins in bigger cities.

A number of scholars have also found that race and ethnicity can play a dominant role in candidate success (Kaufmann 2004; Herring and Forbes 1994; Lieske and Hillard 1984). Other scholars (Keiser 1997, 2003; Grimshaw 1992; Pinderhughes 1987; Orr 2003) have argued that the presence of machine or machine-like institutions severely hindered black candidates from winning the mayoralty in some cities, which may suggest that incumbents are more likely to win, but not necessarily. In a similar vein, scholars have assessed the effect of reformed structures on voting and elections, concluding that they contributed to the underrepresentation of racial and ethnic minorities and the poor (see Welch and Bledsoe 1988 for a review).

Classic scholarship on political machines generally suggests that machine candidates won elections with great consistency (Gosnell 1937; Miller 1968). However, there is no comparative work on machine politics that explicitly assesses whether organization candidates won reelection more consistently or by larger margins than other candidates. In some cases the assumption that machines were electorally dominant was not substantiated with any evidence (Shannon 1969; Banfield and Wilson 1963). In scholarship in which evidence is presented, winning reelection is commonly seen as a defining characteristic of the machine itself (which conflates the organization's tactics with their effects), or de-

tails are presented regarding machine strategies without direct analysis
of electoral outcomes.

Political Monopolies offers a different set of causal factors and measures of successful reelection. This chapter uses election data from nine
cities to analyze reelection patterns. Five of the cities—Chicago, Kansas
City, New Haven, New York, and Philadelphia—represent machine cities. The other four—Austin, Dallas, San Antonio, and San Jose—represent big-city reform politics. As explained in the introduction and the
appendix, these cities were selected on the basis of availability of election
returns. They epitomize the differences between machine and reform
politics and, thus, provide a hard test of the theory that these types of
regimes are theoretically similar. I find that in both types of cities, the
presence of a biased electoral system and a coordinated coalition decrease competition for office and increase the probability of reelection
for incumbents. These factors do affect electoral control.

Data Testing the Effects of Bias

To understand the factors that predict dominance, I estimate the effect of bias and organization on (1) electoral competition and (2) the
probability of incumbent reelection. In the first analysis, the dependent
variable is a measure of competitiveness—the *margin of victory*, the percentage of the vote gained by the winner with the lowest total minus
the percentage of the vote gained by the loser with the highest total. In
two candidate races, this is just the loser's vote subtracted from the winner's. In multimember races (where, for example, ten candidates compete for five seats), this measure provides a conservative estimate of the
winners' advantage because it captures the smallest margin of victory
won. For this analysis, each observation is an election in a given city. The
years included in the analysis are listed in table 4.1 below. To examine
incumbent reelection, I use data on the win/loss record of incumbent
candidates. The dependent variable is dichotomous, coded one if the
candidate won and zero if she or he lost. In these analyses observations
represent individual candidates.

The primary independent variable is the presence of bias and coordination. Chapters 2 and 3 provided a good deal of qualitative evidence
that coalitions in machine and reform cities both employed strategies of
bias and coordinated organizations of resource-rich elites and loyal voters. These chapters described an enormous variety of possible strategies
and approaches for achieving coalitions' goals, some of which were more
effective than others. Unfortunately such rich detail will be lost in the

quantitative analysis—not because it is unimportant, but because finely grained measures of bias types, organizational approaches, and degrees of bias or coordination are unavailable. Furthermore, it is virtually impossible to disentangle the processes and timing of bias from coordination. These components reinforce one another—it is easier to organize effectively when opponents have been eliminated because of bias, and it is easier to enact biased rules when politicians organize effective coalitions. Instead of offering precise and separable measures for the statistical analysis, cities are placed into lumpy categories: whether there is evidence of a high level of bias and coordination, or not. The presence of both variables is referred to as the *bias period* in the analysis, and serves as the key independent variable.

For each of the nine cities, I conducted an in-depth analysis of the city's history to determine the dates of the bias period. First, using historical accounts of party hierarchies in machine cities and the development of nonpartisan slating groups in reform cities, I determined periods of time when a single organization controlled nominations for office in the party or citywide.[2] Second, I used biographies of city leaders, newspaper accounts, and historical analyses to identify years when biasing strategies explored in chapter 2 were employed. This bias period variable is coded one during the stretch of time where organization and bias are present for each city and zero when either factor is missing.[3]

The operationalization of the bias period was straightforward in reform cities because these coalitions tended to use institutional change as a mechanism of bias. The change to a council manager government, coupled with the formation of a nonpartisan slating group, represented the start of the bias period in Austin, Dallas, San Antonio, and San Jose. The bias periods end with the implementation of district elections for council members and the dissolution of the nonpartisan slating group. Because machine cities used less easily quantifiable mechanisms of bias, I relied heavily on experts' accounts of the actions various political coalitions took in office and the strength of the party hierarchy. Primarily drawing on Mayhew (1986), Erie (1988), Larsen and Hulston (1997), and Wolfinger (1974), I looked for evidence that strong party organizations in Chicago, New York, New Haven, Kansas City, and Philadelphia tightly controlled nominations and used public funds (through patronage) to consolidate their organizations. Table 4.1 lists the nine cities and bias periods.

Detailed explanations of the dates selected for the bias periods are offered in the historical chapters explaining the process of bias (chapter 2),

Table 4.1: Monopoly cities used in electoral analyses

City	Bias period	Electoral data
Austin	1954–72	1919–85
Chicago	1932–78	1905–85
Dallas	1942–75	1921–85
Kansas City	1915–39	1869–85
New Haven	1954–68	1901–85
New York	1918–32	1882–85
Philadelphia	1894–50	1853–85
San Antonio	1955–76	1945–85
San Jose	1945–77	1914–85

coordination (chapter3), and decline (chapter 6). A distilled version of events is offered here to outline my choices. In Austin reformers passed a city manager charter with nonpartisan, at-large elections in 1924; in 1953 they amended the charter again, requiring councilors be elected at-large by numbered seats, further biasing the system. Also in 1953 reformers organized a slating group that began nominating candidates for office. In 1971 the reformers lost their unity when the business community fractionalized and began slating multiple candidates for city offices. The lowering of the voting age to eighteen by Constitutional amendment also contributed to reform collapse, putting the end of the bias period at 1972.

In Dallas, a city manager charter with nonpartisan, at-large elections passed in 1937. The Citizen's Council Association (CCA), a nonpartisan slating group, began slating candidates for office in 1941. In 1971 black residents challenged Dallas's at-large system in court, and in 1975 the district court found in favor of the plaintiffs. The CCA dissolved after 1975, signifying the end of the bias period. San Antonio adopted a city manager charter with nonpartisan, at-large elections in 1951. In 1955 a nonpartisan slating group called the Good Government League began coordinating candidates. This organization folded in 1976, and district elections were implemented in 1978. In San Jose, reformers implemented a nonpartisan, at-large city manager charter in 1914, and began slating candidates in 1944. Reformers lost cooperation of a majority of the city council in 1977, following convictions of four councilors. District elections were implemented in 1978.

As explained above, most machine cities did not have clear institutional changes signifying the start and end points of bias. Chicago politicians began engaging in patronage politics and using public funds to build their organizations in the mid-nineteenth century, biasing the system in favor of those in office. Both parties faced factional infighting until 1931, when Cermak unified the Democrats, marking the beginning of the bias period. In 1978, following the death of Mayor Daley, the party factionalized and was unable to maintain unity in the primary election of 1979. In Kansas City, the local Republican and Democratic Parties first began accusing each other of committing election fraud in the late 1880s. The charges continued throughout the first half of the twentieth century, but the parties remained disorganized at the city level until 1914, when Pendergast arranged to share municipal benefits with a rival faction in exchange for unity within the Democratic Party. The machine collapsed when Missouri governor Lloyd Stark spearheaded an investigation of Pendergast for election fraud, and stopped the flow of state and federal dollars to Pendergast's organization. In 1939, Pendergast was indicted for tax evasion, marking the end of the bias period.

New York's local politics exhibited all of the hallmarks of machine bias by the turn of the twentieth century—fraud, coercive patronage, corruption, etc., but it lacked order and unity until Tammany Hall beat out other Democratic factions to dictate nominations starting in 1917. The confluence of bias and organization lasted until 1933, when a large-scale investigation and crackdown on vote fraud undermined Tammany's cohesiveness and stifled the coalition's ability to fix elections. As early as the 1830s, Philadelphia politicians were making use of patronage to secure votes. Philadelphia's Republican machine began its development in the late 1870s, reliant on patronage from the Republican-controlled state government. But feuds among Republican wings existed until the early 1890s, when state boss Matthew Quay installed Israel W. Durham as the local leader, quashing factional divisions. The organization disintegrated when voters passed a new city charter in 1951, following a damaging investigation of the Republican Party's practices. These developments disrupted the organization's biasing tactics as well as its cohesiveness.

In the late 1870s, the New Haven Democratic party was credited with providing more votes to Democratic candidates than there were ballots cast in the election, but generally accounts of election fraud are sparse until the 1970s, when the machine was in decline. Mayhew (1986) reports that in the 1950s the Democrats were organized by Golden and Barbieri in alliance with Mayor Richard Lee, who slated candidates for all city offices and maintained control by exchanging "contracts, insurance accounts, and favorable tax assessments . . . for campaign contributions, and several hundred patronage jobs . . . for salary kickbacks, party support, and party work" (29). The organization was irreparably weakened when Lee retired in 1969, and redistricting shook up the city council.[4] Thus, in each of the cities, the coincidence of bias and organization dictated the coding of the bias period variable.[5]

There are a number of additional independent variables in the analysis to account for the diverse electoral systems in each city. For the machine cities, the analyses include general elections for mayor—a single post elected citywide. All of these elections have at least two major party candidates. For reform cities, all elections for city council (or commission), city manager, and mayor (when this position exists) are included. During most of the time period included in the analysis, the mayor was simply a member of the city council. These elections are all nonpartisan. Additionally, for reform cities, all primary elections are included. It is impossible to test results using only general elections for these cities because many council members and some mayors were elected outright in the primary while other seats in the same election were forced into a runoff. This is made more complicated by the different rules for winning. In Austin and San Jose, for a portion of the time series, candidates were not allowed to win outright in the primary. In these elections, the top $2*N$ (where N is the number of seats) vote getters advanced to the general election. A final challenge presented by reform cities is the different number of officials elected in any given race. During at least some of the years in the study, all of the reform cities had at-large elections, meaning that the entire city was the electorate for all of the council seats. Two of the cities, San Jose and pre-1953 Austin, elected multiple council members at a time. San Antonio, Dallas, and post-1953 Austin used a post system where each candidate ran for a numbered seat. This created a series of citywide single-member elections. San Jose, San Antonio, and Dallas moved to single-member district systems for electing council members in the 1970s and 1980s.[6]

In any given year, a city may have held multiple kinds of elections. For example, in the year 1942, San Jose voters cast ballots in five different elections: the city manager's retention election, a primary election for three at-large seats (a multimember election), a primary election for one at-large seat (a single-member election), and a general election for the two council races.[7] San Jose had the most complicated electoral system of all of the cities; for the most part, observations represent single-member races for councilors or mayor.

The analyses control for the differences discussed above in a number of ways. First, I include the seat type of each election—*mayor, city*

council, commissioner, and *manager*—as a series of dummy variables
in the analyses. City council elections are the most numerous, so this
serves as the excluded category. Second, I incorporate the number of
candidates running for each seat and the number of *seats* available in
each election.[8] I also include dummy variables for the different types of
elections, including *general, primary,* and *primaryNR,* which represents
a primary election in which there was no runoff. In the analyses presented, only the dummy variable for primary elections is included. This
has the effect of pooling general elections and primaries with no runoff
in the regressions. This method was selected because these two races are
theoretically similar as the final election for office.[9] In order to ensure
that these differences are not driving the results, all of the analyses were
repeated using only citywide, final (general and primary no-runoff) elections, with the effect of stronger results in all cases. Given the diversity
of the data, I also tested each regression using different methods for calculating standard errors, including clustering by year, by election, and
by city. I examined each analysis with and without fixed effects for cities to control for unobserved differences across cases. The conclusions
remain the same if they are included, but adding city-level effects means
that machine and reform cities can not be pooled. For this reason I present all of the analyses without fixed effects.[10]

The regressions also incorporate a number of control variables to account for alternative explanations. In the margin of victory analysis, I
add the number of *incumbents* running in the election to control for the
possibility that the effect of the bias period is really just a measure of
an increase in the number of incumbent candidacies. To control for the
possibility that the bias period is coincident with low-interest elections, I
include a *turnout* variable.[11] This measure is constructed as the number
of ballots cast in a given election divided by the total number of potential voters in the city. Potential voters include all persons of voting age
(males only prior to 1920). Noncitizens are included because promoting
naturalization of immigrants can be a method of increasing the size of
the electoral coalition (Erie 1988), and some states allowed alien suffrage in this time period.[12] In a number of places, restricting citizenship
and increasing the difficulty of naturalization and registration was an
important biasing strategy.

I also control for the expectation that the competitiveness of elections
is likely to be different in large versus small cities, but assume that this effect levels off. To capture this, I estimated annual intercensal *population*
using linear interpolation of decade measures and include the natural log

of this figure in the analyses. I add a trend variable representing the *year* that the election was held to control for the possibility that competitiveness increases or decreases over time. In the data collection, strategies of bias are categorized as being predominately machine style (patronage based) or reform style (vote-dilution/suffrage-restriction based). In the analysis this is represented by a dummy variable indicating whether the city is classified as *machine* or *reform*, coded one if the city is a machine city and zero if it is a reform city. Including this variable tests the rival expectation that regime differences drive electoral outcomes. Summary statistics are provided in appendix tables A5 and A6.

Bias Decreases Electoral Competition

Do bias and organization lead to dominance? If my theory is correct, during the bias period competition should decline as the margin of victory increases. Figure 4.1 shows that in every city the margin of victory for winners increased during the bias period.[13]

In order to control for other factors, I regress the margin of victory in a given race on the bias period variable along with the controls described above. Table 4.2 presents these regression results.[14] The results fit well with what is known about local elections. When incumbents run, the margin of victory is significantly larger. Increasing the number of

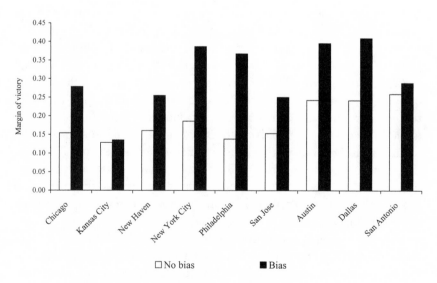

Fig. 4.1: Effect of bias period on winners' margin of victory

Table 4.2: Competition during bias period

Margin of victory		
	Coefficient	Std. error
Bias period	0.060 **	0.017
Incumbents	0.079 **	0.013
Candidates per seat	−0.025 **	0.005
Seats	−0.062 **	0.017
Turnout of eligible voters	−0.589 **	0.062
Year	0.001 **	0.000
Machine/reform	−0.034	0.040
Log population (millions)	0.014 *	0.008
Commissioner	0.035	0.038
Mayor	0.095 **	0.036
Manager	0.009	0.065
Primary	−0.089 **	0.018
Constant	0.405 **	0.053
F	23.95**	
R^2	0.255	
N	973	

Note: Standard errors are clustered by city-election.
OLS regression: $*p < .10$ $**p < .05$

candidates and seats decreases the margin of victory, and turnout has a powerful negative effect on the winner's vote share.

Most importantly, the coefficient on the bias period variable is positive and significant. During the bias period, the average margin of victory in elections increases by about 6 percentage points.[15] This holds even while controlling for changes in turnout, whether or not an incumbent is running, the number of candidates per seat, and potential differences between machine and reform cities.[16] Limiting the analysis to incumbent candidates, I find that they increased their margin of victory by nearly 4 percentage points during the bias period. Equally important, the bias period reduced competition in machine and reform cities alike. Repeating the analysis for each regime type substantiates this claim; both forms see a significant increase in the margin of victory during the bias period. In machine cities, winners increase their margin of victory by nearly 11 percentage points during the bias period and by nearly 8 percentage points in reform cities. When local coalitions dominate governance, they successfully reduce competition in elections.[17]

Bias Increases Incumbency Advantage

These results begin to suggest that both machine and reform regimes were advantaged electorally by organizing effectively and biasing the system. But margin of victory represents only one element in the quest for dominance. A second way to discern the effect of the bias period on coalition victories is to view the incumbents' decision to run for office as strategic. If the bias period really does offer more safety in office, we should observe incumbents running more regularly. To see if this is the case, I regressed the percentage of candidates that are incumbents running in a given citywide election on the bias period. All of the control variables are similar to the previous analyses, except that the number of candidates running is excluded because this should be endogenous. The results are presented in table 4.3.

The results suggest that during the bias period, the percentage of candidates that are incumbent increases by about 3 percentage points on average across the nine cities. More incumbents choose to run for reelection when the system is biased and coalitions are organized.

In addition to increasing the attractiveness of reelection, the theory of political monopoly also predicts that during the bias period incum-

Table 4.3: Bias effect on incumbents' decision to run for reelection

	Percent incumbents	
	Coefficient	Std. error
Bias period	0.034 *	0.020
Seats	0.046 **	0.013
Turnout of eligible voters	−0.338 **	0.093
Year	0.001 **	0.000
Log population (millions)	−0.021 **	0.010
Machine/reform	0.124 **	0.042
Commissioner	0.028	0.043
Mayor	−0.034	0.033
Manager	0.475 **	0.121
Primary	−0.150 **	0.021
Constant	0.111 *	0.060
F	17.82**	
R^2	0.124	
N	853	

Note: Standard errors are clustered by city-election.
OLS regression: $^*p < .10$ $^{**}p < .05$

Table 4.4: Incumbency advantage during bias period

	Incumbent candidate		Incumbent party	
	Coefficient	*Std. error*	*Coefficient*	*Std. error*
Bias period	1.016 **	0.386	1.119 **	0.492
Candidates per seat	−0.058	0.113	−0.119	0.152
Seats	0.158	0.122		
Turnout of eligible voters	−5.651 **	1.669	−1.141	1.302
Machine/reform	1.028	0.851		
Log population (millions)	−0.183	0.162	0.023	0.116
Commissioner	−0.296	0.643		
Mayor	1.323 *	0.760		
Manager	0.275	1.092		
Primary	1.430 **	0.592		
Constant	1.360 **	0.529	1.384	0.743
Wald χ^2	21.90**		6.82	
Pseudo R^2	0.097		0.038	
N	459		180	

Note: Standard errors are clustered by city-election.
Logistic regression: $*p < .10$ $**p < .05$

bency advantage increases for the dominant coalition. Given that incumbency has been shown by other scholars to be an important predictor of electoral success, if the advantage is further enhanced by a biased and organized system, the result will offer support for my claim. This possibility is tested with two logistic regressions, first, using each candidate's incumbency status as a proxy for membership in the dominant coalition and, second, using membership in the incumbent party as the proxy. Because reform cities have nonpartisan elections and keep no records of the organization to which a candidate belongs, this second regression only includes machine cities.

The results presented in table 4.4 suggest that incumbents and incumbent parties have a higher probability of winning during the bias period.[18] Over the entire time period incumbent candidates and incumbent party candidates do well, but they do even better during bias periods.[19] Holding all other variables constant at their mean, the predicted probability of victory for incumbents rises from 79 percent to 91 percent.[20] The effect during the bias period for incumbent parties is more striking. Candidates from incumbent parties increase their probability of reelection from 63 percent to 83 percent. It is also interesting to note that if these regressions are repeated for nonincumbents, the bias period reduces the probability of victory suggesting that the efforts to minimize electoral risk have identifiable beneficiaries (see J. Trounstine 2006).

One important alternative explanation for these electoral results is that incumbents were successfully responding to residents' demands. In other words, these electoral results could indicate the presence of a responsive dominant coalition. The best way to test this possibility would be to control for preferences of voters in the analyses. However, surveys of resident satisfaction rarely exist at the local level and are unavailable for long time spans. Instead, I include measures of the percentage of the population that is persons of color and the proportion of the population that rents its homes in the margin of victory and incumbency reelection analyses. These measures serve as proxies for the distribution of interests in a city. Five-year changes in these percentages are also included. The results of the regressions are presented in tables 4.5 and 4.6.

Table 4.5 presents evidence that the effect of the bias period is strengthened by the inclusion of these demographic controls. Regardless of the changing political context, coalitions in machine and reform cities continued to win by larger margins during the bias period.

Table 4.6 suggests that incumbents' increased probability of reelection during the bias period was not a result of increased stability in city demographics. Historical evidence presented in chapter 5 also suggests that homogeneity of preferences does not explain the electoral outcomes. In both machine and reform cities, despite the regularity with which incumbents won reelection, residents had diverse preferences and supported the governing coalitions' programs with varying degrees of enthusiasm.

Success of a single organization is an important indicator of political monopoly. In the wake of the consolidation of organizations and the implementation of bias in these nine cities, competition declined, incumbency advantage increased, and control of political activity became uncontested. Since 1931 in Chicago and 1953 in New Haven, the Democratic Party has won every mayoral election. In Philadelphia the Republican organization dominated between 1860 and 1950, at times with more than 80 percent of the vote. In only two New Haven elections prior to 1955 did a mayoral candidate receive more than 60 percent of the vote. After consolidation of the monopoly, Lee regularly captured more than 65 percent of the ballots. Tammany Hall governed New York from 1918 until 1932, when the Democratic machine lost to fusion.

Table 4.5: Competition during bias period, controlling for city demographics

	Margin of victory	
	Coefficient	Std. error
Bias period	0.083 **	0.020
Incumbents	0.075 **	0.014
Candidates per seat	−0.023 **	0.005
Seats	−0.064 **	0.017
Turnout of eligible voters	−0.518 **	0.078
Year	0.001	0.001
Machine/reform	−0.086 *	0.046
Log population (millions)	−0.002	0.009
Commissioner	0.014	0.043
Mayor	0.101 **	0.040
Manager	0.024	0.067
Primary	−0.072 **	0.019
% nonwhite	0.185	0.136
5-year change % nonwhite	−0.439	0.463
% renters	0.241 *	0.134
5-year change % renters	−0.595 *	0.305
Constant	0.169 **	0.129
F	13.84**	
R^2	0.247	
N	794	

Note: Standard errors are clustered by city-election.
OLS regression: $*p < .10$ $**p < .05$

During this period, Tammany's margin of victory in general elections climbed in nearly every election.

The effects of reform regime consolidation are similar. Like their machine counterparts, reform candidates won repeatedly, with landslide victories. As a result, in many reform cities, opponents stopped challenging the dominant coalitions in elections. In Dallas, 86 percent of 182 city council members elected between 1931 and 1969 pledged allegiance to the Citizens' Charter Association. This nonpartisan slating group held a majority on the council every year, except during a brief period between 1935 and 1938. San Antonio's Good Government League won 95 percent of the eighty-eight council races between 1955 and 1971. Between 1944 and 1967 in San Jose seventy-five councilors were elected to office; seventy-two were members of the dominant coalition. In sum, when coalitions coordinate successfully and bias the electoral arena, they seek

Table 4.6: Incumbency advantage during bias period, controlling for city demographics

	Incumbent candidate		Incumbent party	
	Coefficient	Std. error	Coefficient	Std. error
Bias period	1.070 **	0.395	1.083 **	0.554
Candidates per seat	−0.046	0.120	0.144	0.217
Seats	0.058	0.138		
Turnout of eligible voters	−3.724 **	1.790	−2.915	1.999
Machine/reform	1.193	1.076		
Log population (millions)	−0.255	0.167	−0.322 *	0.169
Commissioner	−0.036	0.757		
Mayor	1.136	0.870		
Manager	0.676	1.080		
Primary	1.462 **	0.567		
% nonwhite	6.738 **	2.835	2.474	5.175
5-year change % nonwhite	−8.028	8.780	35.091	25.993
% renters	−1.581	2.321	−0.215	2.723
5-year change % renters	7.564 *	4.029	10.460	7.047
Constant	1.154	1.329	0.871	2.275
Wald χ^2	35.90**		15.40*	
Pseudo R^2	0.124		0.133	
N	430		121	

Note: Standard errors are clustered by city-election.
Logistic regressions: $*p < .10$ $**p < .05$

reelection more often, they win reelection more often, and candidates win with larger margins of victory. Given the long bias periods, these results may mean that outcomes were clear well in advance of election day.

Now that we have evidence that the combination of bias and organization allows coalitions to dominate government, the next sections turn to the important questions of when and where monopolies are most likely to arise. Using a larger data collection, I first analyze the political and demographic context of different types of monopolies and then analyze the timing of emergence.

Predicting the Type of Monopoly

The theory presented in chapters 1 through 3 offers a series of predictions regarding when we are likely to see coalitions select certain types of biasing strategies. Evidence presented in chapter 3 suggests that the political context and demographic makeup of a community dictate which groups of voters will become the core of a political coalition seeking power. Coalitions are likely to select their core based on preexisting loyalties, the size of different ethnic, religious, or economic groups, and similarity in policy goals. The political context, the coalition membership, and the goals of political leaders determine not only who will be courted as core members but also which strategies can be used to bias the system in favor of incumbents. I assume that coalitions will seek to implement biasing strategies that maximize deterrence of challengers and minimize maintenance over time. In other words, they will prefer strategies like suffrage restrictions over vote fraud.

The most important constraints facing coalitions in achieving these goals are the extent of the coalition's institutional control and the characteristics of the coalition's core voters and opponents. The more institutional control a coalition wields, the more likely it should be to rely on strategies of bias that are difficult to enact but are highly effective for eliminating competition (such as suffrage restrictions). Coalitions building monopolies in cities with a large population of poor voters and a high degree of inequality should be inclined to use patronage-based strategies. Coalitions that come to power in relatively homogenous cities where opponents can be identified by nonpolitical features like income or race should seek monopolies reliant on suffrage restriction and other mechanisms to reduce minority claims on government.

I offered evidence in chapter 2 that coalitions in American cities have tended to rely on two common bundles of strategies. Machines primarily used patronage to bias the system while reform organizations relied on suffrage restrictions and vote dilution. If these theories of core membership and strategy selection are correct, reform cities should be characterized by high levels of institutional control and a relatively homogenous population by both economic and racial measures while machine cities should exhibit less institutional control and more diverse populations with relatively low socioeconomic status.

Of course, this theoretical proposition is a dramatic oversimplification of reality. It is never true that a political coalition is able to select its core constituency and its strategies of bias with a clean slate. The kinds of rules already in place, the voting tendencies of the residents, and political changes at the state level all would have dictated how organizations sought to keep themselves in power. However, both machine and reform politicians *did* have some choices. Voting loyalties were not fixed, charters were malleable, and control was uncertain when these coalitions rose to power.

To some extent both reform and machine organizations influenced their own destinies. Reformers could have chosen to build patronage regimes, and they did not. In part this was because they sought to spend government largess on other priorities, but additionally patronage would have been a poor mechanism for ensuring loyalty of their middle-class base. It is probably also true that reformers selected this middle-class base precisely because they had little interest in a patronage regime. Whether the core coalition or the goals were drafted first may be interesting, but it is irrelevant to this discussion. In either case reform monopolies should be characterized by a population that has a relatively large, homogenous middle class. Similarly, machine politicians could have sought to ally with those seeking suffrage restrictions. They might have tried to win power by ensuring that the working class was kept out of the political system instead of encompassing their vote base. But they did not. For machine politicians, most lacking inherited wealth, reliance on party organizations for achieving political dominance made sense. Winning in such an environment was easiest by reaching out to groups that represented large shares of the population—in these big cities, working-class and foreign-stock residents were more numerous than the middle-class native whites who would have benefited from suffrage restriction. Both machine and reform coalitions relied on biasing mechanisms that were sensible given the demographic and institutional contexts they faced.

Data for Analyzing Monopoly Strategies

To determine why political coalitions select some strategies of bias over others and when monopolies are most likely to emerge, I collected data on the complete set of 244 cities ever included on the one hundred largest cities list. The dependent variable in these analyses is a *monopoly period* for each city. Because it would have been difficult (if not impossible) to determine the coincidence of bias and organization in all of these cities, I used secondary sources to establish time periods when a single organization appeared to have strong control over city government for at least a decade and relied on tactics of bias (e.g., patronage, suffrage restrictions, etc.). Fortunately, there is a high degree of consensus among historians regarding the periods in which organizations were *most* powerful.

The historical literature on political machines and machine politics is well developed and provides clear examples of dominant biased regimes (e.g., monopolies). I relied primarily on comparative research by Mayhew (1986), Erie (1988), and Bridges (1997) to compile a list of cities with monopolies and the start and end dates of dominance. For example, Erie (1988) offers a concise chart determining the presence of a strong political machine in each of eight cities for the twentieth century; he defines the machine as citywide power centralized in the hands of a party boss, who commanded large electoral majorities, controlled local offices and agencies, remained in power for at least a decade, and exchanged patronage jobs and welfare services for votes (18–19). This chart served as the basis for my determination of the start and end dates for machine dominance in Albany, Chicago, Jersey City, New York, Pittsburgh, and Philadelphia. Similarly, in a study of traditional party organizations, Mayhew determines periods of machine control. Mayhew's analysis reviews all large cities for evidence that a well-defined organization regularly nominated winning candidates for public office and successfully exchanged material inducements for support over a long period. In many cases Mayhew provides precise dates for the rise and fall of machine monopolies.[21] Those same dates are used in this analysis.[22] In some cases I supplemented Mayhew's list with individual accounts of city organizations (e.g., Larsen and Hulston 1997 for Kansas City) to attain the precise dates of the monopoly periods.

I used a similar analysis and coding process for reform cities. I looked for the dates when a city manager charter, at-large, nonpartisan elections, and a cohesive group operated to control local policymaking for at least a decade. Scholars (Bridges 1997; Davidson and Fraga 1988; Mayhew 1986) have provided evidence that nonpartisan slating groups (NPSGs) in the South and West dominated government. For example, in regard to Dayton, Ohio, Mayhew (1986) explains, "[A] good government organization called the Citizen's Committee dominated municipal elections at least through the 1950s" (72). As Mayhew's comment suggests, reform dominance in the literature is associated with electoral success. Additionally, scholars attribute policy goals and political programs to these NPSGs. Bridges (1997) argues that the "leaders of newly formed nonpartisan slating groups promised efficiency and lower taxes, clear lines of authority and administration" (111). In combination, these characteristics qualitatively define an organized group of political actors controlling government activity through the electoral process. I consider these monopoly periods.

It was often not possible to determine the precise dates for the rise and collapse of the monopoly. For a substantial number of cities, Mayhew (1986) explains that a machine had dominated at some point or continued to dominate, but gave no more precise dates. For example, speaking

of Waterbury, Connecticut, he says, "Democratic 'powerhouses' . . . are
said to have operated in the 1960s" (30). Similar to the machine case, I
found a number of reform cities that were monopolized, yet had no clear
way of determining the start dates. The statistical procedure for handling these cases is described for each analysis below. Another challenge
was coding the handful of cities that had multiple periods of control.
For example in New Orleans, a Democratic machine developed after the
Civil War. In 1934, Huey Long replaced the leaders of the organization
with his own men, but a machine continued to dominate. In other instances, like Pawtucket, Rhode Island, a Democratic machine took over
from a Republican organization. In both of these types of cases I coded
the monopoly period continuously. In one case, San Antonio, Texas, a
reform monopoly took over from a machine monopoly.[23] This city is
included in both the machine and reform analyses presented below. All
of the cities along with the dates of their monopoly periods are included
in the appendix, in tables A1–A3.

The independent variables in the analyses are drawn from the Census
of Population and Housing. I interpolate annual values from the decade
measures and then, to measure change, calculate five-year differences in
each measure. According to my theory, one of the important predictors
of strategy selection is intuitional control. Control equates to having
a majority of seats in the legislative and executive branches and either
home rule or a friendly government at the state level. Collecting information on which political faction controls the legislative and executive
branches is extremely time consuming and costly; in some cases the data
are unavailable. Similarly, determining whether or not a given coalition
enjoyed protection at the state level is virtually impossible. As proxies
for these mechanisms, I include a variable noting each city's *home-rule*
status in a given year. I also include a variable designating whether or
not a single party had *unified* control of the state government in each
year because local support from state officials would have been most
likely in such an environment.[24] The theory predicts that cities in which
reformers came to power will be characterized by a greater degree of
institutional control because they adopted suffrage restrictions and vote-
dilution strategies.

Further, I suggested that we should see suffrage restrictions and vote-
dilution strategies selected when coalitions face a relatively homogenous
population. Thus, reform cities should also have less diversity. I use the
proportion of the population that is *nonwhite* (which includes African
Americans, Chinese, Japanese, and Indians) to analyze this claim.[25]

Conversely, I have proposed that patronage-based strategies should be more likely in communities with a high degree of inequality and large poor populations. By this rationale, machine cities should have a higher degree of inequality and a proportion of persons with low socioeconomic status. I am unable to use income measures to represent these concepts because the Census did not begin collecting such data until 1959. Instead I use the proportion of the population that *rents* its home as an indicator of the wealth of the residents. I attempt to capture the relationship between the relative sizes of high and low socioeconomic classes with a ratio that divides the proportion of the workforce employed in *professional* positions by the proportion employed in *manufacturing*. The further away from one the ratio is, the more unequal are the occupational categories in a city. Furthermore, a ratio higher than one means that professionals dominate the economic structure, while a ratio less than one signifies a relatively larger proportion of manufacturers, which are likely to employ blue-collar workers. The theory predicts that machine cities will have a low score on this measure and a score that is far from one.

Because the core constituency in machine cities tended to be white ethnics, these cities should have larger proportions of *foreign stock* (foreign born and native born with at least one foreign parent) residents compared to reform cities. Conversely, reform cities should have larger proportions of *native-born whites* (total population less nonwhite and foreign-stock residents) and a larger middle class.

Political Context Determines Regime Type

Does the political context determine the types of regimes that develop? Do coalitions select strategies that maximize their chances of holding power given their environment? To answer these questions, I compare reform and machine monopolies directly, during their first year of operation, on the factors listed above. This analysis only includes cities for which a start date for the monopoly period could be determined.

The results in table 4.7 offer strong support for the political context hypotheses; coalitions built monopolies using strategies that reflected their core constituencies and levels of institutional control. The table displays mean values on each variable for reform and machine monopolies.

It was suggested above that cities with a ratio less than one and/ or far from one are likely to have a relatively larger population of low socioeconomic status residents. As the table shows, machine cities are characterized by a larger number of renters and by a score on the economic ratio measure that is both low and far from one. As predicted,

Table 4.7: Political context of monopoly

	Reform		Machine	
	Mean	Std. error	Mean	Std. error
% renters	53	0.03	66	0.03
Professionals/manufacturing	1.22	0.33	0.22	0.02
Home rule (% of cases)	89	0.11	12	0.08
Unified state government (% of cases)	100	0.00	65	0.12
% foreign stock	19	0.04	48	0.04
% native white	69	0.04	41	0.03
N	9		17	

Note: Two-sample t-test
All differences significant $p < .05$.

machine cities are also characterized by large foreign-stock populations. On average, machine-dominated cities were composed of nearly 50 percent foreign-stock residents. Offers of patronage and neighborhood-based organizing tactics made sense in this environment. Finally, as anticipated, machines used strategies of bias that were relatively easy to implement because they lacked institutional control, as evidenced by the small proportion with home-rule status and the lower levels of unified government.

In contrast, reform-dominated cities have smaller poor populations and a large proportion of relatively high socioeconomic status residents, a homogenous white population, and all had home rule. These data offer evidence to support the theory that political coalitions select their core constituencies and strategies of bias based on their demographic and institutional contexts.[26]

Conditions for Monopoly

Given that monopolies are rare but not impossible to erect, this section explores changes in a city's environment that might lead it to successfully establish a monopoly. Theories of machine and reform emergence are abundant in urban politics scholarship. Early explanations for the rise of machines (Banfield and Wilson 1963; Moynihan and Glazer 1970; Merton 1957; Scott 1968) focused on the characteristics of the voters most likely to be the targets of machine mobilization—poor immigrants. The argument suggests that when the "private-regarding" population becomes large enough, a machine is consolidated. Other scholars, like

Handlin (1973) and Whyte (1955), focused on the processes of industrialization and the ethnic and class conflicts that developed in response to the rapid changes. These theories predict that changes in economic structure would lead to the consolidation of the machine. A related line of thought posits that businessmen in need of centralized structures of decision making led to the development of machines (Shefter 1978; McCaffery 1992). Similarly, Munro (1933) argues that the division of powers in American cities is the "taproot of bossism" (14). When political authority is officially decentralized, it is likely to be centralized by a boss unofficially.

Finally, a number of scholars have argued that city size is important for machine development. Gimpel (1993) found that large, dense cities are more likely to be monopolized by machines possibly because of their importance to state and national politics and their conduciveness to traditional organizing strategies. This hypothesis is underscored by Lascher's (2005) finding that incumbents are more likely to win reelection in large cities. A slightly different prediction is offered by Erie (1988), who argues that population growth impedes machine building because in these circumstances it is too costly for the machine to organize voters.

Early theories of reform emergence tended to focus on the conflicts born of rapid urbanization and changing demographics. Hofstadter (1955) and Hays (1964), for instance, argue that reform movements reflected a program to regain social status and policy control by upper- and middle-class native-born Protestants and advanced professional groups. An alternative argument by Fox (1977) suggests that reformers came to dominate when the need to cope with industrialization became too great for antiquated structures of government. The clean lines of authority and the bureaucratic efficiency of manager charters would have been most useful for cities in need of professionalized, low-cost forms of service delivery. Similarly, Bridges (1997) argues that the success of reform in the Southwest reflected the need to increase the size of the population and the economy during periods when growth and development were uncertain. While each of these theories offers plausible necessary conditions for the establishment of machine and reform regimes, none clarify the sufficient conditions for consolidation (see Shefter 1978 for a similar line of thinking). Most of these theories are too broad to predict the timing of monopoly emergence.

Alternatively, I have argued that the combination of bias and coordination is likely to result when changes in the political environment threaten a coalition's control over political office or policy goals. For instance, Chicago's machine organized following sweeping wins by local Republicans and in response to Prohibition. Furthermore, I have asserted that machines' centralizing efforts were supported when economic shifts created a business class with a strong interest in stability. Reformers organized when economic elites became interested in public investments in growth and in increasing the efficiency of local government. Increased union activity, slowing growth rates, and demographic shifts also contributed to reform consolidation.

If threats encouraged the consolidation of the monopoly, we might say that stability in the political environment discouraged consolidation. This is similar in some ways to an argument made by Lipset, Trow, and Coleman (1956) in their brilliant treatise on the International Typographical Union (ITU). Lipset, Trow, and Coleman provide a series of predictions regarding when we can expect democracy to be maintained (and development of an oligarchy prevented) by tracing the development of two-party competition in the ITU. One of the conditions they identify is security. When a union or trade faces a threatening environment, the dominant impulse among members and leaders is to limit dissent and offer a united front against the employer, making oligarchic dominance more likely. In cities, a lack of threat should have also made consolidation less likely.

Lipset, Trow, and Coleman further suggest that tendency towards Michel's iron law of oligarchy is especially likely to occur in large organizations that require a high degree of bureaucratization to get their work done. We can use this prediction in the city setting to say that smaller cities should be able to resist monopolization more easily than large cities. This prediction is supported in the literature referenced above on machine development that finds larger cities more likely to be dominated. Lipset, Trow, and Coleman also argue that when constituents are organized into groups with diverse interests, and no one group has enough power to dominate the union, democracy is likely to be maintained. Thus, cities with a high degree of heterogeneity might be more difficult to monopolize.

There are a number of additional predictions offered by Lipset, Trow, and Coleman (1956) that translate well into the city context, but are impossible to test here because of a lack of data. For instance, they expect that oligarchies are less likely to arise in unions that have strong, autonomous local chapters. In city politics we might say that a strong independent bureaucracy or a system with autonomous ward bosses might be more difficult to monopolize, all else being equal. Such division of power within the government would have offered potential challengers access to resources, as well as made the consolidation of the organization more challenging. Similarly, they suggest that the presence of a large number of voluntary associations within the union that disconnect socialization from governance encourages the development of alternative viewpoints. At the city level we could predict that a well-developed civil society should make democracy more stable and monopoly less likely. With better data one, could test these hypotheses, but it is not done here.

Data for Analyzing Monopoly Emergence

In order to analyze the effect of changing political contexts on the development of monopoly, I regress monopoly emergence on the census variables listed above using all 244 cities in the data set.[27] The observations are arranged so that each city has a separate observation for each year of the data collection, 1900–86. Cities are coded zero when they are at risk for monopolization (e.g., have never experienced monopolization) and coded one during their first year of monopolization. After becoming monopolized, the city exits the data analysis.[28] In these models, machine and reform monopolies are analyzed separately because I argue that different political contexts dictated the type of monopoly that formed.[29] The setup used for this analysis is a competing risk model.[30] This means that until a city becomes monopolized, it is at risk of being dominated by either a reform or a machine coalition. Once it is monopolized, the city is no longer at risk for either type, because it exits the analysis.[31] This allows me to predict the factors that increase or decrease the probability that a monopoly will emerge in a given city.

Some of the cities in the data set did not experience the emergence of a monopoly during the selected time period. This problem is referred to as censoring. Some cities entered the data set already monopolized (left-censoring) while others were not monopolized at any time before 1986 (right-censoring). In using logistic regressions to analyze monopoly emergence, the left-censored cases drop out of the models completely and the right-censored cases drop out in their final year of observation.

In the data set, there are thirty cases with clear dates for the emergence of the monopoly (San Antonio represents two of these cases) listed in tables A2 and A3. Three of these cases, Philadelphia, Pittsburgh, and Baltimore, established monopolies just after the Civil War. Because these cases enter the data analysis already under machine control, they are left-censored at 1900—in other words, they exit the analysis before they have a chance to become monopolized.[32] One additional machine case, Cumberland, Rhode Island, was not large enough to warrant inclusion in the census after 1930. Because this city did not become monopolized until 1945, it drops out of all of the analyses, leaving twenty-six cases. Further, there are forty-two cases (listed in table A2) in which the date when the monopoly first developed is unknown, though there is evidence that a monopoly governed at some point during the twentieth century. These cases are also treated as left-censored at 1900. The remaining 178 cases (listed in table A1) are right-censored at 1986. This means that they remain at risk for the entire time period and exit the analysis in the last year of the analysis. Of the twenty-six cases with clear monopoly emergence dates, seventeen are classified as machines and nine are reform.[33] Reform monopolies are treated as right-censored in the machine analysis after their first year of monopolization and vice versa for the reasons explained above. Approximately 40 percent of the cases became monopolized in the same year as another case.[34]

For the independent variables, I use a series of five-year changes in demographic and economic variables to uncover the factors that motivate monopoly building. In the analysis of machine emergence, I include the level and five-year change in the proportion of the population that is *foreign stock* and the proportion of the population that *rents* its homes to represent the coalition's core membership. A decline of these populations should increase the emergence of machine monopolies because such a change would threaten their political control. Similarly, an increase in the proportion of the city that is *nonwhite* should increase the probability of machine dominance.

To capture the possibility that machines emerged in response to an increased interest in political stability among economic elites I examine the five-year change in the *ratio* of the proportion of the workforce employed in manufacturing compared to the proportion employed as professionals. A larger share of the population employed in manufacturing should be an indication that economic elites have larger sunk costs and so should be relatively more interested in a stable and centralized political system. Clearly this measure could have many other interpretations. For instance, an increase in this ratio might be capturing an increase in the constituency most likely to be targeted by the machine—those working in factories rather than those working in white-collar professions. However, because the analysis includes other measures that are better measures of the machine's constituency—foreign-stock residents and renters—it is plausible that this measure is capturing an increase in a city's immobile capital.

I examine population *growth* and natural log of the city's *population* size to test the possibility that growing cities are less likely to develop machines while large cities are more likely to host machines.[35] I include a measure of the *diversity* of the population to determine whether or not more heterogeneous communities are more likely to resist monopolization. This measure is a Herfindahl index (sum of the squared proportions) of foreign-stock, nonwhite, and white native-stock residents. I incorporate two rough measures of institutional control—local *home rule* and *unified Democratic* control over state government.[36] As explained in the previous section, because patronage-based strategies should only be adopted when control is weak, the home-rule coefficient is expected to be insignificant. Democratic control is expected to be significantly positive, reflecting the need for machine organizations to have the support of state government in order to secure a lock on patronage. Finally, I include a series of dummy variables representing the duration of nonmonopolization. One dummy variable is included for each year in the data set. If no monopoly has come to power in a given city up to the end of that year, the variable is coded one. This means that emergence is conditional on having been not monopolized to that point. These variables also allow the probability of monopoly emergence to change over time and account for any temporal trend in the data—e.g., that monopolization is particularly easy in one year or becomes easier over time.

To analyze reform emergence, similar measures are examined. The historical evidence suggests that reformers were most likely to consolidate when they faced threats to their policy program focused on growth and development. We might expect this to be true when there are large and increasing portions of the population that prefer a different focus for city funds. I use the five-year change in the proportion of the residents that are *nonwhite* to represent this population.

I have argued that the presence of economic elites interested in using public investment for growth should increase the probability of reform emergence. There is no ideal measure of this group. However, the evidence presented in chapter 3 suggests that the chambers of commerce and other professional groups were common leaders of reform organizations. In light of this, I include the *ratio* of persons employed in professional jobs to those employed in manufacturing.[37] As a measure of the reform vote base, the proportion of the population that is *native-born white* is also included.

Because I argue that growth was integral to reform consolidation, I include four different measures of this concept: the five-year *relative* change in population, the two-year change in this *growth rate*, the five-year change in the proportion of *homeowners,* and the five-year change in the proportion of the population that is *employed.*[38] I have argued that reformers organized during periods of growth in the South and West. They sought governmental structures that would promote efficient administration and allow public funds to be focused on development; further, they became mobilized in response to threats to their cities' long-term growth prospects. According to this claim, one should expect that reform monopolies will be most likely to emerge when the population and economy is growing overall, but when the growth rate declines.

As in the machine case, I also include the natural log of each city's total *population* and the index of *diversity* to test the notion that larger cities and less heterogeneous cities are more likely to become monopolized. The dummy variables for nonmonopoly duration are also included. Finally, the reform analyses include two measures of institutional control—*home rule* and the presence of a state enacted *poll tax.* As explained in chapter 3, possession of home rule significantly empowered reformers to consolidate their power by allowing them to change the rules of the political game. Further, having a state government restrict the electorate through mechanisms like the poll tax increased the likelihood that reform monopolies would emerge.[39]

I analyze the emergence of monopolies using logistic regressions, but verify all of the findings with Cox proportional hazard models as well. The Cox models allow me to deal with the presence of tied events and censored observations systematically. In general, statistical significance is improved with the Cox models, due to the preservation of cases that are dropped in the logistic regression. However, the logistic regression is much easier to interpret and more intuitive given that this work focuses on the effect of contextual changes on the probability of a city becoming monopolized. As it turns out, for a data set like this one, which has time-varying covariates for many cases across a long time period and a binary dependent variable, these models are mathematically nearly identical, as are the results. The findings from the logistic regressions are presented below. The duration-fixed effects are included, but not presented.

Political Threats Increase Monopoly Emergence

The results in table 4.8 provide evidence that monopolies are more likely to emerge when they face electoral and policy threats, and that they are constrained by their levels of institutional control. There is also evidence supporting the traditional understanding of the characteristics of the core members of machine and reform organizations.

Table 4.8: Factors affecting monopoly emergence

	Machine emergence		Reform emergence	
	Coefficient	*Std. error*	*Coefficient*	*Std. error*
Population base				
% renters	6.76 **	2.76		
% foreign stock	3.86 **	1.41		
Ratio professional/manufacturing			2.06 **	0.74
% native white			13.00	8.30
Log population (millions)	0.60 **	0.20	0.80 *	0.47
Diversity	−12.76 **	4.17	−11.24 *	6.40
Threats to coalition				
5-year change % homeowners			26.62 **	8.28
5-year change % foreign stock	−7.01	4.77		
5-year change % renters	−21.08 *	12.71		
5-year change % nonwhite	7.93 **	3.65	43.04 **	20.03
5-year change % employed			45.49 **	22.32
5-year change ratio manufacturing/professional	0.38 **	0.18		
5-year relative population change	−5.53	3.44	3.60	3.19
2-year change population growth rate			−18.33 **	8.14
Institutional control				
Poll tax			1.63 **	0.75
Home rule	−0.90	0.88	3.74 **	1.52
Unified Democratic state	1.21 *	0.65		
Constant	−3.46	2.45	−8.30 **	2.59
Pseudo R^2	0.26		0.40	
Wald χ^2	104.88**		110.17**	
N	1664		966	

Note: Robust standard errors clustered by city are reported. Duration fixed-effects are included but not presented.
*$p < .10$ **$p < .05$

As we would expect given the conventional wisdom, machines were more likely to emerge in cities with large proportions of renters and first- and second-generation immigrants. But even more powerful for predicting the consolidation of machines is the loss of these populations. The single largest predictor of machine emergence is a declining proportion of residents who are renters. As this population shrank, machine consolidation became more likely. Setting the five-year change in renters at the fifth percentile and all other variables at their mean values, the predicted probability of machine emergence is 0.06 percent. This probability increases to 0.5 percent, when the five-year change in renters is set at the ninety-fifth percentile.[40] A decrease in the population of first- or second-generation immigrants also increases the probability of machine emergence.[41] Conversely, an increase in the nonwhite population of cities inspired machine consolidation. It was the *loss* of their traditional base that led machines to seek control through bias and organization. The threat of defeat provided incentives to these coalitions.[42]

These data also support the argument that a changing economy encouraged the development of machines. As the manufacturing sector expanded, so did machine monopolies. So whether one views this measure as capturing an increase in the need for centralization as a result of industrialization or as a desire for stability from increasingly immobile economic elites, machines appeared to have been a solution. For cities with a five-year increase in the ratio of manufacturers to professionals, the expected probability of machine emergence is about 1.9 percent compared to the 0.9 percent probability of emergence in cities with a shrinking manufacturing sector.[43]

As the theory offered by Lipset, Trow, and Coleman (1956) suggests, smaller cities were more likely to resist monopolization. Large cities were more likely to be monopolized, but growing cities were less likely to see a machine emerge. Similarly, a high level of diversity in a city had a strong negative effect on the probability of consolidation. Diverse cities with increasing populations would have been difficult arenas for machine organization. Machines also appear to have been aided in their quest for dominance by having party support at the state level.

A different set of factors appear to be important for the emergence of reform monopolies.[44] As predicted, reform organizations are more likely to be consolidated when the economy and population were growing, but when the population growth rate declined. A growing proportion of homeowners also inspired reform consolidation. There are a number of possible interpretations of this result. I have argued that an increasing proportion of homeowners motivated reform consolidation to ensure that government could efficiently and effectively respond to growth. But it is also possible that a growing population of homeowners threatened reform policy goals. Reformers' goals included using public funds to develop their cities. Without a monopoly in place, an increased number of property owners might have meant defeat of new taxes to fund development. In fact, in a number of cities, reformers finally organized in pursuit of dominance after the public voted down a bond referendum for a large-scale project like a sewage plant. Yet a third way to interpret this coefficient would be to suggest that it measures growth in the reformer's traditional base—middle- and upper-class residents. However, adding a static measure of percent homeowners is not close to statistical significance. While cities with a large proportion of homeowners were no more or less likely to see reform monopolies emerge, cities with a growing proportion of homeowners were. It was during periods of change that reformers mobilized to dominate government.

When elites saw the future of their cities' health in jeopardy, they mobilized to build dominant regimes. Reform emergence was particularly likely in cities with an economic structure weighted toward professional occupations and large populations of native white residents. The ratio of manufacturers to professionals has a significant, positive effect on the probability of reform consolidation. In these cities, more elites had reason to seek and protect the benefits of development.

From whom would reformers have been protecting their government? The large positive effect of the five-year change in percent nonwhite suggests that an expanding population with social and economic needs might have threatened reformers' electoral success, their policy programs, or both. However, it appears that a city that had an existing high level of diversity tended to be unreceptive to reform domination. While cities in the South and the West became more diverse, reformers changed the political structure of their cities to minimize opportunities for dissent. In line with the effort to limit minority claims on government, reform consolidation was made more likely by having home rule and a poll tax. In sum, like machine leaders, reformers sought to establish monopolies when they faced political and policy hurdles that required cohesion.

Conclusion

In machine and reform cities, organization of coalitions posed a formidable challenge. The vote base of each regime coalition was determined to a large extent by the composition of the potential electorate. In machine cities, the support of white, foreign-stock, working-class residents was necessary to win elections during the machine's rise to power. Sensible politicians invested significant time and energy in mobilizing these voters. In reform cities, the coalition base tended to be white, middle-class residents who shared the developmental focus of reform regimes. In both types of cities, elites who controlled resources by virtue of their elected offices, economic power, or social power, were also key components of the coalition. These regimes became consolidated when politicians faced threats to political or policy goals. Contrary to popular belief, machines built dominant regimes when the population of renters and foreign-stock residents was on the decline.

After coming to power by mobilizing voters and appealing to broad coalitions, machine and reform regimes began to entrench themselves in power. Like business firms operating in a highly competitive market, political organizations seek to create a monopoly. In the cities included in this analysis, they succeeded in doing just that. By attacking competition at each stage in the electoral process—preference formation, the casting of votes, and the transformation of votes to seats—machines and reformers increased the likelihood that they would remain in power. From the years that they governed to the platforms that they endorsed, Dutch Hamann and Richard Daley shared more than traditional urban scholarship would predict. I have argued that they and their organizations also shared a political calculus, to win office and stay there. The differences between the choices that machine and reform politicians made rested on the world that they inhabited. They faced different voters, different institutional settings, and different visions of the future. But, at the end of the day, there has only ever been one local politician. Boss or manager, what mattered is that he knew how to engineer a monopoly.

Effects of Political Monopolies

RICHARD J. DALEY may be the most famous mayor in twentieth-century America. He had immense power and many adoring fans. Ebullient aldermen were known to burst out in spontaneous praise of their leader during council meetings. He was nicknamed "Hizzoner." When Daley passed away, thousands of people stood in line for hours in twenty-below weather to offer him tribute. One man explained, "[A]ll these people are repaying him for remembering them like he did" (quoted in Keegan 1976, 1). This was the same Richard J. Daley who in 1968 handed down an order that would haunt him for the rest of his life. As Chicago hosted the Democratic National Convention and the nation watched riots rip the city apart, Daley instructed his officers to "shoot to kill arsonists and 'shoot to maim or cripple' looters" (Schreiber 1968, 1).

Daley viewed the liberal antiwar movement in the same way that he viewed the civil rights movement and the War on Poverty—as an affront to his power and the stability of Chicago (Cohen and Taylor 2000). As he made clear in his famous order, he was prepared to defend his city at any cost from the success of such revolutionary elements. In large part Daley was able to maintain stability. Chicago never went bankrupt, never lost its business district or its middle class. While other rustbelt cities like Detroit hemorrhaged people and taxes, Chicago was the "city that work[ed]" (*New York Times* 1976, 28). But for some Chicagoans, particularly poor and black Chicagoans, the city did not work quite so well. Daley governed over a period of rapid development and intense segregation. African Americans lived in overcrowded ghettos, were restricted from high-level political positions, were arrested and incarcerated at disproportionate rates, discriminated against in city hiring, and provided with lower quality city services.

San Jose's reform leaders, epitomized by the powerful city manager Dutch Hamann, can also be characterized as having led the city to greatness while leaving some neighborhoods behind. In the post–WWII era, San Jose was changing rapidly. Defense contracts and the mild climate encouraged a massive influx of migrants to the Santa Clara valley. Between 1940 and 1950, San Jose's population grew by nearly 25,000 people. When Hamann was appointed in 1950, he took office determined to build upon this growth, to make the San Jose metropolitan area "one of the . . . most important areas of the West Coast" (San Jose Master Plan 1958, quoted in Matthews 2003, 95). In 1969 Hamann wrote, "There is no question in my mind that San Jose will be the dominant city of Northern California before the next twenty years have passed. The growth that lies before the city will dwarf all that has gone before" (quoted in Stanford Environmental Law Society 1970, 21).

Hamann's work was not in vain. In many ways the foundation for Silicon Valley was laid by his coalition and its bold decisions throughout the 1950s and 1960s (Matthews 2003). Yet, although growth and development were the goals of San Jose reformers, some areas of the city, particularly those that were predominately Mexican American, lacked paved roads, street lights, sewerage systems, and representation on the city council. San Jose's Latinos endured police brutality and discriminatory treatment in the justice system, the school system, and in city hiring (Pitti 2003).

In both San Jose and Chicago, the system of monopoly created by well-organized coalitions and biased systems led to a political arena that made challenging those in power difficult if not impossible. In a healthy democratic system, success in office suggests that the coalition has responded to the needs and wants of the voters. But if political institutions have been biased toward those in power, reelection of the incumbent organization does not mean that residents have exerted control over their elected officials. Chapter 2 provided evidence that dominant coalitions in machine and reform cities tilted electoral outcomes in their favor by shaping preferences, limiting voting options, and influencing the translation of ballots into seats held by the government. Chapter 4 substantiated that bias and organization had identifiable electoral effects as well. But what, if any, consequences did monopoly have for the people living in these cities?

This chapter offers both quantitative and narrative support for the argument that during monopoly periods, the governing coalition had the opportunity and incentive to respond to narrow segments of the population. As was the case in the previous chapter, for the most part this chapter refers to periods when bias and coordination were present at high levels, and compares these to periods in which either or both factors were not present. The choice to use this dichotomous categorization is driven not by a belief that cities only come in two states, but by a lack of nuanced data that would allow for an investigation into the effects of varying degrees of monopolization. Nonetheless, the relative distinction between monopolized and nonmonopolized cities remains a central theoretical contribution of this work. The 30 percent of American cities that met these admittedly high standards for monopolization did have political patterns that looked significantly different from other cities.

First, I present evidence that, once in power, machine and reform regimes ceased intensive mobilization of new voters and selectively courted core supporters to turn out. At the same time, the dominant coalition reduced benefits to some portions of the population and elections became uncompetitive. As a result, during the monopoly period, turnout of eligible voters declined.

Next, I investigate the effects of monopolies more broadly by examining patterns in the distribution of government benefits. I find that compared to cities in which there is no single dominant coalition advantaged by bias, monopolies focus benefits towards governing coalition elites and core coalition members, away from the broader community. In machine cities, party leadership positions, patronage jobs, government contracts, services, and urban policies were focused toward select white ethnic groups. In reform cities, middle-class whites and business constituencies filled elective and appointed offices and were provided expansive growth policies, low taxes, amenities and services in middle-class neighborhoods, and businesslike operation of government. Additionally, for both machine and reform regimes, powerful governing coalition elites were offered a disproportionate share of benefits.[1] I find that during the monopoly period, dominant coalitions spent less overall, reduced differences between expenditure and revenue, met the demands of key coalition members, and increased spending on developmental categories at the expense of the broader public.[2] Successful efforts to win reelection do, in the end, mean that fewer voters play a role in the governing process as security in office liberates coalitions from citizen demands.

Declining Participation Is a Consequence of Monopoly

In order to analyze the effect of monopoly for residents, I begin by looking at patterns of voter turnout during the bias period. In this section I use election data from the same nine cities analyzed in chapter 4. Five of the cities represent machine monopolies: Chicago, New York, New Haven, Kansas City, and Philadelphia. Four represent reform monopolies: San Jose, San Antonio, Austin, and Dallas. A complete explanation of the selection criteria for this sample is provided in chapters 1 and 4. In short, these cities were selected on the basis of available data. The dependent variable, *turnout,* is a measure of the total number of ballots cast in a given election divided by the number of eligible voters. The number of eligible voters includes all persons of voting age (males only prior to 1920). Noncitizens are included for both theoretical and practical reasons. Increasing the citizenship rate was an important strategy for mobilizing voters in machine cities, and a number of cities offered alien suffrage during the time period. Additionally, city-level data on numbers of citizens is not available for the entire time period.

The *bias period* for each city serves as the main independent variable in the analysis. This variable is coded one in years when high levels of bias and coordination were present and coded zero when either condition was not met. The list of years in the bias period for each city is included in table A4. A complete description of the coding choices for this variable is offered in chapter 4, along with more detailed descriptions of additional independent variables that control for alternative explanations for changes in turnout. To account for the possibility that turnout is purely responsive to the competitiveness of elections, I include the *margin of victory*—the percentage of the vote gained by the loser with the highest total subtracted from the percentage of the vote gained by the winner with the lowest total in each election. Also included are: the number of *candidates* running for each seat, the number of *incumbents* running, and the natural log of the total *population* of each city. I add a trend variable representing the *year* that the election was held and dummy variables representing the type of seat for which the election was held, *manager, commissioner,* or *mayor,* with *council* as the excluded category. Finally, a dummy variable is included indicating whether the city is classified as *machine* or *reform.*[3]

In a simple comparison, table 5.1 shows that for most of the cities in this study, the turnout of eligible voters in citywide, general elections was lower during the bias period.[4] Furthermore, this decline in turnout is statistically significant. To more rigorously test the hypothesis that turnout declined during bias periods, I regress the log odds of turnout of eligible voters (ln(turnout/1-turnout)) on the dummy variable for bias period and include the controls listed above.[5] The log-odds transformation of the dependent variable is used to achieve a normal distribution of the dependent variable and to bound predictions between zero and one. The analysis presented in table 5.2 shows that during bias period, the log odds of turnout of eligible voters in citywide elections

Table 5.1: Turnout during bias periods

	No bias (%)	Bias (%)
Chicago	50	49
New York	45	34
New Haven	44	57
Kansas City	34	47
Philadelphia	53	45
San Jose	32	21
San Antonio	17	14
Austin	22	18
Dallas	11	8
Albuquerque*	36	16

* Figures are from Bridges (1997).

Table 5.2: Effect of bias on turnout of eligible voters

	Log-odds turnout of eligible voters			
	Coefficient	Std. error	Coefficient	Std. error
Bias period	−0.38**	0.07	−0.23**	0.06
Incumbents running			0.00	0.03
Margin of victory			−1.36**	0.14
Candidates per seat			0.06**	0.02
Log population (millions)	−0.11**	0.03	−0.10**	0.03
Year	0.01**	0.00	0.01**	0.00
Machine/reform	1.48**	0.14	1.38**	0.13
Commissioner	−0.05	0.10	0.06	0.10
Mayor	0.31**	0.12	0.25**	0.12
Manager	0.55**	0.12	0.67**	0.13
Constant	−2.56**	0.20	−2.43**	0.18
F	113.68**		99.18**	
R^2	0.51		0.62	
N	686		686	

Note: Standard errors are clustered by city-election.
OLS regression: $*p < .10$ $**p < .05$

declines by about 0.38, which equates to about 6 percentage points on average.[6]

Since the analysis in chapter 4 suggested that competition also declined during the bias period, it is possible that the relationship between dominance and turnout is spurious. The second regression in table 5.2 shows that even controlling for incumbents running, the margin of victory, and the number of candidates per seat, turnout declines by about 4 percentage points during the bias period.[7] As dominant coalitions won by larger margins and increased their incumbency advantage, fewer voters were involved. In essence, these regimes could win reelection with only a small share of the eligible electorate voting them back into office.

There are competing explanations for these declines in turnout. Residents might not vote because, as I contend, they are discouraged from participating, or alternatively because they are satisfied with the governing coalition. If the second explanation were true, one would expect those most satisfied with the governing coalition to drop out more rapidly than those dissatisfied. A precinct analysis in San Jose and a ward level analysis in Chicago suggest that the proportion of people turning out to vote declined more drastically in areas populated by *non-core* coalition members.

To conduct this analysis I singled out areas in each city that were part of the core coalition and areas that were peripheral to the organization in power. The neighborhoods were selected using a combination of secondary source materials and census data. I used GIS mapping tools to define the boundaries of the neighborhoods and then assigned precincts to the correct area using polling-place addresses. In San Jose, the core areas, Willow Glen and Hester Hanchett, represent extremely stable, white, middle-upper-class neighborhoods with very high proportions of homeowners. The peripheral neighborhoods, East San Jose, North College Park, and the Gardner area, correspond to residents least favored by the regime. They have remained poor and working-class neighborhoods with high numbers of nonwhite renters since the 1930s. For the analysis of Chicago, I used the heavily African American second, third, fourth, sixth, and twentieth wards to signify residents least favored by the regime, and combined statistics from the working-class, Irish and Eastern European eleventh, thirteenth, and nineteenth wards for the core areas.[8] Table 5.3 shows the pattern of turnout over time in the two types of neighborhoods.

The data suggest that turnout of registered voters deteriorated at a higher rate in areas representing non-core coalition members. While turnout rates declined in the core areas, overall the rate remained fairly

Table 5.3: Turnout varies with regime membership

	San Jose				Chicago		
Year	Peripheral turnout (%)	Core turnout (%)	Mean margin of victory (%)	Year	Peripheral turnout (%)	Core turnout (%)	Mean margin of victory (%)
1938	47	46	1	1931	82	95	17
1946	32	36	13	1959	49	76	43
1958	20	26	59	1963	61	78	11
1962	27	36	12	1977	28	60	32
Total decline	−20	−10		Total decline	−54	−35	

stable. In both cities, these areas averaged higher turnout rates than the city as a whole. One might argue that these patterns represent the greater sensitivity of low socioeconomic status voters to changes in competition. The column noting the mean margin of victory in each election signifies that the relationship is not so straightforward. In neither city is the turnout rate particularly responsive to competitiveness. It is also suggestive that in the earliest election for both cities the peripheral neighborhood turnout rates were about equal to the rates in core neighborhoods. Once the regime collapsed, these areas again turned out at higher rates.

To rule out competing hypotheses, one would ideally test the relationship between dominance and turnout while controlling for socioeconomic status. Unfortunately, accurate data are not available at sub-city levels. I attempt to circumvent this problem using two additional analyses. First, I add controls to the turnout regressions presented above, indicating the proportion of the city that *rents* homes and the percentage of residents that are *nonwhite*. These measures serve as proxies for the residents that would be most likely to drop out of the electorate due to socioeconomic factors. Table 5.4 provides the outcome of this analysis. Adding the controls strengthens the power of the bias-period variable. Independent of the size of the poor and nonwhite populations, the bias period reduces turnout.[9]

The second way I propose to eliminate socioeconomic effects on turnout is to analyze turnout in Chicago's fifty wards for three elections during the bias period, controlling for the demographic makeup of those wards. The analysis pools general elections for mayor from 1959, 1963, and 1971. The dependent variable is the log odds of the turnout of eligible voters. The independent variables in this regression are the percent-

Table 5.4: The effect of bias on turnout of eligible voters, controlling for city demographics

	Log-odds turnout of eligible voters	
	Coefficient	*Std. error*
Bias period	−0.30**	0.07
Incumbents running	−0.00	0.03
Margin of victory	−1.25**	0.14
Candidates per seat	0.04**	0.02
Log population (millions)	−0.14**	0.03
Year	0.02**	0.00
Machine/reform	1.42**	0.16
Commissioner	0.30**	0.12
Mayor	0.49**	0.13
Manager	0.31**	0.13
% nonwhite	−2.73**	0.33
% renters	−0.44	0.43
Constant	−2.70**	0.36
F	78.18**	
R^2	0.66	
N	601	

Note: Standard errors are clustered by city-election.
OLS regression: $*p < .10$ $**p < .05$

age of residents in each ward who are of Irish, Polish, African American, or German descent.[10] I use 1960 census data for 1959, interpolated values for 1963, and 1970 values for 1971. To uncover the relationship between regime membership and turnout, I also add a dummy variable for submachine boss William Dawson's controlled wards. Dawson was the machine's most prominent organizer of black votes.[11] If the theory is correct, African American areas should have a negative relationship with turnout except for Dawson's wards, which should have a positive relationship.

The results in table 5.5 suggest that regime membership was an important component in determining average rates of turnout. Although not statistically significant, as predicted, areas with high proportions of African American residents had lower turnout, except where Dawson organized voters for the machine. The highest African American concentration areas that were not organized by Dawson had 48 percent turnout.[12] However, in Dawson's wards, with a mean of 82 percent black residents, turnout averaged 54 percent. In comparison, Irish and Polish populations have a positive effect on turnout. Moving from the minimum concentration of Irish residents to the maximum increases the predicted turnout from 46 percent to 72 percent. For Polish descendents, the figure goes from 47 percent to 51 percent. In heavily German areas, turnout averaged only 51 percent. This makes sense given that Germans were peripheral to the Daley machine (Erie 1988). Germans had the highest socioeconomic status of these groups, so this relatively moderate level of turnout counters a purely socioeconomic explanation. Due to problems of ecological inference, these results should only be taken as suggestive, but they do contribute to the body of evidence illustrating that dominant regimes selectively mobilize supporters and ignore or perhaps discourage others from participating in elections.

With no viable opposition, a satisfied electorate, and the goal of long-term dominance in sight, coalitions in machine and reform cities changed their focus. They became less interested in mobilizing the maximum number of voters and more interested in maintaining a coalition closer to minimum winning size. Qualitative evidence also indicates that during the bias period, machine and reform regimes selectively mobilized core coalition members and ceased efforts to register and turn out others.

Table 5.5: Chicago turnout by ward

	Log-odds turnout of eligible voters	
	Coefficient	*Std. error*
% Irish	8.66 **	2.56
% Polish	2.11*	1.09
% German	−0.42	2.32
Dawson	0.12	0.18
% black	−0.13	0.33
1959	−0.17 **	0.07
1963	0.21 **	0.05
Constant	−0.26	0.19
F	25.39**	
R^2	0.297	
N	148	

Note: Standard errors are clustered by ward.
OLS regression: $*p < .10$ $**p < .05$

Machines were famed for their unwavering efforts to naturalize, register, and mobilize newly arriving immigrants. But this behavior only accurately describes the early stage of machine building. When machines faced a tough fight for office they sought to maximize their share of votes from the eligible population, and they did so primarily by bringing new voters into an established political system with strong party allegiances. Once they achieved dominance, machines no longer fought laws that restricted certain populations from voting, and they began to ignore newly arriving immigrants, focusing instead on turning out their reliable patronage-based coalition (Erie 1988; Pinderhughes 1987; Grimshaw 1992). The 1900 census in New York reveals that 56 percent of white immigrants were naturalized, compared to only 43 percent in 1920, the middle of the city's bias period. Between 1890 and 1920 the Jewish and Italian proportion of the New York voting-age population expanded rapidly from 10 percent to 30 percent. During the same period, the share of Jewish and Italian voters rose more modestly from 2 percent to 13 percent (Erie 1988).

While machines simply stopped intensive efforts to bring people to the polls, reformers implemented institutional changes that minimized the number of voters. Measures like nonpartisan and nonconcurrent elections, strict registration requirements, poll taxes, literacy tests, and minimal press coverage depressed turnout citywide (Kelley, Ayres, and Bowen 1967; Lee 1960; Alford and Lee 1968; Dixon 1966). Throughout the twentieth century in reform cities, the common trend was declining turnout, but reform coalitions often mobilized their core constituencies to win elections. To ensure passage of municipal bonds and support of the reformers' platform, San Jose's city manager formed high-powered bond committees, held rallies, and invited celebrities to speak on behalf of his proposals and candidates. In 1961 he brought Miss America to San Jose to endorse a bond (Stanford Environmental Law Society 1970). The result of mobilizing only certain segments of the community was that in both machine and reform cities, dominant coalitions appeared to govern with near-complete consensus. They faced little to no competition from elites, and voters offered sometimes close to unanimous support of their leaders.

Monopoly Results in More Narrowly Distributed Benefits

Given that monopolies encounter reduced electoral participation from certain groups, are they then able to reduce services and exclude these groups from the benefits of government? To test this proposition, I analyze city financial patterns, comparing periods of monopoly dominance to both pre- and post-monopoly periods and to cities that never hosted a monopoly. This analysis includes the 244 cities ever to have been listed on the Census's 100-largest-cities list (see appendix tables A1–A3).

If my theory is correct, when monopolies are in power, spending should be targeted toward governing coalition elites as well as the regimes' core constituencies at the expense of benefits that serve the broader electoral community. Support for this claim is provided through an analysis of the proportion of machine and reform city budgets spent during the monopoly period as compared to other periods on three categories of expenditure, representing: (1) elite demands, (2) core constituency demands, and (3) broader community demands.

This analysis relies on annual city financial data gathered from the United States Census County and City Data Book from 1940–86.[13] For the most part, the fiscal measures are provided every five years in the second and seventh year of a decade, and the demographic measures are provided every decade in the Census of Population and Housing. I interpolated values for intervening years for the independent variables. The dependent variables, all based on real measures, are the proportion of direct general expenditure spent on various fiscal categories that serve as proxies for the winners and losers of municipal benefits.

Admittedly, there are no precise measures of expenditures for different types of voters that work across both time and place. I rely on the available census data and arguments made in the secondary literature to select the categories of spending. *Reformers' core* constituents were white, middle-class voters, and, thus, city spending on sanitation services—a major concern of homeowners—is used to represent their demands (Bridges 1997). The base of machine regimes was working-class, white ethnic voters. The machine's most valuable benefit was a payroll job. Consequently, the percentage of city budgets allocated to police and fire expenditures is used to capture the *machines' core* preferences. Since the vast majority of police and fire expenditures go toward payroll, it is reasonable to assume that increases and decreases in this measure indicate expansion and contraction of the city workforce.

One cannot use payroll expenditures directly because the proportions vary depending on the total number of functions a city must handle. Given that every city in the data set handles police and fire functions, this measure operates as the best proxy for the preferences of the machine's core. Further, this measure allows one to distinguish between the different uses of payroll for a machine monopoly. As explained in chapter 2, patronage positions were used to organize the machine and bias the system in favor of the incumbent coalition. But payroll jobs were also provided as benefits for machine supporters.[14] However, police and fire positions are frequently protected by civil service. Though machines had many ways of getting around civil-service requirements, the presence of police and fire unions ensures that in many cities hiring and firing cannot be done on a solely political basis. In this analysis I seek to measure the machines' propensity to increase benefits to their core supporters, not the presence of bias. Using the proportion of the budget spent on police and fire allows me to do this.

Both types of regimes relied heavily on the business class to maintain stability and support progress in their cities. For machine and reform regimes alike, the governing coalition included interests that could finance development and campaigns for office and block proposals that they perceived as threatening; these represent the governing coalition elites. I use expenditure on roads and highways, representative of pro-development spending, to capture spending for *governing coalition elites* (Peterson 1981). Finally, to measure changes in spending on *broader community* goods, I analyze expenditures in the categories of health and public welfare.[15]

In an ideal world, I would have used the characteristics that define monopoly (organization and bias) as my primary independent variables in determining a *monopoly period* for each of the 244 cities in the data set. Due to the severe paucity of municipal election data and the difficulty of measuring machine forms of bias across a large number of cases, there is virtually no way to do this. Instead, I rely on the rich historical research conducted by other urban scholars to determine sets of years that might be considered monopoly periods in each city and then analyze municipal benefit distribution in relation to these periods. A complete description of the process employed is provided in chapters 1 and 4. Clear start and end dates for the monopoly period were determined for twenty-five cases (listed in table A3 in the appendix). Of these twenty-five cases, seventeen are machine monopolies and eight are reform monopolies.

A simple analysis of expenditure patterns displayed in figure 5.1 provides evidence that compared to the periods before and after dominance, machine and reform regimes spent a larger share of their budgets on governing coalition elites and core constituents during monopoly periods.

Reformers increased expenditure on sanitation by approximately 6 percentage points in order to serve their middle-class voters during the monopoly period. Machine regimes reduced sanitation spending during their monopoly periods but increased police and fire expenditures by

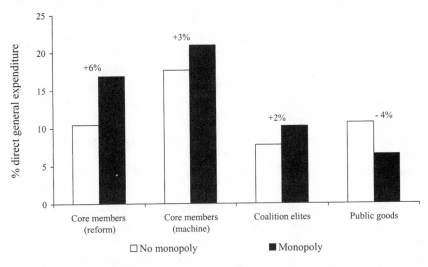

Fig. 5.1: Effect of monopoly period on spending patterns

an average of 3 percentage points, suggesting the importance of payroll jobs for their supporters. In both types of cities, highway expenditures, supported by businesses and developers, increased during monopoly periods by an average of 2 percentage points, while spending on health and welfare declined by an average of 4 percentage points.

In order to test these findings more rigorously I regress the percentage spent in each category on a dummy variable for the monopoly period and include a variety of controls to isolate monopoly as a causal factor.[16] Other scholars have argued that fiscal capacity, functional responsibilities, bureaucratic decisions, and residents' needs are better predictors of government spending than political factors (see Meier, Stewart, and England 1991 for a review of the literature). A measure of *general revenue* standardized to 1982 dollars is used to test the alternative hypothesis that capacity, not dominance, determines spending patterns.

Because cities are subordinate to states and the federal government, a large portion of their revenue comes from intergovernmental transfers. When subventions are tied to specific purposes, expenditure patterns may reflect priorities of higher levels of government rather than political demand. Additionally, extra income from the state or federal government may free up city funds for spending on redistributive functions. The percent of *intergovernmental revenue* is included to control for these possibilities. Along these same lines, a dummy variable noting whether or not the city had *home rule* indicates the flexibility of local officials in changing patterns of expenditure.

To account for the possibility that demographics may drive patterns in city spending, I add a control for the percentage of the population that is *nonwhite* according to the census.[17] Additionally, the size of the needy population may affect expenditure patterns. I include the proportion of the population that is home *renters* to account for this. Another aspect of a city's need might be its size, both geographic area and total population. For instance, as a city expands and incorporates outlying areas, expenditures on new infrastructure might dominate. The regressions include measures of the city's *land area* in square miles, *total population,* and five-year *percent change* in total population to control for this possibility. The measures of land area and total population are logged to account for a leveling-off effect at high values. Finally, I include a *year* variable to capture linear trends in spending,[18] dummy variables for region including *South, West,* and *Midwest* (with *Northeast* as the excluded category), and dummy variables noting whether the city was ever monopolized by a *machine* or *reform* organization.[19] These last two variables allow me to determine whether or not machine and reform cities had different spending patterns from nonmonopoly cities over the entire time period, even when monopolies were not in power.

I present four models below, regressing the proportion of the budget spent on sanitation, police and fire, highways, and health and welfare on the variables described above. The analyses exclude cases in which it is known that a monopoly dominated at some point during the twentieth century, but where I have no knowledge of the precise start and end dates for this monopoly (see table A2 in the appendix). In the regressions on core expenditures (sanitation and police and fire), the monopoly period is specific to the type of regime in question. For instance, in the model for sanitation expenditures, the monopoly period is only coded one during reform monopoly periods; it is coded zero for all other cases during all other years. This allows me to test the possibility that the focused expenditures were particular to the regime's core constituents and not an effect of monopoly in general.

For both machine and reform cities, the results in table 5.6 suggest strong, clear patterns of expenditure. Regimes concentrate resources on governing coalition elites and core constituents at the expense of the broader public.

Both machine and reform monopolies spent significantly more on their core members during monopoly periods. Reformers increased expenditures by more than 6 percentage points and machines by about 3.5 percentage points for the most important constituents. The figures

Table 5.6: Effect of monopoly on targeted benefits

	% DGE spent on reform core		% DGE spent on machine core		% DGE spent on coalition elites		% DGE spent on broader public	
	Coefficient	Std. error	Coefficient	Std. error	Coefficient	Std. error	Coefficient	Std. error
Monopoly period	0.061 **	0.019	0.033 **	0.013	0.022 **	0.008	−0.029 **	0.013
Fiscal capacity								
General revenue (millions)	−0.001	0.001	−0.004 **	0.001	0.003 **	0.001	0.008 **	0.002
Fiscal flexibility								
% revenue intergovernmental	−0.031	0.036	−0.148 **	0.052	−0.062	0.041	0.116 **	0.034
Home rule	−0.010 **	0.004	−0.013 **	0.004	0.005	0.004	0.016 **	0.006
Population needs								
% nonwhite	−0.007	0.021	−0.003	0.016	−0.012	0.019	−0.070 **	0.026
% renters	−0.179 **	0.023	−0.155 **	0.015	−0.176 **	0.024	0.206 **	0.073
Log land area	−0.011 **	0.005	−0.025 **	0.005	0.002	0.004	0.020 **	0.009
Log population (millions)	0.007	0.005	0.022 **	0.005	−0.012 **	0.004	0.005	0.006
5-year relative population change	0.070 **	0.027	−0.116 **	0.039	0.085 **	0.027	−0.085 *	0.051
General controls								
Year	0.001 *	0.001	−0.001	0.001	−0.001	0.001	−0.001 **	0.000
South	0.046 **	0.012	0.037 **	0.007	0.023 **	0.004	−0.027	0.030
West	0.018 **	0.008	0.102 **	0.005	0.031 **	0.007	−0.076 **	0.024
Midwest	0.041 **	0.008	0.038 **	0.004	0.054 **	0.008	−0.038 **	0.014
Machine	0.011 *	0.006	−0.016 **	0.005	−0.011	0.007	−0.041 **	0.014

(continued)

Table 5.6: Effect of monopoly on targeted benefits (*continued*)

	% DGE spent on reform core		% DGE spent on machine core		% DGE spent on coalition elites		% DGE spent on broader public	
	Coefficient	Std. error	Coefficient	Std. error	Coefficient	Std. error	Coefficient	Std. error
Reform	−0.020	0.013	−0.021 **	0.006	−0.036 **	0.011	0.029 *	0.017
Constant	0.187 **	0.062	0.565 **	0.072	0.210 **	0.063	−0.057	0.084
Wald χ^2	2469.80**		26806.15 **		7180.14 **		1835.85 **	
R^2	0.183		0.278		0.330		0.160	
ρ	0.315		0.477		0.348		0.608+	
N	1158		836		1158		907	

Note: Panel-corrected standard errors reported.
+Model corrected for autocorrelation, Prais Winsten method.
OLS regressions: $^* p < .10$ $^{**} p < .05$

may seem small, but represent large sums of real money. The differences between the monopoly and nonmonopoly periods equate to an increase of about $9.4 million on sanitation spending in the average reform city and about $13.7 million on police and fire spending in the average machine city.[20] Both types of regimes also increased spending by about 2 percentage points on the developmental category of roads and highways, a priority for developers and business interests. At the same time, coalitions spent 4 percent less on health and welfare. Splitting the sample by monopoly type confirmed that the effect of monopoly period was statistically indistinguishable for machine versus reform regimes with regard to increased spending on roads and decreased spending on health and welfare. Additionally, monopolies reduced per capita expenditure by about $9.20, even when controlling for revenue, a decline of about 19 percent. This reinforces McDonald's (1985) argument that contrary to the expectations of turn-of-the-century critics of machine politics, these organizations did not expand government to provide for the needs of the urban masses.[21] As machine and reform regimes became secure in office, they turned their attention away from the demands of a broad electoral coalition to serve the preferences of governing coalition elites and key coalition members.

There are a number of interesting results from these analyses for students of city politics. For instance, these data support Peterson's (1981) argument that cities are significantly more likely to spend money on redistributive programs when they have bigger budgets overall and receive significant amounts of aid from higher levels of government. Additionally, having a large population in need of government services (renters in these models) appears to tie the hands of city budget makers significantly, encouraging a reduction in spending on sanitation, police and fire, and roads in favor of health and welfare. As other scholars have found, region remains an important factor in determining spending patterns. Yet even with these controls, the monopoly period remains a significant predictor in expenditure patterns. In their quest for reelection and in service to their organizations, dominant coalitions shifted municipal expenditures toward their key constituencies.

Dominance Increased Benefits for Core Coalition Members

Qualitative evidence also suggests that when regimes successfully dominate the system, they focus benefits on their core constituency and members of the governing coalition. In machine and reform cities alike, dominant coalitions rewarded key members of their coalitions with divisible benefits and policy choices. Monopolies were successful because they were attentive to their base. This is not a small point. All of the coalitions that governed over a monopoly period were reelected to office time and again. Even if the rules of the game advantaged these incumbents, they would not have survived had they not been responsive to some portion of their communities. As William Munro (1933) remarked, "[I]t is the boss who serves as the mediator between poverty and power . . . he is the protector of his people" (19).[22]

In Chicago, the Irish held the mayor's seat from 1933 until 1983, with one brief three-year hiatus. Into the 1970s, the Irish held between one-quarter and one-third of the seats on Chicago's city council, while they made up only about 2 percent of the total city population (Erie 1988).[23] New York's Tim Sullivan, Irish boss of the East Side, governed over a district that was 85 percent Jewish and Italian, but only 5 percent Irish in 1910. New Haven's white immigrant ethnic groups, Italians, Irish, and Jews, accounted for 57 percent of the city's registered voters in 1959, but accounted for 82 percent of elected municipal officials. Of these groups, the Irish were most heavily overrepresented, at 29 percent of the officials but only 11 percent of the electorate (Wolfinger 1974). Because dominant organizations in these cities controlled the nomination process as a mechanism for consolidating their monopoly, it can be seen as no accident that core coalition members were disproportionately slated for office.

White ethnic constituencies also won disproportionate shares of patronage jobs, party positions, and appointments in machine cities. Table 5.7 shows the percentage of government employees identified as Irish in three machine cities. As machines consolidated power, they employed a greater percentage of the total Irish workforce in municipal government. In 1900, Irish shares of government jobs were roughly proportional to their population proportions. By 1930, when machines

Table 5.7: Irish government employment in machine cities

	% employed in local government		% of workforce employed in local government		% of population (1st and 2nd generation)	
	1900	1930	1900	1930	1900	1930
New York	36.6	51.7	5.8	23.6	31.1	8.8
Jersey City	42.4	58.3	5.1	20.8	37.7	3.3
Albany	30.0	41.0	4.6	14.8	32.6	10.1
Average change, 1900–1930	+14%		+14.6%		−26.4%	

Source: Erie (1988); United States Census of Population and Housing, 1910, 1920, 1930

dominated these three cities, Irish patronage far outstripped population shares.

Some scholars have argued that patronage or "bloated public employment" is actually a form of income redistribution (Alesina, Baqir, and Easterly 2000, 220). However, while groups like the Irish benefited from machines' allocations of patronage, during the bias period, machines actually employed a smaller proportion of the total population in government jobs. Analysis suggests that the proportion of residents employed in city jobs declined from 4.3 percent to 3.4 percent on average during machine monopoly periods.[24] Given this, it is unlikely that the machines were simply attempting to redistribute income to all low-income and working-class persons.

Aside from patronage jobs and municipal positions, core coalition members in machine cities benefited from their preferred relationship with dominant regimes in other ways as well. Union members were rewarded with large public works projects and support for labor organizing. Other coalition members, like business groups, frequently requested and were granted lax enforcement of laws governing their conduct or operations, an underassessment of taxes, and liberal business policies (Pinderhughes 1987). Pendergast's general refusal to enforce oversight of nightclubs and prohibition contributed to the birth of some of the world's greatest jazz (Ward and Burns 2000). New Haven's Mayor Lee's first foray into redevelopment was a massive overhaul of the city's parks and recreations programs—projects all to be heavily used by the lower-class residents of the city. He fixed up decrepit athletic fields, built playgrounds, an athletic center, a new clubhouse on the municipal golf course, and a new lawn-bowling clubhouse. In Pittsburgh, the Lawrence organization rewarded African Americans with a fair employment practices ordinance and top-level appointments in the administration.

Machines also supported policies important to their voters. In New York, the Tammany commission that investigated the Triangle Shirtwaist Company fire proposed fifty new laws to protect wages and working conditions for women and children, a boon to their factory-working constituents (Erie 1988). In Albany, where core coalition members were middle class, the machine provided efficient city services, low taxes, and underassessment for homeowners. Such policies came to be adopted by other machine cities as well, especially as their core constituents became home owners. Daley's city "that worked" met the demands of this constituency. He focused on street repairs and beautification, garbage collection and snow removal, low property taxes and preservation of property values.

An important qualification stated in chapter 3 is that machines were careful not to exclude groups of residents from their coalitions outright. This is evident in their allocation of benefits to non-core members. Throughout the monopoly period, machines were skilled at providing symbolic benefits that cost few resources. New York's Boss Sullivan, while keeping Jews and Italians out of elected office and coveted patronage positions, provided food baskets, coal, and sometimes rent money to the new immigrants. He sponsored legislation to make Columbus Day a holiday, took to wearing a yarmulke, and nominated Jews and Italians for minor party posts. Similarly, Kansas City's Boss Pendergast opened political clubs that provided a social outlet for residents who could not afford or were excluded from the city's country clubs. In New Haven the mayor visited at least two schools a week, talking with teachers and reading to the children. In every machine city, bosses provided picnics and ballgames, attended weddings, wakes, and funerals, opened citizen complaint offices, and provided small favors to community members, all as inexpensive efforts to maintain the voters' good will without having to share the most valuable benefit—patronage. These strategies to win reelection were popular and responsive to portions of the community. As mentioned in chapter 1, none of these leaders could afford to rest on bias alone. They worked for reelection as all politicians do, by cultivating a reliable constituency.

Though reform coalitions did not rely on patronage for building their regimes, key elected and appointed municipal positions *were* focused toward core members. Well into the 1980s the overwhelming majority of those who served on San Jose's boards and commissions were part of an old elite network. Political jobs were dominated by a circle of white, middle-class men connected through the city's Catholic boys' high school and Catholic college. Two of San Jose's oldest, whitest, and wealthiest neighborhoods were home to nearly every city council member throughout the entire reform period of 1945–77 (Christensen 1997).

Reformers attended to their core from the beginning of their regimes, focusing on middle-class, white constituents. They offered low, stable tax rates, efficient homeowner services, and clean government. An analysis of library building during San Jose's reform period exemplifies the beneficiaries of reform dominance. Between 1944 and 1962, the most powerful years of the reform administration, four libraries were built. All were nestled within the two neighborhoods that produced all of the city's reform politicians (San Jose Public Library 2003). Similarly, in Austin, all five branch libraries were built in neighborhoods providing wide margins to reformers during the bias period. In San Antonio during the monopoly period, libraries in African American neighborhoods and low-income housing projects were closed. The first new branch to be built since 1930 opened in a newly annexed, affluent Anglo community. Phoenix's reform government conducted a study to determine sites for new libraries that would be most advantageous to their electoral fortunes (Bridges 1997).

Aside from gaining new libraries, middle-class migrants to the West also benefited from reform governments' responsiveness to residential developers. By granting unhindered access to surrounding open space, reform governments provided a plethora of moderately priced, suburban, single-family homes with large plots and beautiful natural surroundings.[25] Reform governments also increased attention on homeowner services. In return, for many years these homeowners loyally supported reform coalitions at the ballot box. However, there were costs to this style of development that would ultimately chip away at reformers' power. Residents faced traffic congestion, environmental degradation, and high costs of living. The loss of agricultural land and the elimination of the orchard industry were encouraged by Hamann and other reform leaders, who offered to rezone agricultural parcels to increase the value of the land for sale (Matthews 2003, 101). This provided a larger sale price to the growers and made more land available for development. That growth had externalities does not minimize the fact the coalitions were providing a substantial benefit to homeowners by lowering the cost of homes and increasing attention to homeowner services.

Dominance Increased Benefits for Governing Coalition Elites

The biggest winners from reform governments were the elite developers, who were so powerful that city planning was often driven wholly by their preferences. In all of these cities, the historical period with the most pronounced development and rapid growth was the monopoly period. This was no accident—the leaders of these regimes were visionaries with long-term plans for their cities, making developers key members of the coalitions. One San Jose developer explained that during the reformers' reign, he was the "closest thing to a power broker that the city had ever had" (Charles Davidson interview 2003).[26] Annexation decisions were based on requests submitted by developers—not on cost to existing residents or the city's ability to provide services to the new areas. Sewer lines were planned by sticking pins in a map when developers requested a connection, and built when enough pins seemed to justify a new line

(P. Trounstine and Christensen 1982). Reform coalitions also subsidized development with public funds. Developers saved about $700 per lot in San Jose compared to neighboring Milpitas due to public funds offered for construction costs, less stringent construction requirements, and low rates on service extensions to the developments in San Jose (Stanford Environmental Law Society 1970). In Austin, when developers paid for street building and utility connections, they were repaid five times the expenditure for ten years, or until the developer's costs were totally recouped with interest. Developers, city administrators, and businesses profited tremendously from these policies. In Phoenix, a 1961 article reported that the new millionaires of the city were primarily housing developers (Martin 1961).

In machine cities, too, governing coalition elites and city officials benefited personally from dominance. Machines in Chicago, New York, New Haven, Pittsburgh, and Albany fashioned powerful governing coalitions of developers, bankers, and unions. They used redevelopment, slum clearance, and corporate development to maintain support from these elites. In Philadelphia, the Republican machine assisted utilities like the United Gas Company and the Philadelphia Rapid Transit Company in establishing economic monopolies (McCaffery 1992). Three brothers connected to the Philadelphia machine, George, Edwin, and William Vare, collected nearly $30 million in city contracts (Committee of Seventy). Many members of the governing coalition—particularly the political organizers, precinct leaders, and ward bosses—received public jobs. Forthal (1946) found that 70 percent of precinct captains in Chicago held public jobs during the mid-1920s. Other members of the coalition benefited from public contracts or partnerships and inside information. In Kansas City, Pendergast's concrete company poured "every cubic inch of material needed for the massive public works programs he relentlessly sponsored for his city" (Ward and Burns 2000, 196). Tammany's Boss Plunkitt was famous for his views on "honest graft." In his words, "If my worst enemy was given the job of writin' my epitaph when I'm gone, he couldn't do more than write 'George W. Plunkitt. He Seen His Opportunities, and He Took 'Em.'" (Riordan 1994, 6).

Machines brokered deals through which businesses provided benefits to politicians, like jobs for constituents, winter coal, or cash, in exchange for favorable policy decisions regarding business operations. In Kansas City, for example, Pendergast received a large cash payoff in exchange for orchestrating the appointment of a superintendent of insurance, who agreed to allow an increase in insurance rates. One journalist wrote of the sheriff's position in Chicago, "Knowledgeable people had a rule of thumb at that time that if a sheriff couldn't step out of office four years later with a clear $1,000,000 in his pocket, he just wasn't trying" (quoted in Cohen and Taylor 2000, 74). So, for many machine elites, dominating the political system and minimizing challenges to the machine's power translated into personal wealth and status.

Peripheral Groups Suffered during Monopoly Periods

While governing coalition elites and core coalition members won benefits from dominant coalitions, other members of the community suffered when public expenditures declined during periods of dominance. The lack of competition generated by the consolidation of the monopoly eliminated the power of peripheral groups to bargain for increased benefits and representation. In machine and reform cities alike, dominant coalitions faced competing demands from poor minority residents seeking integration, better school funding, a halt to police brutality and discrimination, appointment to high-level political positions, and public investment in jobs, housing, and welfare. Simultaneously, middle-class whites and business constituents preferred low-tax, service-oriented policies, and sought continued segregation in housing and education.

During the monopoly period in Chicago (and elsewhere), these conflicts were decided in favor of whites, the machine's core constituency. Using public funds, Chicago's Housing Authority became a veritable model for ghetto building, enforcing segregation, poverty, and racism. In 1957, Chicago's *Daily Defender,* the nation's leading black newspaper, editorialized, "[I]t seems strange that segregation bars are being lowered in the deep South, while in Chicago we are raising them higher!" (11). Daley, like many mayors, expressed strong support for public-housing programs, advocating assistance to people in need. In 1958, Daley traveled to Washington to convince the federal government to allow Chicago to build "low, walk-up structures that would provide apartments for large families, contain small apartments on the first floor for elderly persons, and represent a type of construction that might eventually be sold to private owners" (Buck 1958, 23).

Over time, because of the paucity of funding, the concentration of people, and the enforcement of segregation, housing developments became terrifying places to live, trapping people in prisons filled with violence and drugs. But there was no incentive for the machine to provide solutions because it did not face electoral threats, and so it remained insulated from the reality of the ghetto. Furthermore, some scholars have argued that the machine benefited from maintaining the public-housing system because of the large numbers of patronage jobs it offered (Cohen and Taylor 2000). Continued racial violence at the edges of the ghetto and a close election in 1963 convinced Daley to pull away from efforts to promote integration in service to his white base.

Another example of machines choosing policies that placed the demands of their core supporters over peripheral groups was in the realm of school funding. In many machine cities, a large proportion of the core constituency sent their children to parochial schools (Erie 1988). This frequently made school funding a low priority. During the monopoly period, machines in this data set reduced school expenditures by nearly 6 percentage points.[27] In Chicago the segregation of schools became a major target of black outrage. Led by the Coordinating Council of Community Organizations, the African American community launched an effort in the early 1960s to remove the public school superintendent, Benjamin Willis, for failing to take steps to integrate the city's schools. This culminated in two large-scale boycotts by black students, a number of rallies, marches on city hall, and scathing editorials in the *Daily Defender*. The first citywide desegregation plan was issued almost twenty years later in 1980.

Machines controlled the distribution of benefits carefully. In some cities machines established Byzantine bureaucracies to ensure that only core members would receive municipal benefits. In New Haven, acquiring delivery of some services like tree pruning or waste disposal required attaining a series of permits from offices open at irregular, infrequent times. Such a system makes it possible for the bureaucracy to have a large amount of discretion in providing services, and places the onus for pursuing government benefits on the residents.

There is also substantial support for the argument that machines were highly concerned with who was awarded public jobs (see Wolfinger 1974; Stave et al. 1988). The reliance on patronage jobs as a source of municipal benefits may have had an effect on the administration of city services. There is a large literature on public bureaucracies that shows that staffing bureaus with a high proportion of political appointees makes agencies more responsive to elected officials, but at the cost of less expertise (D. Lewis 2008). There is some evidence that the pattern is similar at the local level (see Stein 1991, for example). Munro (1933) argues, "Misgovernment, in all its iniquites [*sic*], falls most heavily on the poor and on the underprivileged." He explains further, "It is they who have to put up with the dangers and the inconvenience of slipshod building laws, lax health regulations, inefficient inspection of food and milk, uncleaned streets, overcrowded school buildings, and unsupervised playgrounds" (20). Thus, the dominant coalitions' reliance on patronage may have been the source of additional negative outcomes for residents who were peripheral to the monopoly.

In many cities urban renewal represented the provision of benefits to core coalition members and governing coalition elites at the expense of peripheral groups. For every new building that was erected, a slum was cleared, displacing more than a million residents over the course of the federal program (Anderson 1964). These decisions were not made independent of the racial and ethnic makeup of neighborhoods (Hirsch 1983). Although money for urban renewal came from the federal government, the implementation of the programs and the designation of sites of low-income housing projects were handled by local governments. In Chicago, the city council gave neighborhoods the right to "veto the construction of public housing within their borders" (Schill and Wachter 1995, 1295). The result was an extreme concentration of high-rise public housing projects in heavily black neighborhoods. In New Haven alone, Wolfinger (1974) estimates 7,000 households and 25,000 residents were moved to make way for urban renewal. While millions of dollars were spent pursuing redevelopment, the poorest residents in machine cities became poorer. New Haven spent over $200 million in public funds on renewal programs, but by the 1970s had become the fourth-poorest city in the country. By 1989, the infant-mortality rate rivaled third-world countries in some neighborhoods, and the citywide average was the second highest in the nation.

This is not to say that leaders like New Haven's Mayor Dick Lee sought to exacerbate poverty in their cities. On the contrary, Dick Lee was wholeheartedly committed to saving New Haven from its long downward spiral (Rae 2003). However, in many places, the way in which urban-renewal programs were carried out created advantages for some and disadvantages for others because politics and policy remained closed to segments of the population. For example, in New Haven, Mayor Lee's administration organized Citizen Action Committees (CACs) to advise the redevelopment process, provide opportunities for citizen input, and generate support for governmental decisions, but Dahl (1961) argues that "except for a few trivial instances the CAC never directly initiated, opposed, vetoed or altered any proposal brought before them by the mayor and his Development Administrator" (131). Throughout the 1950s, the urban-renewal program governed by New Haven's Democratic machine relied on maps that had been developed decades earlier to determine which areas of the city to raze and replace. The maps that they used ranked neighborhoods from best to worst. Rae (2003) has argued that the hierarchy was "based as much on bigotry as land or buildings" (281). By designating predominately African American neighborhoods as slums and/or risky investments and then demolishing the community, the government instituted a self-fulfilling prophecy for these areas.

In Chicago, black anger against the machine built throughout Daley's years in office, as the monopoly continually slighted the African American community. Issues of police brutality were actively avoided by the Democratic organization. According to the *Daily Defender,* "[T]he Chicago police force is composed largely of men who do not even bother to hide their racial bias, so strong is their hatred of the Negro. And, it is not unlikely that this anti-Negro feeling is a reflection of the people at the top" (1957, 11). In 1960, of 200 lieutenants on the police force, not one was black (*Daily Defender* 1960, A10).

When an important Black Panther leader, Fed Hampton, was shot by Chicago policemen assigned to protect Daley's candidate for state attorney, a prominent African American congressman, Ralph Metcalfe, felt he could no longer support the Daley machine. Metcalfe openly broke with Daley, and when he next faced reelection, Daley slated a high-profile white cabinet member to run against Metcalfe in the primary. Although Metcalfe won, Daley's decision was both meant and taken as a direct assault on Chicago and Illinois's African American communities. To inflame the issue further, after Metcalfe's death in office, a white machine loyalist was selected as his replacement. Similarly, when Daley's death required that the city council appoint an acting mayor, they passed over the African American president pro tem of the city council (Preston 1982). Throughout the monopoly period in Chicago and elsewhere, blacks demanded and were denied appointments to municipal positions. "Mr. Mayor we would like to point out," the *Daily Defender* said, "that in comparison with other cities . . . Chicago is sadly lacking in the utilization of its finest and most well-qualifies [*sic*] Negro citizens in responsible positions in your administration" (1956, 9). By 1970, blacks made up 40 percent of Chicago's population, but only 20 percent of the municipal workforce. As of 1974, Latinos made up only 1.7 percent of the full-time city payroll (Belenchia 1982) but about 10 percent of the population.

Prior to the consolidation of the monopoly, and even during the early years of the machine's rise to power, Chicago's Democratic politicians reached out to the black community. For example, Mayor Ed Kelly built a sizable black following by empowering submachine boss William Dawson, granting him control over the policy racket, appointing blacks to municipal posts, slating black candidates, and targeting blacks for government aid. He defended integrated public housing and schools and banned the movie *Birth of a Nation.*

Similarly, in New York, before the monopoly consolidated, Tammany's bosses expanded vote totals by promising benefits to Jews and Italians. During the 1910s and 1920s, the rising Hague organization in Jersey City actively courted and won the allegiance of new immigrants by converting the city hospital into a medical center and providing free health care to the city's poor. Between 1900 and 1920, competitive party pressures in Albany led politicians to mobilize newer ethnic immigrants from southern and eastern Europe by providing them with jobs and economic relief. Thus, it was only after consolidation of the monopoly that machines narrowed their focus.

Reform Periphery

Constituents on the periphery of reform monopolies also suffered while regimes were in power. Because reformers had spent much energy and many resources on separating politics from government, dissent was eliminated in the very structure of the cities' institutions. By unifying the executive and legislative branches of government and making council seats at-large, all of those in power were beholden to the same constituency. Such a structure made it appear as though the cities were homogenous and unified, but many cities with reform governments had large populations of residents who did not always share reform views. Intense debates erupted over the placement of public works, the location of new roads and freeways, the provision of parks, libraries, and schools, and the role of labor unions in municipal government.

While reform coalitions maintained agendas that promoted growth and development, benefiting business and middle-class whites, they ignored the social needs of many residents and neglected the city's burgeoning physical problems (Abbott 1987). One of the clearest examples of this pattern is seen in Southwestern annexation policies. As cities like San Jose annexed new communities at the behest of developers, poorer communities closer to the center were not provided with basic municipal services. The Latino neighborhood known as the Mayfair District in San Jose flooded in 1952, creating a significant public health threat (Matthews 2003). The same creek overflowed its banks again in 1955, 1958, and 1962. The year that the monopoly collapsed, 1979, the water district finally filed an application to protect the nearly 4,000 homes and businesses in the area from further damage.[28] In the early 1970s, residents of Alviso, a heavily Latino area, blocked a bridge, demanding that crossers pay a toll to pay for needed repairs that the city of San Jose refused to provide (Allen-Taylor 1998).

Austin's 1969 Model Cities program first focused on paving and drainage in center-city neighborhoods. Yet, the predominately African American west side of Austin did not have paved streets in some areas until 1979 (Orum 1987). Meanwhile, city government provided sewerage, streets, and utilities for all of the new developments. In Albuquerque, developers were required to set aside 4 percent of new developments for park land. By 1960, the middle class and affluent neighborhoods boasted fifty small parks and green areas, whereas the poor Valley communities had no public parks unconnected to schools. Some poor and working-class sections of Phoenix lacked municipal water and sewers because they were never annexed. As a result, they only had running water between midnight and 5 a.m. The busy annexation mill in San Antonio doubled the city's size between 1940 and 1950, but leapfrogged over older, poorer, and more heavily Latino neighborhoods. During these years, reformers promised Latino leaders that they would build drainage projects in return for support in bond elections. The bonds passed and the money was allocated, but the projects were never built (Johnson, Booth, and Harris 1983). As late as the 1980s, Mexican American communities in San Antonio and Albuquerque were beset by flooding due to inadequate drainage systems.

Reform coalitions were strategic in their choices to annex and develop. The policies were meant to benefit governing coalition elites and core members in the coalition. Rapid growth precluded development of a public transit system, which would have been highly valuable to low-income residents. New homes and jobs that the reform coalitions brought to their cities did not go to minority residents (Geilhufe 1979). In many places, the newly annexed or developed subdivisions were not open to persons of color. According to a study conducted in post–WWII San Jose, "[A]ll of the subdivisions opened within the last five or six years have written restrictions barring property from occupancy or use by all non-Caucasians except those who are working as domestics in the area" (quoted in Pitti 2003, 88). In the 1960s, when San Jose was the fastest-growing city in the nation, Mexican Americans concentrated on the East Side affectionately called one barrio Sal Si Puedes ("Get out if you can"). It was here that Cesar Chavez began his career organizing the Chicano movement (Pitti 2003, 91). In 2005, Buena Vista, a poorly developed, seedy area, surrounded on all sides by San Jose, was still not annexed by the city. In San Antonio, the Good Government League directed development money to the suburbs, away from older areas that were increasingly strained by the arrival of new low-income immigrants (Johnson, Booth, and Harris 1983).

Many reform governments chose not to build low-income housing, even when federal funds were offered and demand was great. By 1977 the Santa Clara County housing task force declared that about 40 percent of households were in need of housing assistance. A report by the California Builders Association found that increasing developer profits (not increased labor or land costs) contributed most to the skyrocketing home prices between 1967 and 1977. The lack of affordable housing in San Jose meant that low-income residents were often forced to move outside city bounds, first to Alviso and later to Gilroy or Morgan Hill.

Those Latinos who stayed in San Jose lobbied for low-cost housing, improved services, an end to discriminatory housing practices, and better, integrated schools on the East Side. A report of schools endangered by inadequate protection against earthquakes showed that all seventeen schools in serious risk were located in Mexican American communities on the East Side. Latino communities deteriorated relative to white neighborhoods throughout the monopoly period, and segregation worsened (Alesch and Levine 1973). The city responded to these demands primarily with symbolic gestures, creating a Human Relations Board and a program to track the race and ethnicity of city employees. According to Browning, Marshall, and Tabb (1984), San Jose's Model Cities program had a very small budget and was largely used to "insulate city hall from minority demands, to minimize opposition . . . and to divert minority discontent away from city hall toward the leaders of the programs" (217–18). In 1971, San Jose police stopped a black IBM research chemist for a traffic violation and shot him when he attempted to run away. Outraged residents protested in front of city hall and filled council meetings, demanding action (Christensen 1997). But the governing coalition had no incentive to be responsive to minority demands. The institutions that it had created and the culture of nonparticipation that it cultivated kept reformers safely in office.

Inequities in school funding were another legacy of the monopoly period in many reform cities. Until 1953, California law mandated that school district boundaries be coterminous with city boundaries. If a city annexed territory, the school district in the existing territory would be

168

dismantled. As a result, school administrators frequently opposed annexations. At the request of San Jose's assembly representative, the legislature changed the law to disconnect school and city boundaries. The legacy of this change has been extreme fragmentation of San Jose's school systems, and vast inequalities in the school tax bases among the city's different neighborhoods (see Matthews 2003 for a detailed account).

There is evidence that diverse views existed in reform cities throughout the monopoly period. In Austin, during the early 1960s, African Americans joined with sympathetic whites to protest the policies of segregation in the city. They met with city council members, developed ordinances, and offered legal advice to city leaders about how integration could be achieved. At multiple council meetings, the group presented its case. At one meeting in late March 1963, the head of the local chapter of the National Association for the Advancement of Colored People "launched into a wordy tirade against prejudice and discrimination," reading passages from John Howard Griffin's *Black Like Me* (Orum 1987, 259–60). One by one, leaders of the movement came forward to speak, maintaining a filibuster for two full weeks. It is not a tenable position that the city government was unaware of the demands and dissatisfaction of Austin's minority community.

After a disastrous flood in East San Jose in 1952, a newly consolidated Mexican American political group, the Community Service Organization (CSO), began a massive voter-registration drive among Latino residents. In that year alone, 4,000 new voters were registered (Pitti 2003, 167). The response of the white elite makes it clear that they noticed the mobilization. On election day, city leaders dispatched an increased number of poll watchers to Mexican neighborhoods. At one site, four voters were turned away for failing the literacy test. Immediately, CSO sent representatives to the polling place and proved that the challenged voters could in fact read and write English (Pitti 2003).

Later, in the 1960s and 1970s, San Jose residents began to question untrammeled growth, argue for increased debate on planning and growth policy, and ask that the city require any new development to "constitute a 'net benefit' to the entire community rather than promoting growth for its own sake" (a San Jose citizens committee report, "Goals for San Jose," quoted in Stanford Environmental Law Society 1970, 31). During this period, San Jose lost out on the race to secure defense spending because the city had failed to develop adequate infrastructure to support the military's needs (Schoennauer interview 2003). In a 1973 Rand Corporation Study, researchers interviewed residents to determine what kind of living environment they preferred. Interviewees were provided with fifty options that they proceeded to rank from most to least desirable. The choices ranged from things like "a place where people of different races and different ethnic groups can live together—where their children can learn to understand each other" to "a trailer park that is well protected, with small plots, lots of community recreation, little shops within its boundaries" (Christen 1973, 6). Other choices highlighted the importance of the environment, high incomes, or public transportation. The authors of the study found so much variation in the responses that they were unable to draw definite conclusions about the community's preferences. They did find that Anglo and Mexican American residents shared many of the same preferences, but one key difference stood out. Anglos were more concerned about environmental protection while Mexican Americans found a good bus system of utmost importance.[29] The authors also determined that the differences between the preferences of Anglo residents and Mexican American residents were much less stark than the dissimilarities between the city planners and the residents as a whole. Despite the diverse views among community members and elites, dominant coalitions governing in biased electoral arenas responded to a narrowly defined constituency.

As in the case of machines, during periods prior to the consolidation of reform monopolies, politicians sought support from a broader public. During the 1930s, Austin's city council made improvements to the city hospital, opened a new public swimming pool, and launched an intensive drive against syphilis. The city hired a "paid Negro director in charge of recreation for his own people," established a "Negro advisory committee" (H. Stone, Price, and K. Stone 1937, 7), and built a black library and black parks. In the late 1930s, Austin built three public-housing projects with federal dollars, one for blacks, one for Mexican Americans, and one for whites (Orum 1987). In 1949, an additional project for African Americans was built on the East Side.

Of course, Austin was still an extremely segregated city—a deliberate creation by white leaders. However, these leaders *did* assert that a segregated community could be equal. Austin city planners sought to enforce segregation by enhancing city services in only one of the African American neighborhoods, encouraging blacks to vacate other parts of the city. According to the zoning report:

> It is our recommendation that the nearest approach to the solution of the
> race segregation problem will be the recommendation of this district as a

Negro district; and that all the facilities and conveniences be provided the
Negroes in this district, as an incentive to draw the Negro population
to this area. This will eliminate the necessity of duplication of white and
black schools, white and black parks, and other duplicate facilities for this
area. . . . We further recommend that the Negro schools in this area be
provided with ample and adequate playground space and facilities similar
to the white schools of the city. (quoted in Orum 1987, 175)

Similarly, a zoning report in Dallas explained that the "plan that is prepared should provide districts for negroes and Mexicans, giving them
the same facilities as whites, that is, wide paved streets, standard size
lots, and all of the public utilities. In this way, there will be no slums or
blighted districts. . . . " (quoted in Orum 1987, 175).

Neither Dallas nor Austin succeeded at creating separate and equal
facilities. Because of their excluded status and the lack of electoral competition, communities of color had no power to bargain for benefits.
They had virtually no descriptive (much less substantive) representatives in elected and appointed positions. In 1971, Latinos made up only
5.5 percent of San Jose's police and fire forces, but composed 22 percent
of the population, according to the 1970 census. In 1978, the city was
threatened with a loss of federal general revenue funds for the inadequate hiring of Latinos (Browning, Marshall, and Tabb 1984). This
lack of services provided to peripheral groups was in distinct contrast to
other periods of these cities' histories in which peripheral residents were
incorporated into political coalitions that faced risky elections and offered shares of municipal benefits.

Conclusion

In both machine and reform cities, securing dominance made governing coalitions less attentive to the broader public. When the electoral
system became uncompetitive, groups outside of the monopoly coalition
could not easily contest the hand that they were dealt. Biased systems
allowed dominant organizations to reduce the size of their electoral coalitions, conserve resources, and reward key players. During the monopoly period, turnout declined as dominant regimes demobilized voters peripheral to their coalitions. Secure in power, monopolies directed
benefits of municipal government toward core members and powerful
governing coalition elites, while peripheral groups suffered. In nearly all
of the cases analyzed here, those peripheral to the coalition were persons of color. In the reform cities, suffrage restrictions and vote-dilution

strategies ensured that black, Latino, and Asian Americans were limited from participating in the political process. The same outcome resulted in machine cities as an effect of the organizations' maintenance strategies—responsiveness to the preferences of the monopoly's core supporters. Those outside of the coalition were provided symbolic benefits, ignored, and at times attacked by the monopolist in power.

Monopoly Collapse

6

RICHARD J. DALEY, boss of the Chicago political machine, won his last mayoral election in 1975 with more than 77 percent of the total vote, a stunning margin of victory. In the Democratic primary Daley had garnered nearly 58 percent of the total, which would appear to signal that he was in a position of strength. But the fact that Daley had to run in a primary election at all suggests otherwise. The 1975 primary was the first contest within the Democratic Party in twenty years. Daley faced three candidates: a liberal Jewish alderman; a white law-and-order-focused former state's attorney; and a black state senator. Although Daley maintained the machine organization throughout the two elections, he lost crucial support from Jews, labor leaders, African Americans, and white ethnics. The total number of votes Daley received was smaller than the total number of registered voters who chose not to cast a ballot at all (*Chicago Tribune* 1975, A2). Cracks in the machine were visible. When Daley died the following year, the cracks became chasms.

Unable to maintain a unified front, the Democratic Party began to splinter from within. At the same time, an assault on patronage hiring practices by an activist court, mobilization of the black community, and coordination of anti-machine voters spelled defeat for the monopoly. Michael Bilandic, elected in 1977, would be the last monopoly mayor to serve Chicago during this time period. In the 1979 primary, Jane Byrne challenged Bilandic, the machine's choice candidate, and won. Her victory signaled the end of the monopoly period. In 1983, when Byrne and Richard M. Daley (Boss Daley's son) split the white vote in the Democratic primary, Harold Washington became the first African American mayor of Chicago, a victory made possible by the collapse of the monopoly.

San Jose's monopoly came to an end at roughly the same time. Throughout the 1960s, the city grew at a tremendous pace, led by a reform coalition that had dominated governance for decades. The city manager remained the most powerful political official in the city, and the council had become corrupt, exchanging policy for bribes (McEnery interview 2003). Reform leader Dutch Hamann retired in 1969 on the eve of major changes in the political landscape. Minority residents made up an increasingly large proportion of the population and in the late 1960s began to more forcefully demand inclusion in the governing coalition. Simultaneously, neighborhoods were grumbling about the negative effects of sprawling development. The monopoly responded in small ways, drafting a general plan and appointing a few scattered Asian and Latino officeholders. A number of candidates supportive of controlled growth won election to the city council. But the reform monopoly managed to maintain a majority and control for another fifteen years.

Then, in 1977 the reform coalition lost the loyalty of the city newspaper when the paper's Florida-based corporate office hired a new publisher who believed that more diverse views should be represented in the media. He also questioned the intimacy of the relationship between developers and government. For the first time in thirty years the reformers lost the council majority at the November election. In 1978 the city adopted district elections, and the collapse of the monopoly was complete.

Throughout the twentieth century across all regions of the United States in varied institutional settings, local-level coalitions monopolized the levers of government for multiple decades. Yet, eventually each monopoly in this study collapsed. Given their enormous influence and their success at riding the waves of public opinion, why did these monopolies lose power? The short explanation is that challengers emerged, voters supported the opposition, and dominant regimes failed to win elections. A more interesting question asks when and why this pattern of events is likely to occur. My research suggests that the reasons for monopoly decline are highly context specific. Because monopolies rely on different strategies of bias, different forms of organization, and maintain varied degrees of control, no single causal factor predicts collapse. However, certain conditions increase the probability of monopoly decline: by making it more likely that opposition candidates will surface, by increasing the propensity of voters to cast ballots against the monopoly, and by heightening the chances that the governing regime will lose control of government.

I find that an inability to bias the system, a lack of coordination within the governing coalition, a large population of residents excluded from monopoly benefits, and economic stress are the primary contextual factors that increase the probability of monopoly decline. Chicago's monopoly was unable to withstand the combined effects of a factionalized coalition, a large discontented population, and scrutiny of its municipal hiring practices. San Jose's reformers lost control in the face of angry, underserved residents, increased reporting about alternative governing arrangements, and a change in the unity of coalition elites. The collapse of the monopolies changed the structure and policies of governance in both cities. The patterns of decline seen in Chicago and San Jose were replicated with minor differences in all of the monopolies studied here. The remainder of this chapter investigates these claims in more detail. First I present my argument regarding the causes of collapse. Then I summarize existing explanations in the literature. This is followed by tests of the hypotheses derived from the theory and historical evidence from case studies in support of the argument. I examine the makeup of opposition coalitions and the means they use to alter the political arena, the causes of weakened regimes, and, finally, the actual collapse.

The Causes of Monopoly Decline

Throughout this work monopolies have been defined as dominant coalitions which retain power through bias. As one might expect, the concepts of bias and coordination also feature centrally in monopoly decline. A biased system that becomes less so will make it easier for challengers to compete, for voters to mobilize, and for incumbents to lose. For instance, lowering information bias frequently increases the probability that constituents will be mobilized against the regime. Decreasing vote bias tends to increase the likelihood that strong challengers will enter election competitions, and limiting seat bias can increase the chances that the incumbent organization will lose control of government. Often exogenous factors play a prominent role in changes to levels of bias. For many machines, decline followed charges of corruption or vote fraud initiated by higher level governments. In reform cities, the passage of the Voting Rights Act and the court battles that ensued over minority underrepresentation in cities led to changes in electoral systems. Of course, this external intervention was the result of choices monopolies made when capturing and maintaining power, but the timing of the intervention was usually beyond the control of the monopolies.

Similar to the effects of changes in bias, a coalition that fails to sustain coordination is more likely to face opposition candidates, a less supportive electorate, and, ultimately, defeat. Principally important is a loss of cooperation within the governing coalition. When regimes factionalize internally, challengers are both more likely to run and more likely to win because the incumbent is less likely to garner a majority of the votes. The way in which monopolies organize themselves, especially the proportions of voters and elites counted as key members of the coalition, has implications for survival. At the height of power, monopoly coalitions protected by bias provide limited benefits to large portions of their potential electorates. Those excluded from the monopoly's largess offer challengers a natural foundation of support. The narrower the base of the monopoly's coalition relative to the total community, the larger this potential opposition coalition will be. This means that a larger population of excluded residents should decrease the monopoly's stability. It also means that more effective mechanisms of bias make it easier for the monopoly to maintain control with a smaller share of the population. So, we should see benefits more highly concentrated where we see more effective mechanisms of bias.

The shape of the top of the monopoly's hierarchy also has implications for survival. The wider the top of the monopoly's hierarchy (e.g., the larger the number of elites with access to power or resources), the more likely the coalition will factionalize. Monopolies characterized by elites with diverse and conflicting goals are especially prone to this fate. In the years leading up to their decline most reform coalitions suffered from these clashes as their economies became stronger and more diversified. Monopolies with highly centralized power structures are much less vulnerable to internal splits until the leader of the coalition dies or retires, at which point fissures become likely. The death of charismatic leaders adept at suppressing divisions led to the collapse of unity in both Chicago and Kansas City.

Changes in the city's social and economic environment can also contribute to a growing threat. During periods of crises, like economic downturns, the normally apathetic or acquiescent public becomes focused on the failures of the regime and alternative courses of action. Such events shake up all political systems, not just monopolies, making it more likely that the public will be mobilized and challengers will emerge and win. Likewise a decline in city revenues can create distributional problems for the monopoly. During periods of recession, the careful balance the monopoly has crafted between voter demands and resources is threatened. Fewer benefits can encourage supporters of the monopoly to join opponents of the dominant regime.

However, mobilization of opposition can be difficult in such situations. The regime in power may have dominated for a very long time, and residents who are underserved by the political system may not see any benefit in participating. They may not even be aware of the size of the potential opposition coalition, particularly in cases where the media is dominated by monopolist voices. For both voters and challengers, joining an opposition movement is a game of strategy—one only seeks to join when enough other people will join to ensure victory (Karklins and Peterson 1993; Schelling 1985). So, one condition that can increase the mobilization of opposition and the rise of challengers is enhanced information regarding others' preferences and actions. This is why a decrease in the level of information bias in the system tends to mobilize the opposition.[1] A mobilizing force like the civil rights movement can offer a similar impetus.

When confronted with threats to their control, monopolies can take two courses of action in an effort to maintain power—they can try to co-opt the opposition by being responsive in some manner, or they can seek to contain the threat, dig in their heels, and increase their control. Monopolies in the cities studied here often engaged both tactics at different times. For monopolies in the United States, too heavy a reliance on bias or egregious use of force to maintain power almost always results in higher levels of government becoming involved. But if monopolies are willing and able to share municipal benefits in such a way as to secure a majority of votes or relinquish just enough control to maintain authority, monopolies can retain power when threatened. This is what one expects from a democratic system; such behavior pulls coalitions from the monopoly end of the spectrum toward the responsive dominant regime end. Predictably, many monopolies tried this tactic first—but it did not always work.

While it may seem counterintuitive that a dominant regime would ever make the choice not to respond well enough to maintain power, it happened in every case studied here. Monopolies become invested in the institutions that they build, and may find it difficult to adjust or transfer power. Sometimes they miscalculate the danger. The rigid systems of bias insulate regimes from challenges, but they also insulate regimes from information about embryonic threats and make it difficult to change strategies even if decline appears imminent. One of the potential downsides to governing in a biased system is that it may be hard for the monopolist to accurately gauge public opinion. Those dissatisfied with the regime may be reluctant to express their discontent, and because monopolies become focused on maintaining their organization rather than responding to voter demands, they may not recognize a latent threat to their power. Miscalculation is most likely to occur in environments in which information bias is strong and in highly centralized monopolies in which diverse views are not likely to be represented in the governing coalition.

In other situations, the monopoly may simply lack the resources to respond to the challenge; expenditure patterns in cities are difficult to change and there is almost never enough revenue to go around. This is true in part because a large portion of city budgets is spent on the municipal workforce, so altering spending can lead to firing workers. In times of limited or declining resources, monopolists should be least able to extend benefits to a new group of voters.

A second, related instance in which monopolies are unable to offer benefits to new coalition members occurs when the new demands are in direct conflict with the preferences of the monopoly's core constituency. Given the costliness of changing one's reputation in politics it is extremely risky for a monopolist in this situation to decide to abandon its base. But there are examples of this happening. In Pittsburgh, a Republican machine governed from the mid-1860s to the mid-1930s. When Democrats took the nation by storm in the early 1930s, the vast majority of Pittsburg Republican ward leaders and precinct captains simply changed parties. A Democratic machine went on to monopolize city government until the 1960s. Such examples are more the exception than the rule, though; a number of monopolies collapsed because they could not balance the demands of all constituents. This kind of outcome is likely when demographic or ideological shifts increase the proportion of the population outside of the monopoly coalition, and when the peripheral groups present demands that are viewed as zero sum by core coalition members.

In sum, monopoly decline should be most likely when levels of bias are reduced (frequently as a result of exogenous forces), when the proportion of residents excluded from monopoly benefits is large (both because of the monopoly's distributional choices and as a result of demographic shifts), when the governing coalition factionalizes (either because of diverse goals or because of the death of a strong leader), and during periods of economic stress (which focus attention on the failings of the incumbent coalition, hinder the ability of the monopoly to provide benefits to its supporters, and make it difficult to respond to new demands on the regime).

Conventional Wisdom

Traditional accounts of machine and reform decline share some predictions with the theory presented here, but differ in important ways as well. Scholars like Banfield and Wilson (1963), who attribute the rise of machines to the fates of specific immigrant cultures, argue that machines declined when immigration slowed and groups assimilated into the broader "public-regarding" society, eviscerating the machine's base (234–42). Others suggest that rising incomes and education among machine voters led them to reject machines' emoluments (Stave et al. 1988; Dye 1969; Greenstein 1964). These analyses would predict that a smaller proportion of foreign-stock residents and higher incomes would affect machine decline.

Another group of scholars have suggested, in the functionalist spirit of Merton (1957), that machines declined when their services were no longer needed. If, as Ostrogorski (1910) argues, machines won reelection by providing welfare services, then machines might have collapsed when the federal government took charge of this function through New Deal programs (Salter 1935). However, a number of researchers have found that the New Deal allowed machines to consolidate their power by providing additional resources for distribution (Erie 1988; Whyte 1955). Others argue that the primary role for machines was the negotiation of complex relationships between business, governments, and voters emerging out of industrialization (Miller 1968; Shefter 1978; Greenstein 1964). In this case we would expect that a slowing of growth, changing needs among the business elite, or decreasing complexity in the system led to machine decline. Wolfinger (1972) has argued that if this line of reasoning is correct, as city governance has become increasingly complex and power increasingly decentralized, machines should have become stronger over time—an outcome which is not supported by historical evidence. A final functionalist argument is an assertion that candidate-centered elections have made parties less essential for victory (Aldrich 1995) and so less powerful in city politics.

Greenstein (1964) argues that machines declined when patronage supplies became limited either due to civil service or the increasing need for expertise. Additionally, he asserts that direct primaries and nonpartisan elections weakened machines. However, Ruhil (2003) finds that civil service reform was adopted when it became a more politically effective tool than patronage. In his analysis, reformed institutions became a mechanism for securing reelection for previously patronage-based organizations. This suggests that we should be cautious of using the implementation of reform policies and structures as a signal that machines were weak. In fact, Wolfinger (1972) suggests that the primary problem with the litany of reasons for the death of machines is that none of them actually coincides with the collapse of most organizations.

Some scholars (Miller 1968; Dorsett 1968) have argued that machines lost power when voters became frustrated with corruption or political inaction on certain issues. These assessments are an important counterexplanation to the one stated in this work. In effect, these scholars are arguing that the political system *is* responsive. According to this understanding of city history, machines won reelection so long as voters agreed with their policies and platforms; when voters seek alternatives to machine dominance, they are able to elect leaders of their choosing. If these scholars are right, machine decline should be integrally connected to preferences of voters rather than bias or coordination.

Scholars of reform cities have not typically viewed reform organizations as the same type of monopolistic coalition as machines. This means that in most of the literature on reform movements or cities there is no organization to analyze and so no collapse to predict. There are exceptions, though. Browning, Marshall, and Tabb (1984) and Skerry (1995) both argue that reform dominance ended as the result of mobilization of previously disenfranchised persons. Davidson and Fraga (1988) and Bridges (1997) suggest that decline resulted from changes to institutional structures that protected reformers following the passage of the Voting Rights Act. Rosales (2000) argues that the growth of the Chicano middle class inspired change. To this list of reasons, Bridges (1997) adds that reform organizations became the targets of political challenge when they faced severe resource imbalances in trying to provide municipal services to newly annexed neighborhoods.

My theory of regime decline draws on the arguments and evidence presented by these scholars of machine and reform politics, but it is innovative because it successfully explains the collapse of both kinds of coalitions. The emergence of a challenger, a mobilized pool of disaffected residents, and an inability for the regime to respond to new demands spells defeat for monopolies. Changes in the environment that are exogenous to the ruling regime's control can figure prominently in the development of these factors, but to some extent the regimes' own practices contribute to their demise. We should see an increase in the probability of decline as a result of a loss of bias or coordination, demographic shifts, and economic stress.

Quantitative Analysis of Monopoly Decline

To test this theory of decline, I collected data on the 244 cities that were ever among the United States' one hundred largest cities (Gibson 1998). Using secondary sources, I determined that sixty-six of these cities had experienced a monopoly at some point between 1900 and 1980. Of the sixty-six cities that hosted monopolies during the twentieth century, I have been able to determine start and end dates of the monopoly period for twenty-four cities.[2] San Antonio hosted two monopolies for a total of twenty-five cases. These are the same cases used in the spending analysis in chapter 5. Analyzing the decline of organizations requires knowing how long the monopoly was in power, so having both the start and end dates is integral. Figure 6.1 shows the monopoly period for each of these cities in order of their monopoly start dates. The seventeen machine monopolies are represented by solid lines and the eight reform monopolies are represented by dashed lines. The average monopoly on this list was in power for about thirty-five years.

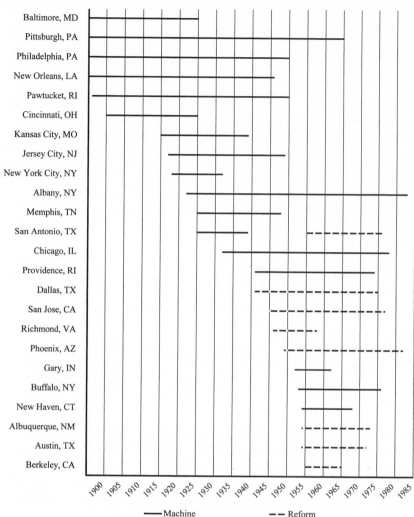

Fig. 6.1: Monopoly periods for cities with certain start and end dates

As is clear from the figure, the monopolies all started before the 1960s and tended to end by the early 1980s. This is likely due in part to the sources used to code monopolies—most were published in the mid-1980s. But it probably also reflects the time contingency of the particular biasing strategies adopted by machine and reform regimes. For instance, after the spread and entrenchment of civil service, building a patronage-based monopoly became more difficult, so it makes sense that few machines emerge in the post–World War II period. Other than this,

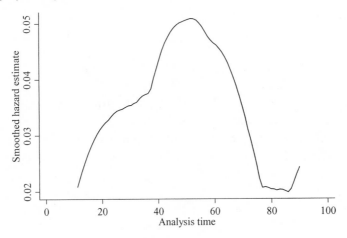

Fig. 6.2: Monopoly hazard rate

there are few patterns to dominance. In some cities, like Pittsburg and New Orleans, monopolies governed more frequently than they did not; in others, like Berkeley or Gary, monopolies were the exception rather than the rule. What is hidden by this chart is the relative strength of the monopolies across time and place. Monopolies are increasingly likely to collapse the longer they are in power, except if they survive past about fifty years. In fact, the hazard rate for monopolies (the risk of collapse at any given time, given survival to that point) is parabolic, as shown in figure 6.2.

What this picture suggests is that it becomes harder and harder for a monopoly to maintain power as the world changes around it, making its strategies of bias and organization less likely to work. But monopolies that can adjust to changing circumstances enjoy a renewed ability to survive.

Data for Analyzing Monopoly Decline

In order to analyze the factors that contribute to monopoly decline, I use these seventeen machine monopolies and eight reform monopolies. The dependent variable is the decline of the *monopoly,* coded zero when the monopoly is in power and one the year it collapsed. The independent variables in the analyses coincide with the three components of the theory—increased likelihood of challenges, environments in which residents are likely to be mobilized, and the context in which regimes can be expected to lose power. I will begin by admitting that these measures only roughly capture the nuances of the argument presented above. For instance, I have no way to distinguish between the losses of different types of bias. Instead, I use the presence of state *civil service* laws as a proxy for a limit on bias in machine cities and a dummy variable noting whether or not the city had *home rule* as a proxy for bias in reform cities.[3] I expect that the absence of bias increases the probability of decline.

Generalizing from the monopolies analyzed closely in other chapters, I include the proportion of the population that is *nonwhite* and the five-year change in this proportion to capture the size of the excluded pool of residents. I would have liked to include data on the resources available to the population of color in these cities, but the data were not available for the time series. To represent periods of economic stress that are likely to mobilize residents and increase the emergence of challengers, I analyze the proportion of the population *employed* and the five-year change in this proportion. I have suggested that the governing coalition may be susceptible to factionalization when elites have conflicting goals. I use the level of and five-year change in *economic diversity* to signify such an environment. This measure is a Herfindahl index (sum of the squared proportions) of the proportion of the city employed in manufacturing, the proportion employed in trade, and the proportion employed in all other industries. Leaders of private industry have a great deal of influence over the politics of cities. I have argued that the cohesiveness required to maintain a monopoly should be more difficult in an economy in which power is more widely spread.

The final component of the theory requires that a monopoly be unable to respond to mobilized demands because of resource scarcity or an underestimation of its opponents. No statistical measure of the latter factor is available in this analysis, but this problem will be discussed at length in the narrative evaluation. For the former factor a measure of the one-year change in total *general revenue* of a city is included. For ease of interpretation, I transform the measure into a dummy variable, coded one if the city lost revenue.[4] Also included is the total *land area* for each city to capture the possibility that an inability to provide services to distant areas weakened the regimes.

In addition to the variables that test the new theory offered here, I analyze a number of variables that assess the functionalist arguments that monopolies decline once they are no longer needed. If, for instance, machines were maintained as a result of their usefulness in assisting immigrants, we should see a relationship between the level and the change in the proportion of the population that is *foreign stock*.[5] I also analyze the proportion of *renters* in the city and the *ratio* of manufacturing jobs to professional jobs (and the five-year changes in these measures) as proxies for the argument that machines lost power when residents became wealthier or when the economy transitioned. The arguments offered for decline in the reform literature are all compatible with my theory, so no additional tests are necessary.

Modeling Monopoly Collapse

Given the small number of cases in this analysis, multiple regression models are not possible. Ideally, one would test the interaction of these different factors, but there are too few observations to run such complicated models. Instead, I estimate a series of simple Cox proportional hazard models to determine the effect of the independent variables on the rate of monopoly decline. I combine the level of each independent variable and the five-year change in the measure in eighteen separate regressions. In each analysis I control for the natural log of the total city *population*. To make the estimates comparable across models, all variables (except dummy variables) are standardized to have a mean of zero and a standard deviation of one.[6]

Event history models, like the Cox proportional hazard model, essentially analyze the occurrence and timing of events; in other words, they analyze change. They estimate the time until some event happens, the time between events, the likelihood that the event will occur at any given moment, or the rate of occurrence. Biomedical statisticians use these kinds of models to estimate things like the probability of death in a given year after a heart transplant. In such cases, the "event" is death and a patient is "at risk" if he has received a heart transplant and is still living. A scientist interested in this question could collect data on patients who underwent transplants, and each year note the number of patients still living and the number deceased. Over time the number of individuals at risk for dying decreases; once a person is dead, he exits the analysis. If the scientist then calculated the proportion of deaths to the number of individuals still alive at the beginning of the time period, she would have an estimate of the discrete time *hazard rate* for the group of patients under analysis.[7]

The scientist might want to know more specific information, though. She might be interested in the hazard rate for each patient—the probability of death for a particular individual in a particular year given that the individual is still living. To do this the scientist could also collect other lifestyle information and model the relationship between these factors and the probability of death occurring. She might want to know, for instance, whether smoking increases the hazard rate for patients who have recently received heart transplants.

In this scientist's study, undoubtedly (hopefully) some patients will not have died while the data were being collected. These cases are "censored." Data can be censored because the event happened before the study began or because the study ended and the individual had not yet experienced the event. The first type of censoring is called left-censoring and the second type is right-censoring. If two or more events occur during the same time interval in the analysis, they are said to have tied.

To analyze her data, the scientist can use a number of different types of models. One option is to assume that the probability of an event occurring at some precise time is arbitrarily small. For these types of data, event history analysis is conducted using continuous time models that estimate the rate at which events occur (instead of the probability) and the effect of independent variables on that rate. Different types of continuous time models make different assumptions about the shape of the hazard rate of one's data. The most flexible of the continuous time models, the Cox proportional hazard model, allows the shape of the hazard rate to vary across time.

This is the type of model I use. In my analysis the "event" of interest is the collapse of the monopoly, given that it has not yet collapsed—in other words, given that it is "at risk." I am interested in the effect of various factors on the rate of monopoly collapse in the twenty-five cities listed in figure 6.1.[8] The observations are arranged so that each city has a separate observation for each year of the data collection, 1900–1986. Cities are coded zero during the monopoly period and coded one in the year that the monopoly ends. After the monopoly collapses, the city exits the data analysis.[9] The precise start and end dates of the monopoly are listed in table A3. One of the machine cases, Albany, New York, collapsed after the end of the data collection; it is right-censored in the following analyses. There are an additional forty-two cases, listed in table A2, in which either the start or the end date of the monopoly period is unknown, though it is certain that a monopoly governed at some point during the twentieth century. In the analyses these cases are treated as left-censored—they exit the analysis before they have a chance to collapse. This is done in order to take advantage of the usable information from these cases—that these cities experienced a monopoly during the twentieth century, but cannot be included as the other cases are because one cannot determine the duration of the monopoly. Approximately 25 percent of the cases collapsed in the same year as another case and are treated as ties in the analyses.[10] I analyze machine and reform monopolies separately because I argue that different political contexts contributed to the collapse of each type of monopoly.

Analysis

Table 6.1 offers evidence in support of the theory. As the population changes—increasing the proportion of the population that is underserved by the regime in power—and as the regime is weakened through internal factions, a loss of bias, and declining revenue, collapse of the monopoly becomes more likely.

Table 6.1: Factors contributing to monopoly decline

	Machine collapse		Reform collapse	
	Coefficient	*Std. error*	*Coefficient*	*Std. error*
Loss of bias				
Home rule			−1.95 **	0.66
Log population (millions)			−2.67 *	1.53
N			198	
Failures			8	
Merit law	1.42 **	0.66		
Log population (millions)	0.09	0.19		
N	598			
Failures	17			
Factions in governing coalition				
Economic diversity	−0.81	0.70	0.82	1.12
5-year change economic diversity	2.61 *	1.55	10.44 **	4.66
Log population (millions)	0.04	0.24	−2.87 *	1.57
N	563		197	
Failures	16		8	
Large population of underserved residents				
% nonwhite	0.90 **	0.28	1.29 †	0.79
5-year change nonwhite	−0.12	0.20	0.61	0.68
Log population (millions)	−0.05	0.36	−3.43 **	1.29
N	563		197	
Failures	16		8	

(continued)

Table 6.1: Factors contributing to monopoly decline (*continued*)

	Machine collapse		Reform collapse	
	Coefficient	*Std. error*	*Coefficient*	*Std. error*
Economic difficulty				
% employed	−3.16 **	0.86	6.02 **	2.36
5-year change employed	0.45	1.31	5.06 *	2.82
Log population (millions)	0.09	0.27	−2.85 *	1.69
N	563		197	
Failures	16		8	
Lack of resources				
Lost revenue	0.78 *	0.45	35.04 **	0.72
Log population (millions)	−0.04	0.23	‡	
Functionalist arguments				
% renters	−0.77	0.53	1.04 *	0.63
5-year change renters	−0.12	0.37	−0.70	0.59
Log population (millions)	−0.001	0.30	−3.30 †	2.03
N	563		197	
Failures	16		8	
Ratio manufacturing/professional	−0.94 **	0.46	−4.33	4.50
5-year change ratio manufacturing/ professional	−0.15	0.95	2.16	4.69
Log population (millions)	0.16	0.28	−2.59 **	1.02
N	563		197	
Failures	16		8	
% foreign stock	−1.10	0.74		
5-year change foreign stock	−0.43	0.69		
Log population (millions)	−0.16	0.59		
N	533			
Failures	13			

Note: Robust standard errors reported; Efron method for dealing with ties.
‡ Model inestimable with inclusion of population variable
Cox proportional hazard models: $*p < .10$ $**p < .05$ $†p = .10$

In both machine and reform cities, a lack of bias increases the probability of monopoly collapse. For machine cities, the presence of state civil-service laws raises the rate of decline, and in reform cities a lack of home rule has the same effect. I have argued that in these circumstances challengers are more likely to emerge, voters more likely to cast ballots against incumbents, and the regime more likely to lose elections. I predicted that increasing the potential for factions in the governing coalition would also increase the probability of decline; increasing economic diversity captures this possibility. The strongest result of these models is the positive effect of a change in this measure. This finding is especially interesting because the models control for the static level of economic diversity. It is a change in the economic environment that makes monopoly collapse increasingly likely. The relationship between an increase in economic diversity and rising hazard ratios for machine and reform monopolies is presented in figures 6.3 and 6.4.[11]

The second component of the theory is that dissatisfied residents must be mobilized in order for regime decline to occur. Table 6.1 offers support for the argument that the presence of a substantial population of residents underserved by the regime in power can increase the likelihood of decline. In both machine and reform cities, the proportion of nonwhite residents has a positive effect on the rate of monopoly collapse. However, the five-year change in this variable does not reach statistical significance in either case. This indicates that a growing black or Latino population was not central to the monopolies' loss of power. This evidence supports my claim that monopolies contributed to their own undoing; it was not only exogenous changes that increased the likelihood of decline. Monopolies appear to be especially vulnerable in both machine and reform cities when populations of color were at least 20 percent of the population. This pattern is shown graphically in figure 6.5.

There is mixed support for my argument that economic trouble facing the electorate leads to an increased rate of monopoly collapse. The level of employment works in opposite directions in machine and reform cities, shown in figures 6.6 and 6.7. Low levels of employment hurt machine monopolies, whereas high levels of employment hurt reformers. For reformers an increase in employment also increases the hazard rate of monopolies. This may have something to do with the type of benefits each monopoly tended to provide. Machines offered public jobs to their core constituents, and used these patronage positions to increase their probability of winning elections. Low levels of employment (a high unemployment rate) could reflect the availability of fewer public jobs or

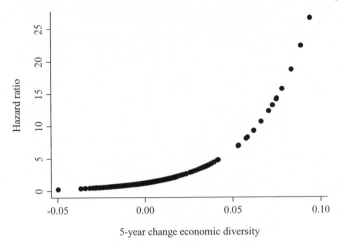

Fig. 6.3: Hazard ratios, economic diversity (machine)

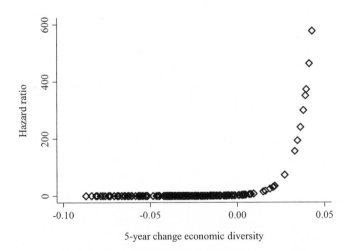

Fig. 6.4: Hazard ratios, economic diversity (reform)

might suggest the presence of a larger number of residents seeking work from the regime in power. Alternatively, for reformers, whose primary platform was economic development, perhaps a healthy economy led voters and elites to seek alternative distributions of power.

The final component of the theory is that monopolies must be unable to respond to changing demands. This context is captured with a measure of revenue loss. In both types of monopolies, a loss in revenue increased the probability of collapse. Resource dilemmas appear to have been extremely consequential for reform decline, but the effect is much smaller and less statistically significant in the machine case. This may be due to missing data—because I only have spending data in the postwar period I cannot estimate the effect of declining resources for six of the machine cases. A second indicator of regime stress is total land area. The aggressive annexation policies of reform regimes created many new unhappy and underserved residents. The positive, significant effect of land area indicates that reformers had a more difficult time maintaining monopolies in cities with larger geographical footprints. I argue that this implies that reform monopolies faced difficulties providing services to outlying areas.

The collection of functionalist arguments suggested that machines should have been weakened when city residents became wealthier and when the proportion of foreign-stock residents declined. Machine monopolies were at higher risk for collapse in cities with smaller foreign-stock populations, smaller proportions of renters, and lower ratios of manufacturing jobs to professional jobs, although the coefficients are not statically significant in two of the three analyses. Furthermore, the change in these measures did not affect machine decline. This suggests that machines were marginally more likely to be stable with a poorer,

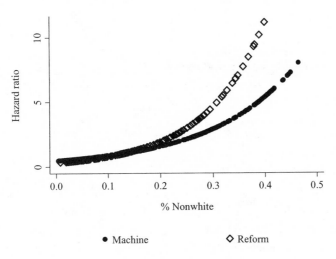

Fig. 6.5: Hazard ratios, % nonwhite

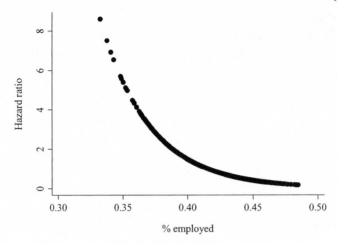

Fig. 6.6: Hazard ratios, % employed (machine)

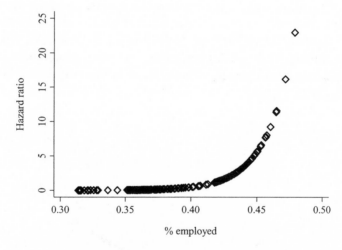

Fig. 6.7: Hazard ratios, % employed (reform)

foreign-stock, and working-class population but that it was *not* the assimilation of these groups that led to machine decline. Additionally, the insignificant effect of population size (and an additional analysis of population growth) suggests that machine monopolies were no more or less likely to collapse in large or growing cities.

For reformers, a large population of homeowners increased the stability of the regime (as indicated by the positive coefficient on percent renters), but a growing number of homeowners had no effect. This provides support for the conclusion that homeowners were key constituents for reform coalitions, and that renters were likely underserved by these regimes, but that changes in the size of this population were unrelated to reform endurance. Finally, the persistent negative effect of population in reform cities suggests that in smaller cities monopolies had higher rates of collapse, perhaps because overcoming collective-action problems among opponents was easier.

Monopolies Respond to Threats

The analyses presented above suggest that monopolies decline because they face particularly precarious positions in terms of resources or organizational cohesion. When they are not under such constraints, monopolists should respond to increases in mobilization by decreasing the proportion of expenditures for their core members, spreading benefits more widely. To determine whether or not monopolists respond rationally to increased mobilization, I measure the extent of concentration of benefits on the core group during the bias period compared to periods before and after the monopolist holds power. For machine monopolies I measure the proportion of the city budget allocated to police and fire expenditures, and for reform monopolies the proportion allocated to sanitation. Chapter 5 presents a detailed discussion of these measures.

If monopolies are more willing to focus benefits on their core constituents when they have achieved more effective mechanisms of bias, then reform monopolies should concentrate benefits more than machines. As explained in Chapter 2, reformers utilized more effective and long-lasting forms of bias by changing city charters to exclude certain types of residents from the electoral process. Machine monopolies primarily relied on using public resources in the form of patronage jobs to organize support for their regimes. Such a tactic was effective, but required more maintenance and a broader base than reform strategies. The simple comparison presented in table 6.2 lends support to this conclusion by analyzing the mean expenditure difference on core members during the monopoly periods compared to the nonmonopoly periods for machine and reform cities.

Reform monopolists increased the proportion of municipal expenditure on their core by about 3 percentage points during the monopoly period, while machines only increased the proportion by 1 percentage

Table 6.2: Weak monopolies spread benefits

	Increase in concentration during monopoly periods	
	Mean value	*Std. error*
Reform monopolies	0.03 **	.007
Machine monopolies	0.01 **	.005

**p < .05

point. The weaker type of monopoly concentrated benefits to a lesser degree. These results support the conclusion that monopolists rationally respond to pressures on their organizations. In machine cities, where monopolists had less certainty about their long-term prospects for maintaining power and were forced to create a more broadly based organization, benefits were concentrated on core coalition members to a lesser degree than in reform cities, where the certainty of reelection was great and representation narrower.

Propping Up the Façade

Historical evidence also suggests that monopolies threatened by mobilization attempted to respond to angry voters. They were particularly sensitive to demands from their core constituencies and junior partners, who were weaker members of the coalition but coalition members nonetheless—voters who became particularly important when elections were competitive. At times, control over the various coalition pieces wavered in both machine and reform cities. When dominant organizations faced internal electoral threats, they moved to co-opt the opposition.

Given the option, bosses tended to adopt the programs advocated by their opponents rather than lose power. So when machine monopolies faced serious threats—especially from within their coalitions—they expanded the circle of constituents who received benefits. After 1963, Mayor Richard Daley began to worry about a revolt from within his white ethnic coalition. Benjamin Adamowski ran a serious campaign against Daley in 1963 and received an overwhelming proportion of the Polish vote (Zikmund 1982). This threat convinced Chicago Democrats to take Polish and other white ethnic demands for segregation seriously, leveling a severe blow to the African American voters, who had consistently supported Daley's candidates. Adamowski promised that as mayor he would safeguard these white communities against black demands. In response, following the 1963 challenge, Daley ensured that white communities were protected by strategic public-housing decisions, governmental acceptance of redlining, and tacit approval of vigilantism against African Americans (Hirsch 1983). While the Daley machine had never been particularly progressive on civil rights, Daley's predecessors had provided real benefits to the black community, especially through the submachine leader William Dawson. The administration's profoundly negative treatment of African Americans following 1963 was a direct response to the demands of junior coalition partners that the machine felt it could not afford to lose, perhaps in part because civil-service reform precluded maintaining a machine on patronage alone, and in part because earlier revolts from the middle class had come dangerously close to bringing down the organization.

But Daley did not ignore the black mobilization completely. Instead he relied on state and federal resources to maintain black quiescence during the War on Poverty.[12] Between 1960 and 1980 in Chicago, 54 percent of black job gains occurred in social welfare agencies awash with Great Society money. By 1980, 60 percent of Chicago's black middle class worked in human services and government. For the lower classes, the machine encouraged enrollment in federal welfare rolls, and then threatened recipients with loss of funding should they support anti-machine candidacies (Erie 1988). Daley also selectively co-opted black issues. When Martin Luther King Jr. threatened a mass mobilization over the issue of slums, Daley publicly asserted a commitment to slum revitalization. As Daley biographers Cohen and Taylor (2000) argue:

> Much of the credit for defeating the Chicago Campaign [King's northern civil rights movement]—and for taking the steam out of the civil rights movement as it tried to move north—belongs to Daley. His response to King and his followers was shrewd: he co-opted their goals; he dispatched black leaders like Dawson and the Reverend J. H. Jackson to speak out against them; and he refused to allow them to cast him as the villain in the drama. . . . [he was able to drive] the movement out of town in exchange for vague and unenforceable commitments (428)

Later, Byrne responded to rising black demands by increasing African American appointments to municipal posts and using political funds to distribute chickens, hams, and food baskets to low-income black families and to make cash donations to black churches. While none of these policies actually responded to black voter demands at the time, they can be seen as an attempt to placate the opposition in order to prevent a loss of power.

Electoral threats in other machine cities generated a similar response of expanded benefits in an effort to maintain control. As Jews, Poles, and Italians slowly mobilized throughout the 1920s as a populist force in New York, Tammany was forced to share municipal largess and adopt new programs. The organization selected Jews as a new coalition partner, providing them party posts, nominations to minor offices, and a greater share of municipal employment, particularly in the school and healthcare systems. Tammany also advocated for municipal ownership of utilities in response to socialist demands. In the 1930s Jersey City's boss Frank Hague staved off revolt among Italian voters by producing a diverse state assembly ticket, board of education, and local judiciary. The Albany machine provided 15,000 jobs to the South End ghetto to reduce minority unrest throughout the 1920s and 1930s. In New Haven, Mayor Lee also bestowed a number of benefits on the African American community—a path later mayors would not choose to follow. According to some accounts, Lee attended to this broader coalition in part because he never felt safe in office and in part because he grew up in a heavily African American neighborhood (Wolfinger 1974). He used patronage to build support in black neighborhoods, took a strong stance against prejudice in redevelopment housing, and drew school boundaries to equalize the proportion of blacks attending the city's two high schools. When a riot occurred in the summer of 1967, Lee was one of the few leaders in the country to direct police *not* to use guns in keeping the peace.

At times this logic of co-optation even meant that the machine would adopt programs seemingly inimical to its purposes. Daley appointed a blue-ribbon reformer to clean up the police department after scandals were uncovered and voters expressed outrage. Royko (1971) explained, "Losing the Police Department as a political appendage might be painful, but it had to be done to save the machine" (121). Pendergast supported Kansas City's change to a reform-backed city manager charter because it was popular with the voters, and he had lost seats in the 1922 election to a reform slate. By endorsing charter change, he responded to voter demand without losing control. He carefully orchestrated the ensuing council elections, won a majority of seats, and then appointed a manager who was supportive of his machine's program. Pendergast also reached out to rising Italian leaders when they demanded incorporation. One young leader flexed his power by kidnapping an Irish ward boss's lieutenants and forcing the ward boss to step down. In return for cooperating with the Pendergast machine going forward, the Italian demanded more protections from the machine in the neighborhood's underground activity. Pendergast was unhappy about the fall of his ward boss, but needed the votes the Italian leader could bring in for the machine, and acquiesced (Larsen and Hulston 1997).

Reformers, albeit to a lesser extent than machines, also attempted to avoid defeat by satisfying the demands of challengers. The first signs of discontent in reform cities began to surface when the negative externalities of untrammeled growth became clear. In the early 1960s, San Jose voters elected pro-homeowner candidates to office and then voted down a bond measure for growth for the first time since the reformers took office. By this point the orchards had disappeared, promises for new schools, streets, and utilities went unfulfilled, police and fire services were paltry, and traffic congestion had worsened. Tax dollars were being spent on growth-inducing capital improvements, not the services that residents desired. Development had not been planned to make efficient use of tax dollars or protect the quality of life. Everywhere reformers promised that their policies would attract economic growth, producing a strong tax base and lower taxes, but in many cases they did not. Between 1950 and 1970 the cost of utilities and property taxes in San Jose went up, not down. During the same period the bonded debt per capita nearly doubled (Stanford Environmental Law Society 1970). Simply put, reform governments had trouble keeping up with the growth that they pursued. In the late 1970s, newly annexed areas of San Jose saw recurrent sewer spills on the weekends as lines were overtaxed. Angry residents became a constant presence at city council meetings, demanding that the city fix the problems.

The governing coalition responded seriously to this threat without undermining its power. The planning commission added two new members in 1962, both nondevelopers, to pacify the public. In 1965 the governing coalition campaigned for and won a new city charter that provided for an elected mayor while maintaining at-large council elections and eliminating the vote of confidence for the city manager (*San Jose Mercury News* 1965). Creating the position of mayor channeled public demands for action and accountability toward a single person, while the at-large elections ensured that the reform coalition would still be able to dominate the council and appoint the now insulated city manager. Additionally, the pay for councilors was increased to $400 per month from $5 per meeting. Increasing the remuneration of councilors was intended to signal that power would be more balanced between the city manager and the elected representatives (*San Jose Mercury News* 1965). However, because the manager retained total control over and access to the bureaucracy, this change ultimately had little effect (P. Trounstine 1985).

A clear example of the shifting levels of benefits provided to different residents can be seen in the development of San Jose's libraries. Prior to the consolidation of the reform regime, between 1900 and 1943 two libraries were built, one in East San Jose and a second in Willow Glen. Both were built within two years of annexing these areas to the old city. Between 1944 and 1962, when the reform coalition dominated government, only the two neighborhoods that housed the reform coalition leaders received new libraries. Between 1963 and 1972, after the dominant coalition faced threats from its junior coalition partners, the annexed communities, six new libraries were built in these areas (San Jose Public Library 2003).

Responding to charges that the at-large system was undemocratic, Dallas reformers initiated a grassroots nominating system by district for their slate. In 1968, they placed a measure on the ballot to expand the council to nine members (from seven), and the following year Dallas's first African American reform candidate was elected to office on the Citizen's Charter Association slate. Austin, too, increased the size of its council and slated minority members for office. But, unlike Dallas, Austin began to share municipal benefits with the challengers as well. Undoubtedly this is because Austin reformers had a much more tenuous hold on power than reformers in Dallas.

By the late 1960s, African Americans had made gains in Austin municipal employment, and one African American leader, Everett Givens, was promised a golf course for his community in exchange for support in an important bond election. Throughout the Southwest, nonpartisan slating groups drafted and elected minority candidates during the 1960s and 1970s. Phoenix reformers nominated African American and Mexican American candidates, taking the wind out of their opposition's sails. Similarly, San Antonio's leaders slated four Spanish-surnamed candidates and began to campaign in Mexican American neighborhoods. San Jose reformers did their part too, appointing Asian American Norman Mineta to the city council in the late 1960s and then a Mexican American councilor, Al Garza, in the early 1970s (P. Trounstine 1995; Christensen 1997). However, in none of these cities did the reformers actually relinquish power to new groups. Appointments of minority candidates were largely seen by coalition regulars and excluded groups alike as token efforts at appeasement. Because they were forced to appeal to citywide constituencies, they could do little for minority communities. Fraga's (1988) research showed that between 1955 and 1975, 84 percent of the candidates elected to San Antonio's city council were the first choice of white voters while only 35 percent and 23 percent were the first choice of African American and Latino voters respectively—even including the minority councilors.

Although each of these examples suggests that more members of the community were brought into monopolies at various moments, in no case was the dominant organization seriously damaged, and nowhere were large segments of peripheral populations incorporated into the monopoly. In many cases the regime maintained power for additional decades after the challenge.

Nobody Can Hold On Forever

For a time (in some cases a very long time), monopolies were able to adjust to threats in order to maintain control, but ultimately declined when they faced rising challengers, mobilized disaffected residents, resource imbalances, factionalization of their coalition, and a loss of biasing mechanisms. Eventually, they all collapsed. When political coalitions successfully bias the system in their favor, they are afforded the luxury of attending to only a minimum winning coalition. Peripheral citizens then organize to bring down the monopoly in power, taking advantage of moments of regime weakness. When monopolies collapse in response to mobilized constituents, it may appear that the cities enjoy well-functioning democratic systems. However, in this study, all of the cases share the distinction of having possessed large numbers of discontented residents, who were vocal and visible long before the fall of the regimes. It is testimony to the power of bias that the monopolies held on for so long in the face of rising discontent. This next section presents an analysis of the makeup of opposition coalitions, a discussion of the factors leading to mobilization, and the eventual causes of regime failure.

Opposition Coalitions in Machine Cities

Over time, machine and reform coalitions tended to exclude large numbers of people from their inner circle of benefits, a practice that was exacerbated by demographic shifts. These peripheral city residents became the base for opposition coalitions. New York's Tammany Hall readily increased spending and debt throughout the early 1900s in response to its core constituents' demands for patronage and services. While all immigrants would have benefited from these municipal goodies, Tammany tended to ignore southern and eastern European immigrants in favor of the older-stock Irish and Germans.[13] As the new immigrants continued to flow into the city, the number of potential constituents excluded from the regime continued to grow as well. Throughout this period, machine exclusion of new immigrant groups encouraged immigrants to develop communal institutions like mutual aid societies that would later serve as organizing tools for Tammany's opponents (Erie 1988).

Tammany's inattentiveness to the newly arriving Jews meant that they tended to find their way into Socialist rather than Democratic alliances. Jews became even more likely to support anti-Tammany candidates after the organization laid off Jewish teachers and social workers during the Depression in order to save Irish jobs. As Tammany was on its deathbed in the late 1920s, Jews, Italians, and eastern European voters actively supported reformers, eventually giving Fiorello LaGuardia a smashing victory in 1933. In Jersey City, too, Boss Hague's organization was eventually brought down by a coalition of Polish and Italian voters supporting a Democratic fusionist, who knew to take advantage of the discontent among those who had been excluded by the Irish. In part it was the outside influence of the New Deal that created the threat to the machine. First Al Smith and then Franklin Delano Roosevelt captured the vote of enormous numbers of new immigrants who then went on to participate in municipal elections, displaying their dissatisfaction with the paucity of benefits provided by monopolies.

New Haven's Democratic organization, secure in its power between 1953 and the late 1960s, provided a disproportionate number of jobs to white European immigrants and placated business and conservatives with extraordinary urban renewal, while low-income housing was eliminated and black neighborhoods suffered degradation. Italians, providing the single largest voting bloc in the city, were shut out of the highest offices. According to the Italian party boss Arthur Barbieri, "[W]e've never been able to get any patronage from [Lee]" (quoted in Nordheimer 1969). Lee doled out the patronage himself through channels over which he alone had control. Italians felt underserved by the Lee machine, and the lack of unity ultimately undermined the coalition. Lee opted not to run for a ninth term, signifying the collapse of the machine. Then, in 1969, the Italian community asserted its power and elected Bartholomew Guida mayor. Finally, in 1989, Mayor John Daniels became the first black mayor of New Haven with support from black activists, businesses, students, community organizers, board-of-education employees, and liberal Yale professors and students (Summers and Klinkner 1990). In the city's black wards, Daniels reaped double the rate of support his Democratic predecessors enjoyed.

In many machine cities, like Kansas City, new immigrant and minority areas were governed by Irish ward bosses. Pendergast's refusal to allow the Italian community to govern itself led to revolt from below. But Pendergast's biggest critics came from white middle- and upper-class residents, who objected to his machine's connection with the underworld and provision of welfare services to the poor. Pendergast's days were numbered when his rivals uncovered evidence of vast scandal, fraud, and corruption, giving constituents a reason to vote out his party. In the late 1930s, a broad-based coalition of Republicans, reform Democrats, and businessmen came together in the Forward Kansas City Committee, bent on getting rid of Pendergast's machine. Their political arm, the Citizen's Reform ticket, swept city and state elections in 1940, and when the Republicans captured more seats in 1942, the Kansas City Democratic machine was officially dead.

Chicago's Democratic machine fared well among white voters, but continually refused black demands and excluded black voters from municipal benefits. By 1976, the dawn of the machine's demise, blacks were underrepresented and paid at lower rates than whites in all sectors of municipal employment except for those areas that were supported by federal funds (Preston 1982). Blacks were also unrepresented in the hierarchy of the machine itself. Aside from a handful of black aldermen and ward bosses, the large population of black Chicago residents did not translate into representation within the political structure. In selecting an interim mayor following Daley's death, the machine-led council passed over their president pro tem, African American alderman Wilson Frost, and selected Croatian Michael Bilandic for the post. The low status of blacks in the organization was, of course, highly dependent on widespread racism among voters and elites, but there was a political logic as well. At least until the mid-1930s, white ethnic immigrants made up a majority of the city's residents. They formed the core constituency of Daley's machine, which in turn served their needs. Blacks were junior partners, if partners at all. By 1975, black candidates began to challenge their secondary status and the machine in elections.

On the most crucial issue to black Chicago throughout the 1960s and 1970s—residential and educational integration—the machine defended its white ethnic core constituents, supporting policies of racial containment and reinforcing segregation. Daley operated covertly to protect white neighborhoods while publicly stating his dedication to represent all Chicagoans equally (Cohen and Taylor 2000). In 1964, in Daley's neighborhood of Bridgeport, a white real-estate owner informed Daley that he was planning to rent his property to a black couple. Responding to the announcement, Daley stated that "every person has the constitutional right to live wherever he wishes." Almost immediately the house was vandalized, rocks, bricks, and excrement thrown through windows, and crowds gathered, protesting the integration. Then, quietly, the renters' belongings were removed from the house, and a realtor re-rented the house to whites. Daley chose not to intervene in the matter (Cohen and Taylor 2000, 322–23). Daley's housing director was widely quoted as saying that Chicago had only "voluntary segregation" (Royko 1971, 78). As Daley biographer Royko explained, the "hungry people who slept five in a bed, not counting rats, and saw the sky through the holes in their roof, might not have agreed that it was a 'voluntary' arrangement" (Royko 1971, 138). Royko goes on to argue that the high level of support the machine received in black wards was the result of threats and coercion. This explains why poor black voters were the last to defect from the machine at a time when members of the middle class had already begun to desert. Poor African American residents had a great deal more to lose by not cooperating with the machine, and it was always unclear whether they stood to gain from an alternative ruling group in power. Daley's mayoral successors, Michael Bilandic and Jane Byrne, continued down the path that he had forged. The machine kept segregation off the agenda, denying that it was a problem.[14]

Alternatively, another group that had received short shrift from the Chicago machine, eastern European immigrants, was poised to gain more from the machine because its demands did not deeply conflict with the machine's core constituency. Polish and Czech communities had long been second in line to the Irish bosses of the organization. They received fewer patronage positions, lower-status leadership positions, and held less power in the County Central Committee. Furthermore, throughout the 1950s and early 1960s, the machine's dedication to urban renewal at the behest of its business elites had resulted in the dispersion of African Americans into working-class white neighborhoods. Adamowski's challenge to the machine in 1963 was a direct consequence of these policies. Adamowski drew heavily from the machine's white ethnic vote by painting "Daley as a liberal, big taxer who was doing too much for the city's poor, especially the fast growing black population" (Green 1995b, 158). Following Daley's death, the Polish community again felt underserved when the machine chose not to slate a Polish candidate for mayor. As they had in 1963, Polish voters put up a fight, splitting from the machine in 1977, 1979, and 1983.

The machine also faced electoral challenges from the black community throughout the 1970s. Black candidates running against or outside of the machine won elections to city council. Jane Byrne, running as a maverick against Mayor Bilandic, captured 63 percent of the black vote, signifying the hope that she would be more attentive to their demands.

She was not, and, thus, lost all of her black support when Washington entered the 1983 mayoral race (Kleppner 1985).

Other Factors Leading to Mobilization

However large the slights by the Chicago machine were to the black community, a number of additional factors were important for creating the conditions that allowed for both Byrne and Washington's victories. In elections during the 1970s, upwards of 60 percent of the eligible black electorate did not turn out to vote. This figure reflects the magnitude of the demographic shifts that had occurred over the previous four decades. White ethnics, the core of the machine, had spread out from the inner city when they could afford to do so. The lower-income white communities that were left saw increasing numbers of African Americans moving into their neighborhoods. Chicago's black population had tripled between 1940 and 1960, and grew 50 percent larger over the next twenty years so that by 1980 blacks composed about 40 percent of the entire population. Over time, the increase in black potential voters and the machine's reluctance to mobilize them created a large base for an opponent to tap. Additionally, the black middle class in Chicago grew during this period, offering political and economic resources to the opposition.

The civil rights movement made this potential pool of anti-machine voters more receptive to mobilization. Daley's very public battles with Martin Luther King Jr. and his intransigence on civil rights issues brought the racism of the machine to the forefront, framing the agenda and providing black and liberal voters with the kind of information that they needed to organize effectively against the machine. Additionally, the civil rights movement spurred increases in registration and turnout that Daley could not control. Accompanied by incredibly focused efforts by community organizations in black neighborhoods to increase voter participation, the movements effectively acted as an exogenous influence, mobilizing discontented residents.

In many cities, increased union activity, particularly among municipal employees, also served to mobilize residents against machines. The coercive system put into place by machine organizations meant that city workers, if mobilized, could potentially be tapped by an opponent. Given that voting against the machine would have cost individuals their jobs, this prospect became more likely when municipal employees became unionized. For the early part of the twentieth century, municipal employees unions were rare. Where they did develop, they frequently lasted only a few years and for the most part were confined to a single

city. This began to change after the First World War, when across the
country police officers and firefighters organized locally, but affiliated
with American Federation of Labor (AFL) nationally (O'Neill 1970).
In the 1930s, the American Federation of State, County, and Municipal Employees organized, also maintaining an affiliation with the AFL.
During the 1930s, teachers unions expanded. These unions grew slowly
during the 1940s and 1950s, but rapidly increased their membership in
the 1960s and 1970s. By the early 1970s, most police officers, firefighters, and teachers in the United States were unionized. Grimshaw (1992)
argues that rising discontent among Chicago's public employees, particularly teachers and transit workers, weakened the machine.

Another factor in mobilizing voters against the machine was the increasing weakness of the machine itself. The Chicago machine faced a
primary challenge for the first time in twenty years in 1975, lost aldermanic and state-level seats in 1969 and 1976, and finally lost the
mayoralty in 1978. In this environment, an anti-machine coalition became increasingly likely to succeed. The death of Daley in 1976 and the
jockeying for power that followed created irreconcilable fissures in the
coalition, which further inspired the opposition to organize. In 1983,
a collection of liberal whites, reformers, and African Americans finally
put Harold Washington in office. With only 12.3 percent of the city's
white vote, Washington's victory was the result of a highly mobilized,
coordinated effort in the disenchanted black community. The Chicago
Democratic machine had been the architect of its own demise.

The Opposition Coalition in Reform Cities

Like machines, reform coalitions lay the foundation for their own
decline by focusing benefits on certain portions of the community while
treating others peripherally. By the mid-1960s, in Phoenix, San Antonio,
Albuquerque, and Dallas, challengers to the dominant coalition claimed
that local government was unrepresentative and undemocratic in its
refusal to support public housing, deal with issues of police brutality,
and provide funding for public health. In 1965 Elizabeth Blessing won
election to the Dallas city council on such a platform with the votes of
low-income residents and the Latino and African American communities. She was aided in her effort because national media had picked up
the story and were running features criticizing Dallas's reigning regime.
This outside influence helped to mobilize the antiregime community by
providing information about alternative arrangements.

San Antonio's antiregime candidates labeled the Good Government

League "a machine," and advocated increased municipal wages and better public works in disadvantaged communities. Throughout the 1950s, 1960s, and 1970s, the proportion of San Antonio's Latino community employed in white-collar occupations expanded dramatically. But because of segregation and racism, these gains were not reflected in residential or educational arenas. This mismatch was one of the driving forces behind Chicano mobilization. Ironically for reformers, the patterns of segregation that kept Latinos confined to portions of the city also made mobilization easier (Rosales 2000).

In all of the Southwestern cities in this study, movements to create district elections were motivated in part by minority communities seeking greater representation in city government. However, it was the presence of white, middle-class homeowners in the call for district elections that won the attention of the governing coalition in many places. As early as 1959, Dallas neighborhood groups began expressing dissatisfaction with the governing coalition. They rallied around quality-of-life issues, and forced a number of the coalition candidates into runoff elections. As was true of machines, the suggestion of weakness in the coalition served to increase organization against the regime. Everywhere in the Southwest, the story is similar. As the governing coalition became safe in office, it focused attention on a few middle- and upper-class white neighborhoods and profits for developers. Newly annexed communities and inner-city minority areas were at best junior partners in these organizations. Outlying neighborhoods felt "overtaxed and underserved" (Bridges 1997, 177). Meanwhile, growth of the city was the driving policy position for most Southwestern governing coalitions throughout the 1950s and 1960s. According to one San Jose city engineer, the leaders saw "growth as the city's destiny" (Schoennauer interview 2003). The kind of growth that Southwestern cities encouraged was vast and lucrative single-family, residential development—not industrial or commercial growth or multi-unit residential development. This had the effect of increasing business for residential developers, bringing large numbers of people into the city, and building clout for the city leaders, as their cities became major population centers. Meanwhile jobs were being created elsewhere.

As explained in chapter 5, this type of development had costs. Taxes were not bringing in enough revenue to provide services to the new residents or to protect against environmental degradation. Three outspoken regime opponents were elected in 1962 on a platform dedicated to neighborhood improvement. One of them, Virginia Shaffer, was nicknamed "Madam No" by reformers, for her frequent rejection of reform policies

(Hayes interview 2003). As an attempt to limit the cost of development, in 1973 voters mobilized a grassroots campaign and won an initiative tying development to school capacity. In the same year, San Jose's first avowed environmentalists were elected to council—Jim Self and Suzie Wilson. Self's campaign manager prepared an extensive analysis of his candidate's voter support (Lokey 1974). He determined that Self's victory in the primary came from increased mobilization in three newly annexed territories. Self's areas of greatest opposition were those older, upper-class, white neighborhoods that had fared well under the governance of the reform coalition. Self's campaign manager notes that the reason for the increased mobilization in the annexed territories was the presence of the ballot initiative on the primary ballot.[15] The reform coalition had sown the seeds of discontent by ignoring demands to relieve overcrowded schools in outlying areas.

The following year, the winner of San Jose's 1974 mayoral election, Janet Gray Hayes, ran on a platform of slow growth and no new taxes. Her tiny margin of victory, 1,225 votes out of 125,000 cast, came from the newly annexed territories and minority communities. In 1978, when district elections were approved, annexed areas, minority, and liberal neighborhoods offered the strongest support (Christensen 1997). Similarly, Albuquerque's People's Committee, opponents to the reform coalition, won three seats on the city council with strong support from newly annexed territories angry at their rising taxes and shoddy services. In Phoenix, an opposition slate running in 1963 vowed not to annex more territory until services were provided for existing neighborhoods. The 1963 election also saw a slate nominating African Americans and Latinos for city council. Turnout increased almost 30 percent from the previous election, as these candidacies presented alternative arrangements of power. A 1975 poll in Phoenix revealed that a large majority of residents disapproved of the institutional setup of citywide elections and part-time councilors with no mayor. Reform coalitions, by actively seeking rapid growth, created the conditions for their own downfall. They orchestrated massive demographic shifts in their own communities, which were exacerbated by the good climate and defense spending in the Southwest (Bernard and Rice 1983), but they then paid minimal attention to the new residents' needs.

Yet, governing coalitions held on, at least in part, because these dissatisfied residents were disorganized, plagued by collective-action dilemmas. Olson (1967) argues that in Austin during the 1960s "challengers could agree that they opposed pro-business incumbents but could not agree among themselves on any form of electoral cooperation or on how they might combine, if elected to form a new majority on the council" (quoted in Bridges 1997, 177). During her first term, San Jose's Mayor Hayes was ultimately thwarted from doing serious damage to the governing coalition's plans by a recalcitrant city council, a strong bureaucracy, and budgetary woes (Hayes interview 1980). As a result, insurgent candidates won isolated victories, but reform coalitions maintained their hold on power.

Other Factors Leading to Mobilization

By the early 1970s, the nationwide environmental movement had increased awareness about the negative effects of unconstrained growth. Additionally, the little victories of antireform forces throughout the late 1960s and early 1970s suggested weakening regimes. In 1964, two members of San Jose's reform coalition announced that they would not seek reelection because of shifting forces at city hall. In 1965, a candidate who had previously represented the old guard of the dominant regime switched gears and ran for office with a coalition of slow-growth supporters, labor union members, and racial and ethnic minorities. By the early 1970s, the council's cohesiveness on growth issues had crumbled. By 1973, three of the seven city councilors frequently voted against developments and occasionally a fourth councilor joined their objection, blocking proposals. While this turn of events did not represent the end of the regime's control, it put a serious damper on its ability to continue with pro-growth policies. Journalist Susan Cohen (1985) explained, "Projects that once were approved in days or weeks began to take months or years to make their way through City Hall" (14). Then, after a two-year investigation, monopoly councilor Al Garza was indicted in 1979 for taking a bribe in connection with a zoning decision. He pled guilty to bribery, conspiracy, and perjury (Harper 2001). The scandal was widely covered in the news, and contributed to the climate of distrust among residents (Hayes interview 1980).

As in Chicago, the Southwest civil rights movement also increased mobilization among minority communities. The Model Cities and War on Poverty programs, while doing little to alleviate the conditions of low-income communities, did force new issues onto the agenda and bring new voters into the process. But these external influences were certainly not the only mobilizing factors in Southwestern cities. In San Jose, in 1969, the reform coalition sponsored a "Fiesta de la Rosas" to bring attention and business to the city. The fiesta was to feature costumed Spanish conquistadors, all whites, accompanied by a Mexican peon and his burro. The party was boycotted by local Latinos, and a mass protest resulted in a widely publicized fight with the San Jose police (McEnery interview 2003). The same group of community organizations that rallied around the boycott later organized politically to fight for low-income housing, opposition to redevelopment and gentrification, and the need for increased minority representation in government (Pitti 2003). In 1977, female municipal employees in city hall and libraries began organizing a movement to achieve pay equity (Matthews 2003). By ignoring, being insensitive to, or attacking minority communities, Southwestern reform governments provided a platform for opponents.

Even with many opposing voices, the major challenges to big-city reform would only come after the regimes themselves had been severely weakened. The pattern is similar to the history of the political machines. When these organizations built their regimes, they biased the system in their favor. As long as bias was in place and the governing coalitions remained unified, challengers would only *threaten* to bring down the dominant regimes. As the regimes weakened, either from internal collapse or exogenous influence, the cacophony of opposition voices was amplified. In many cases the dominant coalitions responded by trying to co-opt the challenge. In more cases they pushed further along the road of exclusion and bias. For a host of different reasons, these regimes in trouble were unable to ride out the challenge, and all came tumbling down.

Weakened Machine Regimes

Building a long-dominant regime resistant to changes in public opinion requires a large number of complicated pieces to come together in the right constellation. Coalitions must bias the system in their favor and consolidate their organizations. Failing to satisfy one or both of these conditions weakens the regime and offers mobilized, discontented individuals an opportunity to challenge the regime.

In each of the machine cities studied here, the governing organization was unable to maintain the same level of bias in the system that had allowed them to dominate the political arena in previous years. These changes were wrought largely by exogenous forces. In some instances (Kansas City and Jersey City), United States district attorneys or state attorney generals brought cases against machine politicians; in others (Chicago and Albany), state governments enacted reforms like civil service, and individuals leveraged the court system to challenge the regime; in still others (New York and Pittsburgh), revenue shortfalls required that machines cut their supply of patronage. Because control over patronage constituted the primary mechanism for biasing the system, this resulted in weakened machines.

Chicago's machine came under fire from all of these external actors, but the most important was a series of court orders that restricted municipal personnel decisions, thereby weakening the machine. Beginning in 1972 with a consent decree signed by Mayor Daley, Chicago was formally prohibited from firing city workers on the basis of partisan affiliation. This decree, named after the plaintiff Michael Shakman, also required the city to notify workers of their rights on a regular basis. This resulted in the filing of more than two hundred lawsuits against the city, many of which led to the reinstatement of fired workers. While the 1972 Shakman Decree did publicize the machine's tactics, it did relatively little to stop the political uses of patronage because it only covered termination, not the hiring of employees. Shakman returned to the court to close this loophole, and in 1979 won a second case in which the court ruled that the machine's hiring practices were unconstitutional. However, the judge did not provide an implementing order for the decision until 1983. This last order, known as Shakman III, resulted in the development of extremely specific directives for hiring municipal workers. At the time, many scholars and practitioners felt that this collection of decisions eviscerated the machine's patronage system.[16] Chicago's machine was further weakened when a series of investigations broke about its uses of fraud to win elections, and nepotism to maintain loyalty within the organization throughout the 1970s.

In Kansas City, anti-machine governor Lloyd Stark limited the machine's ability to operate. Stark removed Pendergast's men from the city payroll and appointed a new election board not beholden to Pendergast, reducing the possibility that fraud could be perpetrated. Stark upset Pendergast's control over vote choice in other ways, too, enacting a registration law and conducting massive investigations into Kansas City's election practices. Stark convinced the legislature to put Kansas City's police force under state control, eliminating the machine's ability to use "legal" force to ensure election victories. The machine did not take these changes lightly. When Kansas City's new police commissioner (appointed by the governor) began an intense routing of the machine's political connections with the underworld, he was physically threatened on multiple occasions. Poisoned candy was placed on his desk, an ace of spades with a bullet hole in it was stuck under his door, and coffin-shaped bi-chloride mercury tablets were placed in noticeable locations (Larsen and Hulston 1997).

In addition to Stark's meddling, the Pendergast machine was further damaged when a coalition of disaffected residents won a populist victory through a 1940 charter amendment that forced a new election for all of the city council seats and the mayoralty. In Philadelphia, too, under duress resulting from a fraud investigation, the machine adopted a new charter that entailed sharp reductions in patronage, banned political work among municipal employees, and consolidated a number of city and county offices. Fraud investigations pursued by authorities outside of machine influence represented a loss of one of the machine's essential biasing mechanisms—control over information about the performance of government and available alternatives. Once machines were unable to maintain this biasing strategy, they were severely weakened and open to attack.

Decline of Machine Organizational Cohesion

While the restrictions on patronage and investigations by outside actors impeded machine operations, regimes were also handicapped when they struggled to maintain organizational unity. In some cases this too was an effect of monopolization. As regimes consolidated power and reduced their coalition size, battles emerged over who would dominate the new, smaller coalition, especially after founding leaders died or retired. In a famous early study of machine decline, Zink (1930) found that for three of the twenty bosses he studied "greedy underlings" brought them ruin (57). Four other bosses lost power because of disloyalty in their ranks. Seven of the machines collapsed when the boss died. This was what happened in Chicago. The biggest blow to Chicago's organization came from Daley's death in 1976. Daley controlled patronage nearly completely by uniting Democratic Party leadership with the mayoralty. He also kept a tight rein on nominations for elected office, preventing rogue challengers from moving up the ranks of the hierarchy.

Because Daley had groomed no successor, after his death there was no one to keep such exacting control over the organization. Daley suffered from a stroke in May of the previous year, so Chicago's machine elites had already begun to think about the future of the organization after he was gone. They were keenly aware of the potential problems that would ensue if they allowed the organization to splinter. To prevent this, they sought to orchestrate an agreement to divide power among the various blocs jockeying for control. The party selected George Dunne, the Cook County Board president and forty-second ward committeeman, for the position of chairman of the Cook County Democratic Organization. After his election, Dunne announced that he would also accept the mayoral nomination, but it quickly became clear that the political winds were blowing against this aspiration, and Michael Bilandic was drafted to fill Daley's unexpired term. According to the *Chicago Tribune,* "Daley's unique hold on political and governmental affairs and his national reputation as a kingmaker stemmed largely from his controlling the two posts. Many administration leaders have said, in the aftermath of his death, that no one should ever again hold both positions" (Mehler 1976, 1).

Democratic officials intended that the two men, Bilandic and Dunne, would share control of the organization. Had they allowed the machine to reappoint a boss, they might have been able to maintain power. The new lack of centralized control opened the door to a massive rupture in the factional unity of the organization as well as its maintenance of relationships with regime elites. In their attempt to determine who would succeed Daley as mayor, the Democratic aldermen revealed deep divisions between Irish and Polish voters and elites as well as the African American faction of the party. Bilandic won the nomination as well as the general election, but then faced a factional challenge again when Jane Byrne opposed him in 1977 with the support of an angry coalition of Polish, black, and anti-machine voters and elites (see Green 1984; Kleppner 1985). Bilandic had never truly captured the support of the party's ruling elite, and so was vulnerable to an electoral threat. Byrne's mayoralty exacerbated fissures in the party. Worse, through various policy decisions and erratic behavior, Byrne lost the backing of the media, business and union leaders, firefighters, teachers, transit workers, Latinos, and blacks in her attempt to govern Chicago (Preston 1982). As mayor, Byrne actively fought Dunne's power and eventually succeeded at convincing the Democratic Central Committee to replace him. The new chair, Ed Vrdolyak, further decentralized the organization by empowering ward bosses, who, like Vrdolyak himself, had been "kept of the periphery of power by mayor Daley" (Kleppner 1985, 132). Both Bilandic and Byrne were ineffective mayors, unable to manage the city bureaucracy and unable to build cohesion among the ward politicians.

Many scholars have argued that the presence of these divisions in the machine were apparent before Daley's death, citing, for instance, the fact that Daley's handpicked successor for William Dawson's congressional seat broke with the machine in 1971 over issues of police misconduct. The presence of independent and highly visible black leadership was certainly important for the mobilization of the black community and the decline of the machine, but it is unlikely that the machine would have so completely lost control without its internal fissures. Washington's electoral victory in 1983 was a direct result of the division in the white ethnic vote between Boss Daley's son, Richard M. Daley, and Jane Byrne. Daley captured the south side/Irish coalition, and Byrne won the Polish votes on the north side. With his newly mobilized block of black voters, Washington swept in for the victory. Similarly, in New York, Tammany suffered from internal divisions, as LaGuardia's southern and eastern European coalition capitalized on a split in the Irish vote. Likewise, Pendergast only succeeded in engineering his Kansas City machine when he subdued the factional fights between his Goats and the opposing Rabbits. It was no mistake that an old, disgruntled Rabbit returned to head up the coalition that spelled his defeat.

Divisions in the governing coalition were disastrous, but in Chicago and elsewhere machines also faced difficulty when they lost support of elites in the broader political arena. Boss Pendergast probably best exemplifies such a fate. After Pendergast slated Stark for the governorship, Stark turned on Pendergast in furtherance of his own political ambitions—to win election to the Senate. Stark believed that his best chances for victory lay in destroying Pendergast's machine, and with the power of the state government behind him, he did just that. Tammany was also damaged by a loss of support at the state level when a Republican legislature refused to grant the city government annexation and taxation powers. Perhaps more troubling for Tammany was losing favor with Roosevelt, who handed New Deal patronage to Tammany's opponent, LaGuardia. Machines were also in trouble when changes beyond their control in the political environment altered the constellation of important elites. One of the things made clear by Byrne's mayoralty was that Daley's death had restored status to the powerful ward bosses in the machine. Byrne's realization of this fact is what led her to abandon her reform platform and ask forgiveness from the party regulars. On the other hand, when a machine could maintain unity and support of elites, it could fend off attacks to its power. In Chicago, Washington's first bid for the mayoralty (in 1977) brought in only 10 percent of the vote, 4 percent more than African American candidate Newhouse had won in 1975 (Grimshaw 1992). Neither candidacy united the black community, and neither gained the support of black politicians within the machine, who feared the costs of supporting a losing anti-machine candidate.

Reform Organizational Splinters

Like machines, declining reform coalitions were threatened by a loss of unity, eroding support from key elites, and elimination of biasing mechanisms. Factions in the governing coalition weakened regimes. In Dallas, a split in the nonpartisan slating group broke conservative Republicans from the reform coalition. The leader of the factional group, Earle Cabell, ran for mayor and won the 1961 election (Fairbanks and Underwood 1990). His opposition slate forced several dominant coalition candidates into runoff elections for council seats as well. In addition to factions among politicians, Dallas's reformers faced factions in their governing coalition elite. Cabell won financial backing from a number of organizations previously dedicated to the regime. Cabell also won the endorsement of the newspaper, and, as in San Jose, when the regime lost control over the news, it was seriously weakened.

In the early 1970s, San Antonio's Good Government League (GGL) suffered from fatal divisions between the city's older "moneyed interests," concerned with revitalizing downtown, and suburban developers and north side business owners who wanted to continue expanding the city's borders (Johnson, Booth, and Harris 1983, 24). The developers split from the GGL and ran opposition business slates in the 1973 and 1975 elections. These divisions provided an opening to mobilized, discontented citizens. In Albuquerque, the reform regime faced a difficult challenge from an opposition slate that included endorsements of previous regime members. These elites sought a different distribution of leadership and benefits in municipal government, and felt they could do better outside of the dominant coalition than they could within it.

Factions in the governing coalitions also arose in San Jose, dividing the business community. In particular, the passage of a 1978 statewide ballot initiative, Proposition 13, undermined cities' reliance on property taxes as their main source of revenue. This had the effect of changing the constellation of important elites at the local level. Where residential developers once dominated the political coalition, suddenly industrial development, downtown businesses, and retail developers became more important players because they generated jobs and sales taxes. Because of the incompatibility of their standard vision with the new elites, the reform coalition was weakened by the changing circumstances. The new elites supported a different platform and coalition. San Jose's first post–Prop 13 mayor, Tom McEnery, focused on urban renewal and placed new limits on sprawling development as a direct result of these changing circumstances. He had wide support among neighborhood groups and minority residents pursuing a change in the status quo *and* from business leaders pushing for downtown development and industrial growth.

Reform Bias Weakened

A number of reform-biasing instruments lost their impact during the 1960s and 1970s as a result of both endogenous and exogenous factors.

In San Jose, as in other reform cities, having monopoly control over the public discourse was fundamental to maintaining power. In the late 1970s, the reform coalition lost control of the city's newspaper when the parent company of the *San Jose Mercury News* forced out the publisher, Joseph Ridder, a dedicated reform booster. He was replaced by his nephew, who sought to open the paper to dissenting voices. Because they had eliminated all competing newspapers in order to consolidate power, the reformers had no effective option for keeping a lid on the news. Phil Trounstine, the paper's political editor, argued that the movement for district elections in 1978 succeeded in large part because, for the first time, the *San Jose Mercury News* fairly and accurately portrayed the negative and positive rationale for the change. The paper published a large pull-out section profiling each district that would be created under the new charter (P. Trounstine interview 2003). In protest, the city manager organized "a 'march on the *Mercury News*' by the city's business elite to lobby the newspaper to oppose district elections" (Christensen 1997). It is likely that the increased information offered to voters played a prominent role in the approval of the district system.

Perhaps the most damaging change reform coalitions faced was the elimination of key biasing mechanisms as a result of the passage of the 1965 Voting Rights Act and its 1970 and 1975 extensions. The new federal laws led to the abolition of literacy tests and poll taxes and provided a legal basis for neighborhood groups and minorities to challenge their city governments' at-large elections. The Supreme Court case establishing this latter precedent, *White v. Regester* 412 U.S. 755 (1973), was filed by black and Latino plaintiffs challenging the Texas legislature's reapportionment plan of 1970. The court found that establishment of multimember districts in Bexar (home of San Antonio) and Dallas counties was unconstitutional because they diluted the voting strength of Mexican Americans in Bexar County and the voting strength of African Americans in Dallas County.

In *White v. Regester,* the ruling against multimember districts applied to state legislative seats; however, in both Dallas and San Antonio, the case provided an impetus for minorities to mobilize against city at-large elections as well. In San Antonio, following on the heels of the *White v. Regester* decision, the Mexican American Legal Defense and Education Fund filed a challenge with the Justice Department requesting a review of the city's 1972 annexation, which brought nearly 40,000 new white residents into the city's political boundaries. The Justice Department agreed that the annexation diluted Mexican American voting strength and recommended that the city either change its method of electing councilors or face forced de-annexation of the territory and an indefinite suspension of its elections (Booth 1983, 195). By referendum the city adopted a change to district voting in 1977.[17]

In San Antonio and elsewhere, the change to district elections shifted the electoral process away from the city's voters and toward the city's residents. In a districted system, regardless of the level of participation in elections, all geographic areas of the city are guaranteed a seat on the council. Interestingly, the movement for district elections in some Southwestern cities was driven by whites, seeking greater influence for their outlying communities. They aligned with minority interests to achieve the desired outcome. In other cities minorities led the charge for districts and minority inclusion. In all of the cities studied here, district elections were adopted by reform governments under duress. According to Bridges (1997):

> Proponents of district elections argued that government would be more democratic, accountable, representative, and accessible; that the costs of campaigns would be lower and that public policy would be more equitable if districts were adopted. Opponents argued that local government was not broken and so needed no fixing . . . [some] saw Armageddon approach as districts would bring corruption, ward politics, social division, and "brown power." (195)

The dominance of reform governments was not easily challenged, however. District elections were defeated at the polls in every city prior to passage and only placed on the ballot once it became clear that governments might face legal action or lose coming elections. In all of the cases studied here, the loss of at-large elections came after governing coalitions had already been substantially weakened by electoral losses and factionalization. The change to districts turned out to be the nail in the coffin of reform regimes, rather than the catalyst for their demise. When reform coalitions were forced to discard their biasing mechanisms, when they lost a unified front due to challenges, and when they no longer had the support of governing coalition elites, they were forced to confront the increased competition resulting from the mobilization of discontented residents, and they failed to preserve the regime.

Regimes in Trouble

The logic of regime building presented here suggests that as soon as dominant organizations succeed in ensuring their power over the long term, they immediately begin to endanger their chances by sowing seeds of discontent. When a regime is unable to maintain its biased system, the only way to survive the increase in competition is to offer benefits to the challengers, thereby co-opting the opposing movement. This process is how one typically thinks competitive elections should work. Candidates bid for voter support by offering benefits to a broad coalition of supporters. The tougher the competition, the more people that have the potential to be included in the governing process. As was detailed earlier in this chapter, in a number of the cases, dominant coalitions responded to challenges at the polls by increasing benefits to meet the demands of previously excluded groups. They maintained power where they were able to find an equilibrium position that balanced demands and resources. This effectively moved coalitions away from the monopoly end of the spectrum of system types and toward responsive dominant regimes. Where machine and reform coalitions could not or chose not to expand their inner circle, they lost power. In these cities, bias alone was never sufficient to maintain control.

Plagued by the scarce resources of city government, to extend benefits to an additional set of demanders meant either raising more revenue or cutting benefits for existing supporters. At various moments, machine monopolies were beset by recession or cuts in state and federal funding. Without additional revenue to maintain the support of voters, the machine was in dire straights. For example, Daley's reliance on federal resources to maintain his coalition left him vulnerable to changing urban policies. Federal cutbacks in the 1970s and early 1980s worked to further mobilize angry black voters. Recession in the 1970s required Daley and then Bilandic and Byrne to cut patronage and shrink services. This, in combination with the weakened organization and mobilized anti-machine voters, all but spelled defeat for the Chicago machine. In New York and Jersey City, the 1929 Depression had a similar effect. A decline in city revenue coupled with greater demands for welfare spending upset Tammany's equilibrium. The bosses were unable to increase revenue because banks refused to extend additional credit. LaGuardia brought down the machine in 1933 as a result. Hague, on the other hand, secured federal resources with control over New Deal programs, and held on for another twenty years.

In other cases, the reason for a lack of incorporation of opposition demands had nothing to do with a city's fiscal situation and everything to do with its political coalition. The primary reason the Democratic machine in Chicago did not respond to African American demands in a satisfactory way was because they would have lost their white ethnic base as a result. Whites demanded segregation, and blacks demanded integration. The zero sum nature of their group preferences meant that the machine could not find a way to represent both sets of preferences. The black population also expressed demands that were incompatible with the machine itself. Empowering the African American population politically would have undermined the power of the organization because blacks were not part of the machine's core coalition. So, while Daley accepted War on Poverty funds to placate black voters, he never considered achieving the federal mandate of maximum feasible participation. Additionally, the machine in its final stages became so immersed in its factional battles that it literally failed to recognize the threat that first Byrne and then Washington posed. Reaching out to the mobilized black voters was not a path the machine chose.

One of the major reasons that black discontent was so severely underestimated by the Chicago machine was the insulation of the regime as a result of its own practices. Daley apparently refused to visit the high-rise ghettos his administration had built through public housing projects, instead relying on black machine operatives to tell him about their conditions. The few black aldermen who might have spoken accurately about the conditions in the black community were too fearful of Daley's repercussions to be honest about the anger in their communities, the crushing poverty, and the ways in which the city government should respond (Cohen and Taylor 2000).

In short, machines did not offer to co-opt the opposition when they did not see their demise on the horizon. According to his biographers, "Pendergast's arrogance gave him a false sense of invincibility" (Larson and Hulston 1997, 130). When the machine faced rising discontent, an inability to maintain a biased system, and insufficient resources (political or economic) with which to co-opt the opposition, it lost power. By focusing benefits on narrow coalitions, factionalizing under the safety of bias, and then ignoring demands made by challengers, machines were the architects of their own demise.

Like machines, dominant coalitions in reform cities responded to increased challenges at the polls by attempting to co-opt their opposition when they could, but they often did not respond well enough. For instance, in both San Antonio and San Jose, the dominant regime slated minorities for city council positions; however, for the most part, policies and priorities remained unchanged. In these cases, reformers were able to appease the opposition movements for a time, but eventually they faced rising demands that did not mesh with their core members' preferences. In San Jose, the slow-growth movement that eventually brought down the reform monopoly was at odds with the preferences of the dominant developer-led coalition. The reform regime enacted controlled-growth policies but never adopted the strict limits on development that would come after they lost power. The federal rulings that inspired the adoption of district elections in all of the reform cities studied here more rapidly brought about outcomes that were likely in the long run, given the rising discontent.

Like machines, reform coalitions had purposefully isolated themselves from the swings of politics through institutional structures that removed most decision making from the public arena. This insulation allowed them to ignore small shifts in public opinion, and when the rising neighborhood and civil rights movements gathered momentum, many reform regimes were caught off guard. San Jose's powerful city manager Dutch Hamann once was quoted as saying, "You can criticize me all you want but don't forget the people of the community thought what I was doing was good or they could have dumped me. The urban sprawl here is no different from any other place. Urban sprawl was created by the demands of people" (quoted by Rogers 1999, 1A). But eventually Hamann saw the writing on the wall, and resigned office before the new slow-growth coalition had a chance to remove him.

In some cases, both machine and reform, many factors beyond the control of the coalition itself weakened the regime and its ability to respond to challenges. But in other cases, political monopolies were the architects of their own decline; the choices they made generated conditions that increased the probability of collapse. Biased systems offered machine and reform regimes the freedom to pursue municipal policy that benefited monopoly members at the expense of large segments of the population. When regimes failed to maintain unity, lost their ability to rely on bias, and/or were unable or unwilling to incorporate new demands, they ceded power. In all of the cases studied here, after many decades of security, monopolies in reform and machine cities lost control. Some declined at once with a massive sweep of elected offices by the opposition; others relinquished power more slowly, integrating new voices and faces into the coalition until they no longer resembled their former selves.

The Rise and Fall of Bosses and Reformers

IN NEARLY 30 percent of the United States' largest cities, a single coalition governed for more than a decade, relying on bias to maintain power. This set of cities spans every region of the country, every year between 1900 and 1985, and includes governments defined as political machines and others representative of municipal reform. At the end of the day, the myriad differences that scholars have noted between bosses and reformers can be seen, primarily, as alternative strategies for building political monopolies. Representative democracy has not always functioned well in American cities.

The similarities between machine and reform regimes become clear when we take a step back from historical details and political rhetoric. Both kinds of coalitions came to power by mobilizing voters, identifying core members, and coordinating a governing coalition. Politicians in both types of systems developed and maintained structures of bias that favored incumbents at all stages of the voting process. They selected these strategies based on the political contexts they faced and the extent of their control over key institutions, which differed across time and place. In cities where large numbers of working-class immigrants lived and voted, coalitions used patronage to build dominant regimes; elsewhere, in cities characterized by low levels of income inequality and smaller minority populations, politicians relied on suffrage restrictions and vote dilution to capture and hold power.

The safety of a secure future allowed machine and reform coalitions to focus their energies on a small, satisfied coalition of residents. They continued to mobilize core supporters while ignoring or suppressing the turnout of others. Granted freedom by the biased systems, machine and reform coalitions survived with only a fraction of the larger community's support. Dominant coalitions in machine and reform cities steered the benefits of municipal governance to their core members and regime elites, while other identifiable groups were left on the periphery. As these regimes solidified control, the distinction between the coalition to which they were attentive and the electoral coalition that had brought them to power became increasingly stark.

During these periods of dominance, incumbent coalitions were wildly successful, capturing nearly all of the elected positions at the local level and winning by wide margins of victory. But under this veneer of power, the structures of dominance began to give way. Excluding large numbers of residents from the governing process, machine and reform regimes were unwittingly the architects of their own demise. Shifting demographics, rising social movements, division among elites, changing electoral systems, and economic transformations began to push these monopolies toward decline. At some times and in some places, the coalition in power assuaged the challenge by responding to the demands of their opposition. Where they lacked the resources to do this effectively or simply refused to expand their circles of influence, the dominant coalitions lost power. None could hold on forever, and eventually these regimes relinquished their hold over political systems.

In the End

Following the collapse of machine and reform regimes, the political arena changed shape and direction. Competition was rekindled, voter participation increased, and benefits were distributed more broadly in both machine and reform cities. Races for city posts became more closely contested in Austin, Dallas, San Antonio, San Jose, Chicago, Kansas City, New Haven, New York, and Philadelphia following the end of the monopoly period. As machine and reform regimes crumbled the average margin of victory declined by nearly 9 percentage points in these cities. Equally important, the end of the monopoly period increased competition in both machine and reform cities. The decline of dominant regimes also had the effect of broadening electoral participation as new voters were mobilized by the opposition and the incumbent coalition struggling to maintain control. In the nine cities listed above, turnout of eligible voters increased by an average of 3 percentage points in the elections following monopoly collapse. This relationship remains significant after controlling for other factors that might influence mobilization, such as the number of candidates running and the closeness of the election.

Opposition coalitions in machine and reform cities alike promised and delivered increased benefits to groups that had long been ignored or given short shrift by the regimes in power. These voters were mobilized against dominant coalitions with the expectation of increased benefits. Harold Washington's election as mayor of Chicago turned out nearly

73 percent of eligible black voters, a 34 percentage point increase since the most recent election with an African American candidate. Washington's responsiveness to his coalition was evident. Of the new municipal employees hired in 1985, 64 percent were black and more than 10 percent were Latino (Freedman 1988). Using executive orders to side-step an uncooperative council, Washington initiated affirmative action in government contracting, expanding minority shares more than 200 percent (Simpson 2001). To increase neighborhood power, Washington channeled Community Development Block Grant funds to community organizations; to increase government accountability and transparency, he signed a freedom of information act.

In reform cities, too, the collapse of the dominant coalitions resulted in changes to local governance. Competition was increased, campaigns became more issue focused, councils more racially diverse, and benefits more widely shared (Bridges 1997). The pure pro-growth regimes were brought to an end as cities enacted limits or controls on development, drafted comprehensive growth plans, and preserved open space. Development was refocused inward rather than toward outlying areas. San Jose's post-reform administration spent $1.3 billion between 1977 and 1998 on downtown redevelopment projects. A new tax was levied on developers to pay for capital improvements and services—a vastly different scenario than in earlier decades, when city hall had subsidized development on the urban fringe.

San Jose's neighborhoods received increased attention and sympathy from the city council, which had become a diverse and professionalized legislature as a result of district elections and a pay-rate change allowing councilors to work at their positions fulltime. In 1980 (the first district elections), women won a majority of the seats. One of the new members was African American and another Latina. Previously unrepresented neighborhoods also won positions on the council. Over the course of the next two decades the council became more concerned with social issues: enacting a living wage, a health initiative, a tobacco tax, and affordable housing programs. Neighborhood group meetings were initiated, offering access and assistance to communities interested in making changes (Hammer interview 2003). Plans were drafted to build new libraries in communities neglected for half a century by the reformers. Between 1973 and 1981 the government built libraries in older annexed communities. In 1999 the heavily Latino areas of Alviso and the Central City received branches. Minorities also made significant gains in city employment. As of 2003, Latinos represented 26 percent of the fulltime municipal labor force and Asians 11 percent. Each group composed about a third of San Jose's residential population in that year.

After the Fall

It is significant that after the collapse of monopolies, a broader set of constituents were offered municipal benefits. However, in many cases the fall of monopolies set in motion periods of intense factionalism during which gridlock was common. In Chicago, the election of Jane Byrne signaled the end of the machine monopoly. She sought to shake up city government by replacing Daley- and Bilandic-appointed department heads and revamping power within the city council. But after she was elected she found that she lacked the ability to enact policy through the city council or initiate changes in the bureaucracy without the cooperation of the machine's aldermanic leaders. So after winning office as a reformer Byrne returned to the fold of the dying machine (Simpson 2001). During her term she faced consistent opposition on the council, criticism in the media, and difficulty removing machine-loyal municipal employees because of the prohibitions on politically motivated firing defined by the Shakman Decree.

Byrne's troubles negotiating the entrenched machine paled in comparison to the hurdles faced by Harold Washington in his first term as Chicago's mayor. When he took office in 1983 Washington had only twenty-one allies on the city council—and twenty-nine opponents tied to the old machine. All but four of Washington's supporters were black and all but four of his opponents were white. Nearly every controversial vote in the council was decided against Washington along these political and racial lines (Simpson 2001). Washington's willingness to use his veto power ensured that during this period of divided government few changes were made to city governance through municipal ordinances. By his second term of office, Washington had consolidated a clear majority on the council, but the factionalism and racial divisions reemerged after Washington's untimely death. Washington's successor, Eugene Sawyer, was forced to assemble "a new coalition . . . to pass each separate proposal because . . . he did not have a majority bloc to support him" (Simpson 2001, 232).

In San Jose, the years both before and after the collapse of the monopoly were tumultuous. The underpinnings of reform dominance in San Jose began to give way in the early 1970s as antimonopoly candidates won seats on the council. This decade represented a period of transition, with the council majority shifting issue by issue as the members sought to gauge the pulse of both voters and elites. Unlike the case of Chicago, the reform monopoly managed to survive these shifting coalitions for some time because of the structure of reform government. The council-manager system largely suppressed political battles and mitigated the effect of convulsions in public opinion on city government. The strength and independence of the bureaucracy ensured that a shift in city policy required a strong antimonopoly coalition. This emerged with Janet Gray Hayes's 1978 reelection and a five-to-two slow-growth majority on the council (Hayes interview 1980). It was reaffirmed after the first district elections in 1980. But the stability was temporary.

Throughout Hayes's second term, the slow-growth coalition splintered on various issues. At one point Hayes joined the remaining monopoly councilors to extend development in protected areas, and in 1982 a new debate erupted between slow-growth and pro-growth forces over how to handle the city's aging and overextended sewage-treatment facility. Pro-growth forces won the fight as the city ultimately agreed to spend more than $100 million for expansion. The new city government faced other challenges as well: in 1979 and 1980 a push to redevelop downtown was stymied by land-assembly hurdles and contract troubles; city workers went on strike in 1981; and in 1984 the city lost more than $60 million in bond investments (Hayes interview 1980; Matthews 2003; Christensen 1997).

In both San Jose and Chicago, the collapse of the monopoly initiated periods of turmoil. Chicago's mayors Byrne and Washington presided over intensely factionalized councils and parties. San Jose witnessed a jagged move toward a slow-growth path for the city. Both cities would emerge years later in the hands of newly consolidated but refocused pro-growth coalitions. San Jose's new coalition governed from 1982 to 1998. It was inaugurated by Mayor Tom McEnery with a strong council majority and continued by Mayor Susan Hammer. Under McEnery, the city manager became subordinate to the mayor for the first time in the city's history. Chicago's new dominant regime headed by Richard M. Daley (Boss Daley's son) has been in power consistently since 1989. Daley has taken over with a broader coalition than his father organized. Esther Fuchs (1992) argues, "Daley has understood that the city's demographics have changed, that taken together the minorities have become a majority of Chicago's residents and that the mayor cannot govern effectively without their support" (8). Daley has also been responsive to demands to reform the old machine system, agreeing to civil service limitations and freedom of information acts.

The question is whether either of these modern coalitions represents a new type of monopoly. Some analysts have argued that they do. For example, in a piece entitled "The New Daley Machine," Simpson et al. (2004) show that Daley has been in power for more than eighteen years, enjoys the support of nearly three-quarters of the city council at least 90 percent of the time, and garners large campaign contributions from local elites. But according to the theoretical frame offered in chapter 1, none of these pieces of evidence allows us to determine whether or not Daley leads a monopoly. Instead we should look for the markers presented throughout this work: evidence of cohesive coalitions reliant on bias to maintain power. As a result we should see evidence of declining participation and policy focused toward a narrow base. We need a deeper analysis of the ways in which the political process remains closed to certain members of the community, and we need to link patterns of municipal policymaking to these structures and strategies of bias.

Alternative Versions of Monopolies

Scholars of urban politics and political parties alike argue that "the great urban machines, like the dinosaurs, were temporary. The last of the great party machines was Chicago's, and it declined after the death of Mayor Richard J. Daley . . . in 1976" (Hershey and Beck 2003, 55). The world looks a good deal different today than it did in 1900 or 1950, when most machine and reform monopolies arose. An increasing number of cities are governed by nonpartisan district elections, powerful bureaucracies, and hybrid mayor-manager systems with term limits. Suffrage is basically static and civil service is the norm. Graft and corruption have moved below the surface, and many cities have laws promoting transparency in governance. Campaign costs have risen exponentially (Krebs and Pelissero 2001) and voter mobilization in local elections by political parties has all but disappeared in some cities (Welch and Bledsoe 1988). It makes sense, given these changes, that machine and reform monopolies would be unworkable today.

There is evidence, though, that even in the period that is the focus of this study, machine and reform regimes were not the only forms of monopoly. Orville Hubbard, the "Dictator" of Dearborn, Michigan, ran an operation that drew on strategies of bias and mechanisms of coordination found in both machine and reform cities (Good 1989). Good explains that, like machine bosses, Hubbard required his department heads to pay for his election campaigns, and liberally employed threats of public ridicule to force elites into agreement. Similar to reformers,

Hubbard operated in a nonpartisan city and made sure he controlled access to the news media. Like machine politicians Hubbard interviewed all new city employees, but like reformers he also built a strong civil service system. Hubbard's system was hierarchically organized, with each of his department heads responsible for a geographic area of the city and appointed commissioners engaged in electioneering. His reliance on strategies of bias meant that he could be responsive to the demands of a narrow constituency. Because of the enormous tax base provided by Ford Motor Company, city services were well run and property taxes low. But more importantly, Hubbard kept Dearborn "white" during his thirty-six-year tenure. To his core coalition members, united by a virulent fear of black suburbanites, Hubbard was highly responsive. Yet, throughout this period a significant segment of Dearborn residents and the thousands of African Americans who worked in the city did not support segregation. Additionally, Hubbard antagonized the municipal workforce, limiting their pension benefits, continually denying pay raises, and vetoing city contributions to the pension fund. He refused to allow affordable housing projects to be built within the city even when they had broad public support and he developed discriminatory taxation systems that arbitrarily raised taxes for some and cut them for others (Good 1989).

The strategies for winning and holding power were combined in different ways in Dearborn, but the results were similar to the cases studied throughout this book. Monopolies come in many different packages. The absence of machine or reform regimes in today's cities does not preclude the presence of modern monopolies. Incumbent politicians and coalitions should still be able to rely on information bias, vote bias, and seat bias to entrench themselves in power. To the extent that urban political systems are closed to certain groups of residents via bias, we should continue to expect policy outcomes to favor some residents over others.

What form might bias take in today's cities? It would appear difficult for modern politicians to silence the media in today's electoral context, given the increasing number of outlets for news and information in the technological age. However it *is* possible that incumbent coalitions can make access to information about the government or opportunities for replacing the government difficult. Sharpe James, the head of the Democratic coalition that governed Newark from 1986 to 2006, routinely denied access to reporters, spread campaign messages using public funds, and paid a local newspaper $100,000 from city coffers to print positive news about the government (Ekdahl 2007). Marshall Curry explained the difficulty reporters faced in gaining access to James, saying, "The second time I had my camera confiscated, a *Star Ledger* reporter was telling me to just put it away. He said 'Don't fuck around with these guys. Be careful.' For a reporter to tell you to be careful indicates to me that there was some institutionalized consequence that they were aware of" (Marshall Curry interviewed and quoted in Ekdahl 2007, 26). Only ten states require voters to be informed of the date of elections and location of their polling place by mail in federal elections, and even fewer require the information to be provided for local contests (Wolfinger, Highton, and Mullin 2005). Where information is not provided, fewer voters tend to participate. When access to information is unequal, the system is biased and incumbents are likely to be aided.

Incumbents may have other informational advantages as well. It is possible that collusion between county/state prosecutors and city leaders, or a lack of resources to conduct investigations, limits the likelihood that allegations of wrongdoing will be made public. It is also highly likely that disproportionate campaign funds limit challengers' ability to publicize all of the relevant information about incumbents. By 1990 mayoral elections in San Jose had become million-dollar affairs. Low-cost door knocking was relegated to a supplemental campaign strategy, as media saturation and phone banking became the norm. Because money is such an important component of winning elections today, variation in campaign finance laws might offer meaningful distinctions between more and less biased systems. For example, limits on campaign spending can impede challengers relative to incumbents because challengers need to spend money to increase their name recognition (Jacobson 1997). Recent research on New York City found that a change in campaign finance law that increased public financing and restricted the ability of corporations to donate money in municipal elections led to an increase in the influence of labor and nonprofit organizations in elections and policy outcomes (Higgins 2007). This suggests that the need to raise campaign contributions has the potential to bias the system both toward incumbents and toward those constituents who have the financial means to contribute, violating standards of political equality (see Gilens 2005).

More directly, public resources used to enhance an incumbent's probability of winning are an indication of a biased system. This was the case in San Francisco when city assessor Doris Ward illegally used taxpayer dollars to fund her reelection campaign (L. Williams and Finnie 2002). Incumbents can also raise and spend campaign funds unlawfully, as the New Jersey Law Enforcement Commission accused Sharpe James of doing in Newark from 1988–94 (Ekdahl 2007). Philadelphia's city council has had a number of "pay-to-play" scandals in which political favors were found to have been traded for campaign contributions (Ekdahl 2007). These kinds of strategies enhance the power of incumbents relative to challengers, make it difficult for residents to learn about available alternatives, and make it less likely that quality opponents will emerge.

Similar to the advantage offered by larger war chests, according to established research nonpartisan elections offer advantages to incumbents because of the decreased cues available to voters. However, today in most cities, whether elections for city government are partisan or not, a single party holds a large advantage among the voters. This means that even in partisan contests, cues may be unavailable, particularly in primary elections. So incumbents may benefit in the vast majority of cities as a result of limited visibility and information in local politics and elections. Other institutional features may contribute to this low-information, low-turnout environment, including nonconcurrent elections (Hajnal and Lewis 2003) and council manager structures (Bridges 1997; Oliver and Ha 2007).

With regard to vote bias, election fraud perpetrated by insecure incumbents or their supporters surely still occurs, though proof is hard to obtain. Even from the days when fraud was supposedly rampant, we have few pieces of strong evidence. This is obviously because only unsuccessful fraud makes it into the news. But it is also likely to be true that claims of fraud were and are, to some extent, a political tactic used to strengthen laws limiting ballot access (Minnite 2007). But verification of fraud does appear every so often. Washington DC Mayor Anthony Williams's reelection campaign committed 5,533 violations of city election law (*Washington Post* 2002). A 2006 investigation by the *Poughkeepsie Journal* reported that 2,600 dead people had voted in New York. Democratic Party workers were found guilty in East St. Louis for vote buying in 2005 (Shaw, Moore, and Hampel 2005). In Daley's most recent election for mayor, challengers complained because he paid college students $100/day to get out the vote for the mayor (Spielman 2006).

For the most part, though, election irregularities tend to be chalked up to administrative error rather than purposeful deception. Still, polling places may be moved to less accessible locations, voters may be harassed or forced to wait in long lines, and identification may be required unnecessarily. Except for felons and noncitizens, formal suffrage restrictions no longer exist. Yet, most local governments do have laws or structures that make it relatively more difficult to vote. Registration requirements and a lack of information provided to voters regarding poll locations, candidates, or ballot measures tend to decrease turnout particularly among less educated voters. All of these scenarios can bias the system in favor of incumbents if the people who drop out of the electorate would tend to support the opposition.

The most powerful vote-biasing mechanism used by political machines is still potentially available—patronage. A recent investigation by United States attorney Patrick Fitzgerald revealed that Chicago's city government relies on political affiliation to hire and fire workers (Associated Press 2005). Simpson et al. (2004) report that numerous municipal employees are also engaged as party workers, many of whom pay a voluntarily "special tax" on their salaries (9). Cities like Newark and Philadelphia have much larger patronage workforces than cities with bigger populations and there is evidence, particularly in Newark, that these employees have been pressed into political service (Ekdahl 2007). Ekdahl finds that "invitations to [James's] fundraising events were inserted into municipal employees' pay stub envelopes." Police officers "with a generous new contract" denied James's opponent access to public meeting places (Fund 2002, A18). Public-housing tenants were threatened with eviction for supporting the opposition candidate (Fund 2002). After the Newark firefighters union supported James's opponent, the department's funding was cut by 20 percent and firefighters were forced to rotate between firehouses (Ekdahl 2007).

These examples may not reflect the practice in most city governments today. The implementation of civil service, the unionization of municipal employees, and a series of court rulings banning political hiring and firing, have made using public employees as political operatives more difficult. This means that incumbent coalitions must rely on different mechanisms to utilize government resources for organizing support. In some cities, nonprofit organizations provide this link today. A new layer has been added between the government and the patronage employee or service beneficiary, but the effect may be the same—an increased advantage for the incumbent coalition. Marwell (2004) finds that nonprofit community-based organizations (CBOs) in New York City mobilize their clients in exchange for government contracts—just like voters were once mobilized in exchange for patronage jobs. Marwell argues that CBOs "fill the gap left by defunct political party organizations in poor neighborhoods" (269). The North Ward Center in Newark has played a similar role, providing campaign work and mobilizing voters with the understanding that the organization will be a continuing beneficiary of city largess (Ekdahl 2007; Casciano 2007).

In the DC metro area, Frasure and Jones-Correa (2005) also find that CBOs work as intermediaries between residents and bureaucracies. Through these links, CBOs gain access to government resources, and bureaucracies are better able to serve community members. Although Frasure and Jones-Correa do not discuss the possibility that residents engaged in these organizations might be more likely to support the incumbent coalition, it is not hard to imagine that it happens as these organizations "seek and maintain good relationships with local governmental actors" (17). However, we should be careful categorizing these strategies as bias, because distributing benefits like jobs or services to supporters *can* be a reelection strategy that reinforces the electoral connection. As explained in chapter 2, particularistic benefits do not bias the system per se. They work as bias when recipients are coerced into political work or support. To determine whether this occurs in these cases requires deeper research into these organizations and the political activities of their members.

Seat bias produces an advantage for the incumbent coalition in the translation of votes to seats. Gerrymandering is one example of this type of bias, and it still occurs at the city level. In Chicago, one incumbent's ward was saved following the 2000 census by including a "stair-shaped stretch across the Dan Ryan [Expressway]" (Spielman 2006). Philadelphia is reported to have some of the most egregiously gerrymandered districts in the country (Ekdahl 2007). In a different type of seat bias, city councilors in Lynwood, California, refused to schedule a recall election after a petition garnered the requisite number signatures. The *Los Angeles Times* reported that the Lynwood council stripped the city clerk of her election duties when she attempted to schedule the recall (Becerra 2007)

Chapter 2 presented evidence that reform governments in the middle of the twentieth century were able to maintain power despite significant opposition by using at-large elections for city council. Today most cities use at-large elections for at least some of their council seats, and the conventional wisdom is that at-large seats are more competitive than district seats; they are harder and more expensive to win (J. Trounstine and Valdini 2007). This environment may aid incumbents, but it may not. However, because all councilors face the same electorate, at-large elections may make it easier to foster cohesion on councils. If this is the case, at-large elections may aid coalitions in meeting the second necessary condition for building a monopoly—coordination.

Like classic monopolies, building an organization requires a stable block of supportive voters, disciplined politicians, and a coordinated governing regime. In general, developing and maintaining a centralized coalition may be difficult in today's cities, but still achievable. In Houston, one political observer notes, "For a long time, the story was that Houston was tightly controlled by three guys who met all the time in Suite 8F in the old Lamar Hotel. Today, business leaders will jokingly say we've become much more democratic; there's about 20 guys in the group."[1] Ekdahl (2007) finds virtually no evidence in Newark of divided council votes or mayoral vetoes during Sharpe James's reign, and in Chicago thirty-two of the city's fifty aldermen support Mayor Daley 90 to 100 percent of the time on divided roll-call votes (Simpson et al. 2004). This leads Simpson (2001) to refer the Chicago council as a "rubber stamp." Simpson et al. (2004) explain that Daley was assisted in achieving this solid coalition by appointing nineteen of the fifty aldermen to fill vacant seats. In Newark, James relied on a slating system in the city's nonpartisan elections to build cohesiveness among the council and mayor's office (Ekdahl 2007).

Given that parties have become much less important for building coalitions and loyalties, we might predict a number of different avenues for organizing voters and elites in modern cities. Community organizations, religious institutions, or unions with ties to elected officials might serve to coordinate coalitions (see Wong 2006, for example). In these cases, substituting nonpolitical linkages for the grassroots network of parties allows local incumbents to build a stable base. Alternatively, individual leaders may build organizations around their own candidacy, and, if popular enough, use endorsements and campaign funds to garner support from other elected officials. The current Mayor Daley probably fits this description, although to some extent he continues to rely on patronage workers for voter mobilization.

So, at the end of the day, is it likely that Daley leads a form of modern monopoly? The answer is probably yes, but a weaker monopoly than his father led. The theoretical frame in chapter 1 defined a monopoly as a coalition that maintains power by creating political arrangements that minimize the need to be responsive. The current Daley has quite clearly been more responsive than his father to various groups. In order to win reelection in 1991 he cultivated support among liberals and later among Latinos by using policy stands, appointments, and by garnering strategic endorsements (Krebs and Pelissero 2001). Daley has even reached out to the city's black community in limited ways (Krebs and Pelissero 2001). These strategies for reelection served to increase the electoral connection between Daley and his constituents, and as of 2006, on the heels of a major corruption scandal, his approval rating was 56 percent among residents (Spielman 2006). Given his popularity with his constituents, it is not possible to conclude that bias is the only or even primary force driving Daley's electoral success. But his use of typical biasing strategies to protect incumbents suggests that the system is not a level playing field for opponents and that it is closed or at least limited for certain types of residents. As a result, who participates in government and how government benefits are distributed are likely to be affected. Simpson et al. (2004) show that Daley has been inattentive to black residents in Chicago, choosing instead to focus governance toward the global economy, Latinos, and whites.[2]

Overall this suggests that in Chicago building and maintaining a monopoly may be difficult today, but still possible. In particular, the strategies of bias Daley's father relied upon have been less effective for his son; as a result the current mayor has been forced to rely more heavily on responsiveness to voters. In essence, while he may lead a monopoly, his core coalition is larger than was his father's. In his analysis of modern Newark, Ekdahl (2007) draws a similar conclusion. In order to keep winning, Sharpe James had to deliver to a broad base of constituents. However, the examples offered above suggest that politicians clearly still employ strategies of bias even though the patterns of dominance are not likely to reflect the traditional machine and reform formats. It is probable that because most cities feature reform-style institutions today, modern monopolies look like hybrids of these older forms. Furthermore, politicians are likely to develop new strategies for insulating their power and inhibiting the rise of opposition.

Consequences of Different Types of Monopoly

This work focused on analyzing the similarities between political machines and municipal reformers, but throughout highlighted the ways in which the organizations differed. It has argued that the differences reflect the vagaries of monopoly building in particular institutional, economic, and demographic environments. But the distinctions may run deeper than this. Although the patterns are similar, the magnitude of effects does vary on some measures for machine versus reform monopolies. The results in chapters 4, 5, and 6 can shed light on these distinctions. For instance, the analysis in table 4.3 reveals that compared to reform cities, more incumbents chose to run for reelection in machine cities. This is interesting in light of the results presented in tables 4.4 and 4.6, which show that there was no significant difference between machine and reform cities with regard to incumbency reelection rates. So while machine incumbents were running more frequently, they were not necessarily being reelected more often. This may be related to the types of people who tended to hold elected office in the two types of systems. Many machine officials were professional politicians while reform officials were often businessmen who were more likely to rotate in and out of government.

Tables 5.2 and 5.4 suggest that machine cities also saw consistently higher turnout rates, perhaps because of the organizational structure of machines themselves. Where reformers created a small electorate through electoral rules, machines were forced to coordinate cohesive coalitions in growing, diverse cities. To win in this environment, parties were organized hierarchically, and lower-level machine workers were rewarded for bringing in votes. This in turn generated higher turnout that persisted throughout and following the monopoly period.[3] The differences in structure also led machine governments to pursue a less dramatic shift in resources. Because their strategies of bias tended to be weaker and their electoral coalition larger, machine governments were less free to focus benefits on their core members. The results in tables 5.6 and 6.2 show that spending patterns changed less dramatically in the machine case.

Not only are there some important differences between machine and reform monopolies, there may be long-term consequences to having been governed by one type or another. To see whether or not this is the case, I analyzed a modern series of social, economic, and political indicators in cities that had been governed at some point by a reform or machine monopoly and in cities that had never been monopolized by one of these two types according to the categorization listed in appendix tables A1–A3.[4]

The data I use for this modern analysis span the years 1986–2002 and come from the United States Census of Governments and the International City County Manager's Association survey.[5] As dependent variables I used median household income, proportion of population with a college degree, the total value of cash and securities held by the city government, total per capita taxes, per capita property taxes, total revenue collected, total expenditure, and total outstanding debt. To determine whether there were lasting political effects, I analyze the consequence of monopoly on the proportion of incumbents seeking reelection and the proportion of incumbents who win reelection. For all of the analyses, the main independent variables are dummy variables noting whether a city ever had a machine monopoly or a reform monopoly.[6]

These regressions yielded a number of interesting results. The most prominent pattern is that cities that were once governed by a reform monopoly continue to have different political and economic patterns, particularly in comparison to cities without any monopoly. In the years between 1986 and 2002, reform cities had significantly larger populations, had a larger proportion of college graduates, collected less total revenue, had lower per capita property taxes, spent less overall, and had lower levels of cash and securities than nonmonopolized cities. In addition, compared to cities that were once dominated by machines, reform cities had a larger proportion of college graduates, smaller government revenues and expenditures, and lower levels of assets. There was no significant difference between reform monopolies, machine monopolies, and nonmonopoly cities with regard to total taxes per capita, median income, or outstanding debt.

Unlike the finding during the monopoly period, in this analysis, reform cities witnessed a higher proportion of incumbents running for reelection than both machine cities and nonmonopoly cities. But reform cities were no more likely to see incumbents actually win reelection. Generally speaking, then, the legacy of reform dominance is smaller (although not more efficient) governments, a better educated (but not wealthier) population, and incumbents who are more likely to seek reelection (but not to win). It is hard to draw any substantive conclusion from these current patterns—except perhaps that reformers succeeded in preventing the growth of government. Cities that were once dominated by machines today look little different from cities where no monopoly came to power.

These data suggest that the type of monopoly can matter for politicians, for a city's residents, and for the structure and patterns of governance. However, on a number of indicators both during the monopoly period and after the collapse of the regimes, the differences between machine and reform organizations are not particularly meaningful. The more important distinction is between cities in which monopolies are in power and cities in which they are not.

Implications beyond These Cases

The concept of political monopolies and the explanation of the factors contributing to the rise and fall of regimes are important beyond the urban arena. We cannot assume that the same factors and dynamics at work in urban politics are operating in the same way at the national level. But the similarity of goals and constraints faced by political actors in U.S. cities and those faced by similarly situated actors in many national polities suggests that insights gained from the study of urban politics might find parallels in, and shed light on, the comparative study of national politics.

Students of national politics in the United States may be predisposed to thinking of institutions as being less amenable to the kinds of biasing mechanisms outlined at the local level. But other countries can and do change their fundamental electoral laws, regulation of the media, and patronage practices in ways that look much more like U.S. cities than like the U.S. national government. A great deal of work is actively engaged in the analysis and explanation of transitions between democratic governments and authoritarian regimes. In the preface to their recent book, Acemoglu and Robinson (2006) propose the following fundamental puzzle: "Why is it that some countries are democracies, where there are regular and free elections and politicians are accountable to citizens, whereas other countries are not?" (xi). The research presented here contributes to this discussion in a number of ways. To start, this book has provided evidence that even in established democratic systems, a lack of accountability can be an endogenous consequence of reelection-seeking politicians. Additionally, there can be substantial variation in the degree to which free and fair elections are carried out at the subnational level. These conclusions support the dominant view in the study of regime change that democracy ought to be measured in degrees rather than as a discrete category (see Acemoglu and Robinson 2006 for discussion). The findings in this book contribute to this process by investigating the mechanisms by which representation fails to function in democratic systems. The conditions that motivate those in power to attend to their constituents and the conditions that undermine the electoral connection may be applicable in nondemocracies as well. For example, the theory of political monopolies suggests that one could analyze the types of bias employed in authoritarian regimes and the degree to which power is maintained through bias. Where authoritarian regimes rely on less successful mechanisms of bias and are thus more worried about being deposed, they may be more responsive to residents' demands.

My analysis offers insight into the factors that encourage the selection of certain political institutions, rules, and procedures over others during periods of transition, and the timing of those changes. For example, chapter 3 suggests that the preferences of the governing coalition and the socioeconomic status of residents lead some regimes to focus on restricting the electorate and others to focus on coercing it. As for timing, this analysis has concentrated on the factors that affect the presence of bias and the degree of coordination among elites in the development and collapse of monopolies. Perhaps in other political settings, too, factors like a high degree of institutional control and political threat can increase the probability of monopoly emergence, while economic diversity can increase the probability of decline.

Chapter 6 presents evidence that strong economies had different effects for machine versus reform monopolies. High levels of unemployment increased the probability of machine collapse, whereas high and growing levels of employment were troublesome for reformers. For scholars studying the effect of economic growth on the fall of authoritarian regimes or the emergence of democracy, this finding might suggest that the effects can differ by regime type. At the very least, my research supports findings in non-U.S. contexts that the path toward representative democracy is often far from linear.

The research presented here can contribute to the debate over the effect of democracy on development. In many of the cities studied here, monopolies governed over periods of intense growth and progress. With streamlined control, consolidated power, and little effective opposition, these regimes built some of our modern-day metropolises. But compared to cities in which no monopolies ever governed and during years in which monopolies were not in power, monopolies did no better (or worse) at keeping levels of debt or taxation lower, levels of assets higher, or at maintaining superior employment rates or higher incomes. This set of findings is consistent with work in comparative politics showing that regime type (e.g., democracy vs. authoritarian) is basically unrelated to growth (Przeworski et al. 2000). In other words, "there is no trade-off between democracy and development" (Przeworski et al. 2000, 178).

Additionally, the basic pattern described in monopoly cities may in part or in whole describe political patterns elsewhere. A political group coordinates a winning electoral coalition, relies on strategies for perpetuation of power that undermine the electoral connection, and concentrates on rewarding a small core of supporters. The degree to which rewards can be focused would depend on the extent of a particular politician's access and control over policymaking, but we could imagine similar outcomes in diverse settings: a single congressional district, a union, or a school board, for example. As Fenno ([1978] 2003) explained, once in office most incumbents become conservative, protecting their base rather than reaching out to new voters. The discussion of Republican dominance in Congress between 1995 and 2007 offered by Hacker and

Pierson in *Off Center* (2005) reveals a similar set of processes. As was mentioned in chapter 1, I have only analyzed cases in which the political coalition achieved control over the whole government, but fruitful future research might be concerned with identifying variations in the degree of power and concomitant results.

The analysis in this work also speaks to the extensive debates over how democratic representation works and how well it works. A good number of scholars are skeptical of the power of democracy and elections to generate optimal outcomes. Among other things, experts disagree about the capacity for citizens to fulfill the duties that democratic theory requires of them; they argue over the role of elections versus intermediaries like interest groups in disciplining politicians; and they debate the degree to which citizens versus elites influence policymaking.

Alexis de Tocqueville (1956) was one of the earliest scholars to praise the responsiveness of municipal politics. "The existence of the townships," he argued, "is, in general, a happy one. Their government is suited to their tastes and chosen by themselves . . . The political education of the people has long been complete. . . . If the government has faults . . . they do not attract notice, for the government really emanates from those it governs" (61). To Tocqueville, local politics epitomized participatory democracy. Indeed, work by Oliver and Ha (2007) finds that "suburban voters are a generally satisfied lot" and that issue positions tend to be the strongest determinant of voter support (400). We might conclude, then, that incumbents are likely to be returned to office in local elections because they are responsive to their constituents. The trouble is that participation in local elections hovers between 10 and 25 percent of eligible residents in a large number of places.[7] Oliver and Ha agree, arguing that local elections "are dominated by a nonrepresentative group of 'stakeholders' " (393).

In such an environment, access to the ballot box and to information regarding candidates and government performance becomes all the more important for shaping election and policy outcomes. Whereas most debates over participation and representative democracy assume that individuals have the option to learn about politics, elections, and government, and to select government officials who reflect their preferences if they so choose, my work suggests that in a biased system these opportunities are unavailable. Some scholars will argue that even if information is accessible, and even if elections are free and fair, people may not have the motivation or ability to participate in meaningful and productive ways. At the end of the day, we might be awfully bad at governing ourselves. This could in fact be the case. However, the presence of bias will reduce whatever possibility does exist for meaningful representation, be it through direct citizen involvement, intermediaries, or a small stratum of elites. The evidence presented throughout this book shows that government is more responsive to larger numbers of people when monopolies are not in power.

Lessons Learned

So what are the lessons to be learned from these chronicles of urban monopolies? Given that rational politicians are likely to continue to seek ways to ensure their longevity, what kinds of things might we do to minimize the bad effects? One approach to figuring this out is to identify the contextual factors that increase or decrease the probability of monopoly governance. Lipset, Trow, and Coleman (1956), in their study of the maintenance of democracy in the International Typographical Union, provide a long list of features that enhance democratic competition and limit the development of oligarchy. For example, they argue that less centralized administrations offer more people access to resources and make a larger number of decision areas subject to choice, thereby increasing the probability of opposition. Applied to cities, we could say that the greater the autonomy of the constituent parts of government, the less likely a single person or faction will govern. Similarly, the results in chapters 4 and 6 suggest that uncooperative state governments limit monopoly emergence and maintenance. Strong bureaucracies and municipal employee unions may have the same effect. Lipset, Trow, and Coleman (1956) also find that democracy is likely to be preserved when no one group is strong enough to maintain power. The data in chapters 4 and 6 support this conclusion—diversity, both demographic and economic, harms monopoly. Similarly Brierly and Moon (1991) show that diversity inhibits the formation of stable coalitions. Monopolies (and oligarchies for Lipset, Trow, and Coleman) are least likely to emerge and survive in small communities.

This evidence indicates that one potential avenue for limiting the occurrence of monopolies is to encourage small, diverse communities, and governments in which authority is divided. Unfortunately, we may have little control over the first two factors, and the third, creating fractured governing structures, does little to produce responsive government. A more fruitful approach might be to determine institutional contexts that encourage elected officials to improve, rather than subvert links to voters. This means we must focus on limiting strategies of bias, and concentrate on finding mechanisms to ensure that viable opposition arises when needed.

First, we must preserve the free flow of information. We can encourage multiple sources of news, and laws that require governmental openness. We need to protect the independence of prosecutors and communal organizations. Encouraging slates and parties has the potential to provide cues and mobilization to voters, as does publicizing endorsements. At the very least, all residents should be informed of the time of elections and the location of their polling places, presented platforms by candidates, and, where relevant, information about ballot initiatives. Second, we must ensure that elections are free and fair, that municipal employees are not coerced into working for incumbents, and that all votes are counted and cast without threat or bribery. By making it straightforward for candidates to enter races and for residents to register to vote, we make alternative options easier to select. At some point we might consider mandatory media space for candidates and perhaps even public campaign financing. We can not tolerate a recurrence of suffrage restrictions, and we need to vigilantly oppose violations of the one person, one vote system. Districts appear to work well in cities for maintaining diverse views; proportional representation might work even better.

What we should *not* do is confuse longevity in office with a lack of representation, or seek to undermine the authority of our governing officials. The answer is not to have weaker government, but to have better government. As an example of the former, term limits may deter a single politician from entrenching himself in power, but can also undermine the link between voters and politicians by preventing officials from becoming experienced leaders and encouraging termed-out office holders to pay less attention to their constituents. Another misdirected approach to preventing monopoly would be to limit the ability for politicians to coordinate with each other. Doing so only offers an environment in which factionalism reigns and effective, responsive governance is made more difficult. This is not to say that figuring out the best way to structure government is easy or clear cut. But to the extent that we can enhance the electoral connection through institutional arrangements, we must make this choice.

APPENDIX

Data Appendix

When I set out to write this book I had visions of a grand data collection. My wish list of variables included everything from detailed information about challengers in city elections to newspaper endorsements for all candidates to subcity patterns of police deployment and economic health. I discovered quickly what scholars of city politics have known for a long time—there is no centralized depository for city-level data, and many local governments do not maintain historical records.

In order to have the best chance for collecting comparable data over a long time span across many cities, I decided to collect data on large cities. This maximized the chances that the cities would appear in census collections as well as have the administrative capacity to maintain records. Between the years 1790 and 1990, a total of 259 places have been included on the United States Census's one hundred largest cities list (see Gibson 1998). After excluding the fifteen places that were annexed to other cities on the list, such as Brooklyn, New York, I was left with a total of 244 cities in my data set. Even among these remaining cities, data are missing for a variety of reasons. In some years cities were not yet established or were not large enough to warrant the collection of statistics by the Census Bureau. Frequently, the Census did not tabulate data for cities with a population smaller than 25,000.

For all 244 cities, I collected a set of demographic and economic variables from the United States Census. For the years 1900–1930, these data were encoded from paper copies of the official census. For the years 1940–83, data were drawn from electronic data files available through the Inter-university Consortium for Political and Social Research (ICPSR).[1] There are only a handful of census categories that were both useful for my analysis and available for the entire time span. For instance, I would have liked to include data on poverty levels and median income in my analyses, but the census did not ask persons to report income prior to the 1950 census and federal poverty guidelines were not established until 1964. Similarly, my analyses would be vastly improved by separating persons identifying as Latino or Hispanic from whites, but these data are not available prior to 1970.[2] Another omission is the proportion of residents lacking citizenship. There are a number of reasons why I do not include this measure in the analysis. The first is that the census did not ask individuals about their citizenship status in 1960, so the time series is incomplete. Further, the data that are tabulated at the city level vary widely over time. In some years the census provides citizenship status for only white men of voting age. In other years data are not broken down by race, gender, or age, making it impossible to construct a comparable measure over time.

In light of all of these hurdles, I selected eight census categories for collection: total population, number of renters, number of foreign-stock residents (combines foreign-born and residents with at least one foreign parent), number of persons employed, number of "nonwhite" residents (includes African Americans, Chinese, Japanese, and American Indians), and number of workers employed in manufacturing, professional, and trade occupations. These three occupational categories were the only categories aside from agriculture that were collected consistently for the one-hundred-year period and available in the digitized version of the County City Data Book.

My analysis of the electoral effects of bias and organization relies on a subset of the larger data collection. An ideal research design would have allowed me to gather election returns for all 244 cities in the data set or at least a random sample of cities including those with and without monopolies. This proved to be extremely difficult. My first step was to request data from city politics scholars who had published analyses with reference to election results from multiple cities. Most of these data sets were not available. In light of this, I chose to narrow my focus to cities that had hosted monopolies according to the secondary literature. This allowed me at least some analytic leverage, given that there are many years in my study when each city is not monopolized. Further, this focus allowed me to investigate the process of monopolization. But this also means that my conclusions are limited to the population of cities with established histories of monopoly. My analysis in chapter 4 cannot say with certainty that the presence of bias and organization in all cities always leads to electoral dominance. Nor can I explain anything about coalitions that are electorally successful for reasons other than bias and organizational cohesiveness.

I successfully collected data for four reform cities: Austin, Dallas, San Antonio, and San Jose,[3] and five machine cities: Chicago, New York,

New Haven, Kansas City, and Philadelphia.[4] While this collection of cities does capture a lot of variation, these cities are not a random sample of the larger data set. They are not even a random sample of the cities that were monopolized. It is possible that the cities for which I was able to obtain data had the most well established histories of monopoly. For this reason my conclusions should be said to explain the effects on municipal elections when a very powerful organization biases city government. It would not be appropriate to say that these nine cities explain political patterns in all or even most cities in the United States. However, with all of the normal caveats about generalizations, I feel comfortable using these nine cities to make inferences about dominant organizations, as they are strong representations of machine and reform monopolies.

For each of the nine cities, I collected available election data by candidate for the period of 1900–1985. The time span captured periods before and after a coalition biased the electoral system in each city. For three of the machine cities, Philadelphia, Kansas City, and New York, I collected additional election returns prior to 1900 to provide sufficient data before the bias period. The dates of the bias periods for all cities in the analyses and the years for which election results were attained are presented in table A4. For machine cities, only general elections for mayor are included in the analysis. Reform city data includes primary and general election returns for city council members and mayors when they had this position. Readers should note that San Jose's manager faced a vote of confidence, and this is treated as an election for the seat. I use these data to estimate the effect of bias and organization on margin of victory, incumbency advantage, and turnout.

There are two potential endogeneity problems with my measures of the bias period variable used in chapter 4. The first is specific to the selection of the bias period for machine cities. If scholars were more likely to report the coercive use of patronage and fraudulent behavior when certain political coalitions were winning elections, the dates of bias and electoral success could be coincident. A simple analysis of articles from the *New York Times* suggests that the reverse might be more likely. Searching for the terms "fraud," "election," "mayor," and "New York" for three different time periods, I find that fraud was more commonly reported when Tammany was losing elections. The bias period, starting in 1918, represents a period of relatively fewer reports and more wins for Tammany. Even with this evidence, one still might be skeptical that it is possible to untangle historical reports of bias and organization from electoral success in machine cities. For this reason, the conclusions regarding the electoral effects of bias and organization may be considered more reliable for reform cities because the measure of bias is exogenous to electoral outcomes.

The second endogeniety issue is with my research design itself. In order to make the most of my data analysis, I collected election returns from cities where I suspected a monopoly governed in the twentieth century. It is possible that the combination of bias and coordination did not result in electoral success everywhere, but that where monopolies formed, these factors were integral. What this means is that there may be some cities where bias and coordination were present, but coalition members were not electorally advantaged by these factors. Without a larger data collection that includes nonmonopolized cities, I cannot distinguish for certain between this possibility and my theory that the presence of bias and coordination are sufficient for long-term control. However, even with these problems in mind, the analysis presented is still useful for showing the electoral dominance of these organizations.

For citywide financial figures I relied on the United States Census. The Census began collecting some fiscal figures as early as 1850 for large cities. This census of governments was conducted approximately every ten years for cities until 1942. No census was taken between 1942 and 1957. In 1957 the Census began a more systematic data collection occurring every five years. These data were consolidated by the Department of Commerce and digitized for the years 1944–77. I use this collection, supplemented by data from the 1983 City County Data Book. I did not collect data from the earlier censuses because it was unclear how much analytic leverage I could gain by interpolating income and expenditure patterns over ten- to fifteen-year periods. Limiting my distributional analysis to the postwar period means that my statistical results cannot speak to patterns in the five monopolies that collapsed before 1945.[5]

Data Collection

Table A1: Cities with no evidence of machine or reform monopoly in the twentieth century

City	State	City	State	City	State	City	State
Birmingham	AL	Des Moines	IA	Grand Rapids	MI	Portland	OR
Mobile	AL	Dubuque	IA	Saginaw	MI	Allentown	PA
Anchorage	AK	Sioux City	IA	Warren	MI	Altoona	PA
Mesa	AZ	Kansas City	KS	Duluth	MN	Carlisle	PA
Tucson	AZ	Leavenworth	KS	Minneapolis	MN	Easton	PA
Little Rock	AR	Topeka	KS	St Paul	MN	Erie	PA
Anaheim	CA	Wichita	KS	Jackson	MS	Johnstown	PA
Bakersfield	CA	Covington	KY	Natchez	MS	Lancaster	PA
Fremont	CA	Newport	KY	St Joseph	MO	Williamsport	PA
Fresno	CA	Baton Rouge	LA	St Louis	MO	York	PA
Glendale	CA	Lafayette	LA	Lincoln	NE	Newport	RI
Huntington Beach	CA	Metairie	LA	Omaha	NE	Warwick	RI
Los Angeles	CA	Shreveport	LA	Las Vegas	NV	Columbia	SC
Oakland	CA	Augusta	ME	Concord	NH	Chattanooga	TN
Riverside	CA	Bangor	ME	Dover	NH	Knoxville	TN
San Diego	CA	Bath	ME	Manchester	NH	Nashville-Davidson	TN
San Francisco	CA	Gardiner	ME	Nashua	NH		
Santa Ana	CA	Portland	ME	Portsmouth	NH	Amarillo	TX
Stockton	CA	Annapolis	MD	Bayonne	NJ	Arlington	TX
Aurora	CO	Frederick	MD	Elizabeth	NJ	Galveston	TX
Colorado Springs	CO	Hagerstown	MD	Hoboken	NJ	Garland	TX
Middletown	CT	Andover	MA	Passaic	NJ	Houston	TX
New London	CT	Barnstable	MA	Auburn	NY	Lubbock	TX
Norwich	CT	Beverly	MA	Binghamton	NY	Salt Lake City	UT
Washington	DC	Boston	MA	Elmira	NY	Alexandria	VA
Wilmington	DE	Brockton	MA	Hudson	NY	Arlington	VA
Fort Lauderdale	FL	Cambridge	MA	Lockport	NY	Fredericksburg	VA
Hialeah	FL	Chelsea	MA	Newburgh	NY	Lynchburg	VA
Jacksonville	FL	Chicopee	MA	Oswego	NY	Petersburg	VA
Miami	FL	Danvers	MA	Poughkeepsie	NY	Portsmouth	VA
St Petersburg	FL	Fall River	MA	Troy	NY	Spokane	WA
Atlanta	GA	Gloucester	MA	Utica	NY	Tacoma	WA
Columbus	GA	Haverhill	MA	Watervliet	NY	Wheeling	WV
Honolulu	HI	Holyoke	MA	Yonkers	NY	Madison	WI
East St Louis	IL	Lawrence	MA	Charlotte	NC	Milwaukee	WI
Peoria	IL	Lowell	MA	Fayetteville	NC		
Quincy	IL	Lynn	MA	New Bern	NC		
Rockford	IL	Marblehead	MA	Wilmington	NC		
Springfield	IL	Middleborough	MA	Akron	OH		
Evansville	IN	Nantucket	MA	Canton	OH		
Fort Wayne	IN	New Bedford	MA	Chillicothe	OH		

Table A1: Cities with no evidence of machine or reform monopoly in the twentieth century (*continued*)

Indianapolis	IN	Newburyport	MA	Cleveland	OH
Madison	IN	Plymouth	MA	Columbus	OH
New Albany	IN	Salem	MA	Springfield	OH
South Bend	IN	Somerville	MA	Toledo	OH
Terre Haute	IN	Springfield	MA	Youngstown	OH
Burlington	IA	Taunton	MA	Zanesville	OH
Davenport	IA	Detroit	MI	Tulsa	OK

Table A2: Cities with evidence of dominance during the twentieth century, with unclear start and/or end dates

City	State	Type	City	State	Type
Montgomery	AL	Reform	Schenectady (end 1965)	NY	Machine
Long Beach	CA	Reform	Syracuse	NY	Machine
Sacramento	CA	Reform	Greensboro	NC	Reform
Denver	CO	Machine	Raleigh	NC	Reform
Bridgeport (end 1981)	CT	Machine	Dayton (start 1915)	OH	Reform
Hartford (start 1953)	CT	Machine	Steubenville	OH	Machine
Waterbury (end 1975)	CT	Machine	Oklahoma City (end 1971)	OK	Reform
Tampa (end 1945)	FL	Machine	Harrisburg	PA	Machine
Augusta (end 1946)	GA	Machine	Pottsville	PA	Machine
Savannah	GA	Reform	Reading	PA	Machine
Lexington (end 1935)	KY	Machine	Scranton (end 1965)	PA	Machine
Louisville	KY	Machine	Wilkes-Barre (start 1955)	PA	Machine
Worcester	MA	Reform	Cumberland (start 1945)	RI	Machine
Bay City	MI	Machine	North Providence	RI	Machine
Flint	MI	Machine	Charleston (end 1945)	SC	Machine
Camden	NJ	Machine	Corpus Christi (end 1973)	TX	Reform
New Brunswick (start 1935)	NJ	Machine	El Paso	TX	Reform
Newark	NJ	Machine	Fort Worth	TX	Reform
Paterson	NJ	Machine	Norfolk (end 1965)	VA	Machine
Trenton	NJ	Machine	Virginia Beach (end 1966)	VA	Machine
Rochester (end 1925)	NY	Machine	Seattle	WA	Reform

Table A3: Cities with evidence of dominance during the twentieth century, with clear start and end dates

City	State	Monopoly period	Type
Phoenix	AZ	1949–82	Reform
Berkeley	CA	1955–65	Reform
San Jose	CA	1945–77	Reform
New Haven	CT	1954–68	Machine
Chicago	IL	1932–78	Machine
Gary	IN	1952–62	Machine
New Orleans	LA	1895–46	Machine
Baltimore	MD	1865–1925	Machine
Kansas City	MO	1915–39	Machine
Jersey City	NJ	1917–49	Machine
Albuquerque	NM	1954–73	Reform
Albany	NY	1922–83	Machine
Buffalo	NY	1953–76	Machine
New York City	NY	1918–32	Machine
Cincinnati	OH	1900–1925	Machine
Philadelphia	PA	1894–50	Machine
Pittsburgh	PA	1865–65	Machine
Pawtucket	RI	1896–1950	Machine
Providence	RI	1941–74	Machine
Memphis	TN	1925–48	Machine
Austin	TX	1954–72	Reform
Dallas	TX	1941–75	Reform
San Antonio	TX	1925–39	Machine
San Antonio	TX	1955–76	Reform
Richmond	VA	1946–58	Reform

Table A4: Monopoly cities used in electoral analyses

City	Bias period	Electoral data
Austin	1954–72	1919–85
Chicago	1932–78	1905–85
Dallas	1941–75	1921–85
Kansas City	1915–39	1869–1985
New Haven	1954–68	1901–85
New York	1918–32	1882–1985
Philadelphia	1894–1950	1853–1985
San Antonio	1955–76	1945–85
San Jose	1945–77	1914–85

Table A5: Summary statistics, election-level data set

Variable	Observations	Mean	Std. deviation	Minimum	Maximum
Margin of victory	978	0.30	0.27	0	1
Bias period	980	0.46	0.50	0	1
Incumbents	980	0.64	0.74	0	5
% incumbents running	979	0.25	0.29	0	1
Candidates per seat	979	3.09	1.85	1	15
Seats	980	1.15	0.64	1	5
Turnout	973	0.19	0.16	0.001	0.91
Log-odds turnout	973	−1.89	1.37	−6.59	2.28
Log population (millions)	975	−0.82	1.04	−3.43	2.07
Machine/reform	980	0.20	0.40	0	1
Commissioner	980	0.03	0.18	0	1
Mayor	980	0.26	0.44	0	1
Manager	980	0.01	0.11	0	1
Trend	980	103	26.73	1	133
Primary	980	0.17	0.38	0	1
PrimaryNR	980	0.47	0.50	0	1
General	980	0.36	0.48	0	1

Table A6: Summary statistics, candidate-level data set (incumbents only)

Variable	Observations	Mean	Std. deviation	Minimum	Maximum
Won	465	0.75	0.38	0	1
Bias period	465	0.44	0.50	0	1
Candidates per seat	465	2.73	1.50	1	10
Seats	465	1.83	1.44	1	5
Turnout	465	0.21	0.16	0.001	0.91
Machine/reform	465	0.22	0.41	0	1
Log population (millions)	463	−1.25	1.24	−3.40	2.06
Commissioner	465	0.04	0.19	0	1
Mayor	465	0.28	0.45	0	1
Manager	465	0.02	0.14	0	1
Primary	465	0.17	0.38	0	1

NOTES

Introduction

1. Although Booker lost in 2002, it was the most serious challenge James had faced in over a decade. Four years later Booker won the mayoralty after James pulled out of the race at the last minute. James's stated reason for retiring was that he opposed dual office holding and wanted to focus on his position as state senator. Given that James had held both offices for seven years and given that he declined to run for reelection to the state senate the following year, it is a strong possibility that the strength of Booker's threat inspired him not to seek a sixth term.

2. A monopoly is defined as a single coalition maintaining control over government for at least a decade by using strategies of bias.

3. These figures are for 1940 for Pawtucket and 1932 for New York.

4. Some scholars consider this a positive outcome. Reducing attention to the public may mean that politicians are freed from pandering and can focus on making "good" public policy. I operate under the assumption that a political system that is attentive to the preferences of a majority of the population is part of the definition of a healthy democracy.

5. A note must be added here regarding the use of the term *monopoly*. Some readers will immediately have thought of work by Peterson (1981) and Teibout (1956) which asserts that all cities are forced to compete because capital and populations are mobile. Thus, one might imagine that this book is an attempt to argue with this point. As will be explained in the coming chapters, political monopoly refers to a lack of competition within a city; not a lack of competition with other cities. The competitive regional environment identified by Peterson and Tiebout may constrain all cities, but the political system within a given city may nonetheless be monopolized by a single coalition.

6. See Alesina, Baqir, and Easterly (2000) for a similar argument.

7. Erie (1988) argues that reliance on the public sector for economic advancement kept Irish Americans in the lower rungs of the middle class for longer than other white ethnic groups. This suggests that the belief that machines represented immigrants' best opportunity for increasing socioeconomic status was mistaken.

8. This distinction is from Holli (1969). See Connolly (1998) and Finegold (1995) for discussion of the diversity among reform movements. My focus on structural reform ignores the traditions of the Progressive Reformers, who sought corporate regulation and labor protections, and municipal populists, who sought reform in service to the poor and immigrant classes. Further, I am less concerned here with the intellectual foundations of reform than with the ways in which it became implemented in city politics.

9. For examples of reformers advocating for governance by "better men," see Bridges (1997, 110–13).

10. Finegold (1995) argues that reform movements in Chicago, Cleveland, and New York frequently drew support from immigrant and working-class voters, who viewed the machine as oppressive and reform platforms as extremely progressive. However, in many of the cases he analyzes, Finegold finds that the programs and policies developed by experts in the reform tradition were implemented in much more narrow and cost-effective terms at the behest of business elites in these coalitions.

11. Most of the sources that I relied upon for determining cities with histories of dominance were published before 1990 and focused on earlier time periods. For this reason, if a city's monopoly period began after 1980, it is not captured in my data set.

12. I was able to determine clear dates for the emergence of a monopoly in an additional five cities (but could not determine the end date of the monopoly in these cities). Of the thirty cases in which I know the start date for the monopoly period, nine of the cases can be classified as reform and twenty-one as machine.

13. For example, I attempted to collect data on the location of sewerage overflows in San Jose for the twentieth century. While the city has records of the overflows, they are filed using a data system that notes the pipe number, not the location of the pipe. The Department of Sanitation informed me that they had no map of the pipe numbers and that collecting the data would require requesting each record by pipe number. I did not pursue this option.

Chapter One

1. There is a growing literature that argues that responsiveness to voters can produce less effective governance than nonresponsiveness. See, for instance, Canes-Wrone, Herron, and Shotts (2001), who argue that politicians will sometimes "pander" to public opinion, disregarding private knowledge that following public opinion will lead to suboptimal outcomes. Their theory suggests that this is most likely to happen in close races and when the pandering is likely to go undetected. So it could be that an uncontestable market (because it increases incumbent safety) increases the probability of good outcomes in the long run. The evidence in later chapters shows that certain subpopulations did suffer during monopoly periods. I consider this to be a problematic outcome.

2. See Ansolabehere, Snyder, and Stewart (2000) for evidence that vulnerable incumbents focus on creating links to voters. Downs (1957) argues that an incumbent party that always chooses policy based on the majority's preferences can still lose to a challenger under a specific set of conditions, most importantly when the electorate lacks strong consensus and the challenger does not commit to a specific policy until after the government acts. Even still he concludes, "Thus majority rule does not always prevail on specific issues, but it usually does in a two-party system whenever the majority strongly favors a certain policy" (74).

3. The analogy between economic and political monopolies breaks down quickly after these basic similarities. The economic study of monopoly is well developed, and I do not draw on this literature here. The association I make relies on this very basic popular/ journalistic understanding of monopoly.

4. For a discussion of responsible parties, see "Toward a More Responsible Two-Party System: A Report of the Committee on Political Parties," *American Political Science Review* 1950.

5. Some politicians will not be interested in seeking reelection over the long term for any number of reasons. This is likely to be true particularly if they are interested in

specific policy outcomes that can be achieved by influencing other officeholders. I am not explaining the behavior of this subset of politicians.

6. A substantial literature has shown that at-large elections are deleterious to minorities. See, for example, Davidson and Korbel (1981), Engstrom and McDonald (1981), or Polinard et al. (1994).

7. In the instance that the monopolist has a super-encompassing interest in the private economy, it will also be constrained by effects of policies on the economy (McGuire and Olson 1996).

8. Cities are not sovereign governments unless they are granted independence by the state legislature. Most large cities have some degree of home rule, giving them control over taxation and revenue collection, expenditure, zoning, electoral rules, structure of governing institutions, etc.

9. Suffrage restrictions are increasingly effective the more they rely on immutable characteristics. For example, the white primary in the South was more restrictive than literacy tests because while people of color could not change their skin, they could learn to read (this of course ignores the unequal application of the test for blacks and whites).

10. Political machines were not successful at building patronage monopolies until they won large shares of resources, like jobs, from the state and federal governments, suggesting that they were unwilling or unable to tax their own residents heavily enough to provide the necessary jobs without external funds (Erie 1988).

11. A more precise prediction is that the level of inequality should dictate the extent to which the monopoly is a redistributive regime. This parallels the prediction generated by the Meltzer-Richard (1981) model that inegalitarian societies should be more redistributive. There is a large body of empirical research that has found that the inverse is true—societies with less income inequality are more likely to have substantial redistribution policies. Of course, if redistribution leads to less inequality over time this result is not surprising. Iversen and Soskice (2006) show that institutional structures have a strong effect on the redistributional programs of government irrespective of the relative proportions of socioeconomic classes. By analyzing the demographic makeup of communities when monopolists first take control of cities, I endogenize this relationship. Monopolists structure government to prevent or promote redistribution, which may lead to differences in inequality over time.

12. A number of scholars have found that Southwestern and reform-dominated cities lacked the large numbers of foreign-born immigrants and the identifiable working-class present in machine cities. See, for example, Knoke (1982), Bridges and Kronick (1999), and Gordon (1968).

13. See Miller 1982 for a similar argument focusing on political machines.

14. Scholars have offered both theoretical (Groseclose and Snyder 1996; Frohlich 1975) and empirical (Hinckley 1972) evidence in opposition to Riker's theory by primarily focusing on the federal level. These works tend to evaluate situations in which the building of coalitions is a repeated game and thus argue that maintaining oversized coalitions is less costly in the long run. If competition ceases to have a meaningful effect on the behavior of politicians, the incentive to reduce the size of the coalition may remain. Further, since the constraints on budgeting are heavier at the local level, it is unclear whether or not these models would predict similar oversized coalitions in cities.

15. For a formal derivation of these predictions, see Ginkel and Smith 1999.

16. Carlos and Kruse (1996) make a similar argument regarding economic monopolies.

17. It is also possible that voters may shift their preferences in such a way that the regime cannot or will not respond to their new demands. This is theoretically similar to the demographic shift—it just requires no new people to threaten the regime.

Chapter Two

1. However, what one team or player sees as a benefit may not be universal. Some may seek short-term advantages while others seek to maintain the competitiveness of the league over the long-run.

2. It should be noted that a system in which the incumbent enriches himself in such an exchange (instead of using the money for his campaign) is just corrupt—not biased.

3. Royko suggests that the council put up little protest to this loss of power because it meant less work for them.

4. In a modern study of corruption, Meier and Holbrook (1992) find that increasing turnout and competition decreases incidences of corruption.

5. A search of the *Chicago Tribune* for articles containing the words *fraud, election,* and *mayor* turned up 334 articles between 1849 and 1950.

6. It is likely that the surge of Democratic popularity brought many new voters into the electorate; however, this ward was predominately African American, and blacks did not abandon the Republican ticket in large numbers elsewhere until 1936.

7. There were exceptions to this, though. Erie (1988) reports that the O'Connell machine in Albany padded voter rolls to transform a two-to-one Republican lead into a solid two-to-one Democratic lead in six years.

8. Erie (1988) argues that because city governments had limited resources, an expanding electorate made retaining office tenuous. He provides examples from places such as New York and Pennsylvania, where machine leaders supported suffrage restriction in order to limit demands on their organizations.

9. It is important to note that suffrage restrictions were not confined to states and cities where reformers came to monopolize cities. All of the states that housed political machines had at one time or another limited the right to vote to certain groups (whites, property holders, men, etc.). The point here is that reformers benefited from these restrictions because their political opponents were denied the opportunity to participate in elections.

10. This was found unconstitutional by the state government (Bridges 1997).

11. Progressives made registration somewhat easier in other respects. They decreased the amount of time one needed to register before the election from three months to forty days, increased registration locations, and standardized the process.

12. The act included a grandfather clause that allowed anyone currently enfranchised to vote. It is likely that the generational turnover following the passage of this act aided the San Jose reformers immeasurably in the passage of the reform charter in 1915.

13. San Jose City Clerk record of elections and San Jose Commission 1985.

14. One observer of San Jose politics half jokingly referred to this crowd as the Bellarmine/Santa Clara mafia.

15. *Austin Daily Statesman*, December 27, 1908, quoted in Bridges (1997).

16. Reformers were unsuccessful at unseating Long. She continued to win elections even after the charter change was enacted because she was extremely popular with voters.

17. Mayor George Starbird paraphrasing manager Hamann in a 1972 speech given at the San Jose Rotary Club; transcript entitled "The New Metropolis," available at the San Jose Public Library.

18. U.S. Attorney General, objection letter to city of San Antonio, April 2, 1976.

Chapter Three

1. *Home rule* is "defined as the ability of a local government to act and make policy in all areas that have not been designated to be of statewide interest through general law, state constitutional provisions, or initiatives and referenda" (Krane, Rigos, and Hill 2001, 2).

2. There are of course many exceptions to this broad characterization. The most notable is the formation of Republican machines that focused on the middle class as their core constituency. In these cases immigrant groups became the periphery and were only courted when the machine faced potential losses. See Erie (1988) for a discussion. Also, in this study the machine in Albany represents a slightly different machine organization. The core voters in this city were homeowners.

3. Allswang (1971) provides data through 1932. He codes precincts, not wards, by their ethnic identity. His procedure is impeccable, allowing him to determine stable ethnic enclaves from 1918–32. I used his designations from 1932 and coded a ward to represent an ethnic group if he noted at least two precincts within the ward as representing a single ethnicity. I confirmed his designations and coded Irish wards using two additional sources, reports in the *Chicago Tribune* of wards with particular ethnic character and 1960 census data. Ideally, I would have interpolated census data at the ward level for all of the years in my analysis, but the data are not available in the federal census at the ward level by country of origin for 1930, 1940, or 1950. The ward coding is as follows: Irish, 11, 14, 16, 18; Czech, 21, 22, 23; Polish, 10, 12, 13, 26, 35, 28; German, 43, 45; Black, 2, 3, 6; Native American, 19, 49; Jewish, 24, 31, 39; Italian, 20, 25, 42. It is likely that some of these wards housed mixed ethnic communities. Especially for eastern European groups, reports of the period commonly categorized a ward as containing a number of different groups. Luckily for my analysis, since I argue that all of these groups were part of the Democratic machine, the diversity does not undermine the conclusions.

4. For comparison, Allswang (1971) estimates the African American Democratic vote for president in 1932 and 1936 at about 6 percent (70).

5. There is substantial evidence that many of these votes were fraudulent. It is possible that Pendergast only targeted the black areas because they were less likely to protest illegalities given their subordinate position in Missouri life, but it could also have been that Pendergast saw black voters as a valuable constituency for his machine. There is currently no conclusive evidence for either account.

6. Quoted in Robert Fairbanks, "The Good Government Machine: The Citizens Charter Association and Dallas Politics, 1930–1960," in Fairbanks and Underwood 1990.

7. These percentages are undercounts if the city directory listed only adults. Unfortunately, the census did not aggregate figures for the adult population in cities for 1940 or 1950 so a more accurate percentage is not available.

8. Yu (1991) reports that turn of the century reformers in San Jose *were* allied with labor, against Chinese and then Japanese immigrants. Additionally, there are reports of San Jose's reform leaders winning support from labor boss Abe Reuf of San Francisco in the early 1900s. This alliance appears to have been instrumental in getting the Hayes

brothers elected to higher-level government offices. Once the Progressive movement became a more powerful force at the state level, the Hayes brothers openly broke with the Southern Pacific machine of which Reuf was a part. In municipal politics the brothers and their newspaper consistently criticized the machine.

9. See Krane, Rigos, and Hill 2001 for details on dates of these changes.

10. The cities include Chicago, Kansas City, New Haven, New York, and Philadelphia.

11. *Boodle* was a slang term for bribes.

12. Arguments regarding the tyranny of machine politics held a great deal of sway in the Southwest even though local level machines throughout the late nineteenth century and early twentieth century were relatively weak. Because municipal reformers were taking cues from their Eastern counterparts (many of them were actually migrants from the East and Midwest), their platforms looked as through they were battling Boss Tweed in their own cities. To some extent the dominance of the utilities and railroads in the Southwest gave weight to these arguments, but no to-be reform city in this study had an organization worthy of being called a political machine when the reformers came to power, except San Antonio. However, all of the cities did have some petty corruption involving "rings" of politicians and businessmen, and inefficient spending practices. The cities also had fewer voters likely to object to the demands of the reformers, paving the way for their success.

13. Several state-level developments made this possible. Until 1902 state law required charter revisions to be approved by a three-fifths majority. This was changed to allow a board of fifteen elected freeholders to propose revisions that need only be accepted by a simple majority vote. But the city council retained control because its approval was needed to authorize the election of freeholders. In 1910 San Jose reformers lobbied the city council to hold an election for freeholders to amend the charter. The council refused. In 1911, as part of the Progressive package of Constitutional amendments, the state allowed signatures of 15 percent of the electorate to force an election of freeholders, who would then submit a charter to the electorate. This amendment also allowed a two-thirds vote of a city council to elect the board of freeholders. This would have been an important advantage in cities where reformers had won a supermajority of the council seats.

14. Reed had served as executive secretary to Governor Hiram Johnson (Brooks 1917).

15. The system was changed from an at-large system to a designated-place system in which candidates are elected citywide but run for specific seats (or places). There is no direct evidence for the motivation behind this change. One historian writes that "the true intent of the proposition was to get rid of Emma Long and prevent blacks from being elected to council" (Orum 1987, 221). Regardless of the intent, place systems have the effect of advantaging citywide organizations that can prevent their candidates from running against each other. They also make it easier to target strong opposition by making it possible to pit the organization's best candidates against them. Place systems with majoritarian requirements also advantage candidates with large campaign funds.

16. These figures are from the 1900, 1910, and 1920 censuses.

17. The number of eligible voters rose faster during this period, from 605,819 in 1905 to 2,228,302 in 1931, a 268 percent increase.

18. In Kansas City, polls were purposely run extremely inefficiently in order to discourage the nonfaithful from voting. Stools were provided to all known organization voters to make them more comfortable.

19. The Hayes brothers owned San Jose's dominant newspapers and were credited with the early charter reform victories.

20. Ironically, this populist reform provided incredible strength to Anthony "Dutch" Hamann when he took office. Hamann was popular with the voters, and when he won every single vote of confidence, council members could hardly remove him.

21. According to the *San Jose Mercury* coverage of the election, older and less prosperous sections of the city voted for the amendments and against the incumbents. Wealthier and recently annexed sections favored incumbents and opposed the amendments and thus "stood by the administration." The amendments had been placed on the ballot by councilman Clark Bradley, who later voted against the reform faction on many measures, including the appointment of Dutch Hamann. From this scanty bit of information the most one can conclude is that a number of factions supported the removal of incumbent forces from office, including the Progress Committee, some council members, and the poorer, older sections of the city.

22. The city council minutes on Hamann's appointment provide no explanation for the opposition votes. The newspaper coverage of the event simply reported his appointment and praised the council for its wise decision (*San Jose Mercury News* 1950a).

23. Chairman of the Citizen's Committee quoted in Bridges 1997.

Chapter Four

1. Fleischmann and Stein (1998) find no clear relationship between campaign funds raised and electoral outcomes.

2. I would have preferred to measure this control using primary election returns, but the data were not available for the entire time period for all of the cities.

3. I tested a number of different constructions of this independent variable including using only the strength of the organization as the defining feature for reform cities (e.g., making organization the most relevant feature) and using the presence of a friendly governor in power for machine cities (e.g., making control over institutions the most relevant feature). This had the effect of lengthening the monopoly period for some cities and shortening it for others. In most cases the differences were a matter of one or two years and the conclusions from the analysis were not substantially altered. I also created separate variables for the implementation of reform charters and the organization of the nonpartisan slating group for reform cities to see if I could disentangle the effects of these two factors. I was unable to conduct a similar analysis in machine cities because I could not find a way to measure machine uses of patronage and fraud independent of the machine organization. In general the organization variables outperformed the bias variable, suggesting that the most relevant factor for enhancing the probability of reelection is coordination.

4. Rae (2003) argues that the Democratic monopoly continues today. Indeed, the patterns of electoral politics support his conclusion—turnout has continued to fall and margins of victory have gotten larger. However, he also presents evidence that the organization did not maintain unity after the early 1970s. In keeping with my definition that monopolies should result from a combination of organization and bias, I have selected 1968 as the final year of the bias period.

5. There are potential endogeneity problems with these measures that are discussed in the data appendix.

6. Dallas retained two at-large seats and converted eight council seats to district seats.

7. In the election for the three at-large seats, two of the candidates were elected outright in the primary and two advanced to the general. In the general election for this third seat, one candidate was elected. In the primary election for the one council seat, no candidate was elected outright, so two candidates advanced to the general election, where one candidate won.

8. In alternative specifications, I use the total number of candidates running instead of the number per seat. The effects on the coefficients of interest are very small. In all analyses, I only included candidates that received at least 5 percent of the total vote.

9. In alternate specifications, I tested using primary elections as the excluded category. In all of the analyses, the relationships remain the same. However, including the primary, no runoff variable in the margin of victory analysis drastically reduces the effect and significance of the bias period (though it remains positive). This is because by definition primaries with no runoff have larger margins of victory, as the candidate must receive a majority.

10. Year fixed effects overlap with the bias period variable, so they are not included in the analyses.

11. Turnout is also likely to be affected by the dependent variable in the margin of victory analysis. There is no efficient way to deal with this; however, running the analysis without the turnout variable does not change the conclusions nor does running two stage least squares, instrumenting turnout with the set of variables used in the turnout analysis below.

12. For a discussion of states with alien suffrage, see Keyssar 2000. Additionally, the 1960 census did not ask individuals about their citizenship status, so a complete time series is not available.

13. Figure 4.1 only displays the margin of victory in citywide elections.

14. The dependent variable in this analysis is a proportion. I tested alternative means of dealing with this, none of which changed the substantive conclusions. Using a logit transformation of the margin of victory yields a coefficient of 0.34 (0.12) on the bias period variable. With all other variables held constant at their mean values, this equates to a 6 percentage point increase in the predicted margin of victory during the bias period. This transformation is undesirable, though, because it means uncontested races are excluded from the analysis since they have a margin of victory of one. Using a generalized linear model instead increases the effect of the bias period to 0.36 (0.09) which equates to a 7 percentage point increase in the margin of victory during the bias period. Given that these results are so similar to the OLS analysis, and given that the OLS analysis is easier to interpret, I present the OLS results.

15. Restricting the analysis to citywide elections increases the effect of the bias period to about 7 percent.

16. I did not have data on campaign expenditures or quality of candidates to be able to test these alternate hypotheses.

17. It should be noted that, in general, city elections are not very competitive. The mean margin of victory in the data set is 29.6 percent. In the OLS analysis, the bias period increases the predicted margin from 27 percent to 33 percent (all other variables held at their means).

18. These analyses include only citywide elections. Using all of the elections reduces the effect of the bias period in the incumbent candidate analysis to 0.47 (0.27). It does not change the incumbent party analysis.

19. I use the Stata program, Clarify, developed by Tomz, Wittenberg, and King (2003) to simulate the effect of bias and organization on the probability of winning.

20. Reform incumbents increase their probability of victory from 75 percent to 89 percent during the bias period. Machine incumbents increase their probability of victory from 89 percent to 95 percent during the bias period.

21. For example, of Kansas City, Mayhew (1986) says, "Pendergast's Democratic machine dominated politics in the 1920s and 1930s. It . . . reached out like Jersey City's Hague machine to take over the state government during the New Deal. But a reform group won power in Kansas City in 1940 . . . " (100). This quote suggests that 1939 should be the final year of dominance for the Kansas City machine. To find the start date, I culled historical scholarship on the Pendergast organization. Scholars agree that during the early 1900s, the Democratic Party was factionalized between two wings, the Goats and the Rabbits, until 1914 when Pendergast subsumed the fights by divvying up patronage among the leaders. From this point on, the Democratic Party operated as a single nominating organization. Thus, 1914 began the monopoly period for Kansas City in this analysis.

22. In many cases, Mayhew describes the rise of the organization by decade, "early '30s," for example. In the cases where he used the modifier "early," I used the first year of the decade as the start of the monopoly. Where he used the modifier "late," I took the last year of the decade as the start date. In cases where he noted that the organization arose "mid-decade" or used no modifier at all, I used the fifth year of the decade.

23. Urban scholars can no doubt think of many more cases in which a reform group took power after a machine collapsed (perhaps even assisting in its collapse). For instance, Cincinnati or Kansas City might come to mind. However, in neither of these cities did the reform group maintain power citywide for more than a decade. In both cases the reform organizations faced persistent factions that retained control over parts of the city and government.

24. The data on state partisan control are from Burnham (1985).

25. Regrettably, this measure only includes Mexican ethnicity for 1930. A question about Latino heritage was not asked again until the 1970 census. In this analysis, first- and second-generation immigrants from Spanish-speaking countries are incorporated into the foreign-stock measure. Census categories for race are problematic in many ways. For a history of the political process of census enumeration, the development of the racial categories, and the problems associated with using census measures, see Nobles 2000.

26. The same predictions follow from scholarship in the economics literature studying the politics of redistribution. Alesina, Baqir, and Easterly (2000, 1999) find that politicians who represent the interests of the poor but need votes from the middle class to win elections will use patronage to redistribute income rather than providing public goods or pure cash transfers. They argue that cities with higher levels of ethnic fractionalization and income inequality are more likely to have large public payrolls and, therefore, utilize an inefficient mechanism for redistribution. This conclusion builds on work by Coate and Morris (1995), which finds that when voters lack information about the benefits of public projects and the preferences of politicians, some officials have incentives to choose inefficient policy outcomes. Underlying the Alesina, Baqir, and Easterly conclusion is the assumption that in more homogenous communities, public goods are more easily agreed upon and, thus, government policy more efficient. Thus, machine cities, with high levels of diversity and income inequality, and politicians who represent the poor should be more

likely to develop large public bureaucracies. The difference between these predictions and mine is one of purposes. This economic literature argues that patronage should be viewed purely as a benefit for working-class voters. In chapter 5, I offer support for the conclusion that patronage did serve as a benefit for machines' core constituents, but argue here that the maintenance of a large, politically oriented public bureaucracy served politicians' reelection interests first and foremost.

27. See chapter 1 for a detailed discussion of my data-collection rationale.

28. I also repeated the analyses allowing cities to reenter the data set after the collapse of the monopoly. The substantive results do not change. I have chosen to present the results in which I prohibit reentry for theoretical reasons. My analyses allow for two basic states: cities can be unmonopolized or monopolized. It is quite likely that once a city has been monopolized, even if the regime collapses, the state to which the city returns is not exactly equal to the state of the city prior to monopolization. It would be possible to complicate the model adding additional types of states, but the evidence that I have collected and the theory I present do not account for this diversity. Thus, the most appropriate model is the one presented.

29. Thus, I expect that they have different hazard rates and different meaningful covariates.

30. This model may be problematic in that it assumes that until the moment a machine or reform organization becomes dominant, the city could become either a machine or a reform monopoly. Perhaps instead one might say that some cities, if they were ever to be monopolized, would have to fall into one category and not the other. The difficulty is that there are no characteristics that would allow one to categorize each city's type that are exogenous to these models. Further, it is unclear how one would go about setting a threshold of these combined characteristics that was anything but totally arbitrary.

31. Chapter 6 discusses the transition from monopoly back to a competitive system.

32. In alternate tests using Cox proportional hazard models, this specification allows me to take advantage of the usable information from these cases—that these cities did, indeed, develop a monopoly during the period I study, and not after it ended.

33. Three of the machine cities, Cincinnati, New Orleans, and Pawtucket, developed monopolies right about the turn of the century. Because the data analysis includes five-year lagged variables, cities that become monopolized before 1905 would be excluded from the analysis. In order to maximize the available data, these cities are coded as becoming monopolized in 1905.

34. In alternate Cox analyses, I use the Efron method for dealing with ties. This method uses a weighted sum of the cases at risk when calculating the probability of exit, and has been shown to be the best method in data sets with a small number of cases and large number of ties (see Hertz-Picciotto and Rockhill 1997) for analysis.

35. In alternate specifications, I use the nonlogged measure of the city's population. The substantive conclusions remain the same, but the logged version performed much better, suggesting that there is a leveling off of the importance of city size for the emergence of monopolies.

36. A few of the machines in the sample are Republican, suggesting that they would benefit from unified Republican control at the state level. However, the vast majority of the sample is governed by Democratic machines, so only this measure is included in the analysis. Using a dummy variable signifying unified control by either party is not significant.

37. A measure of the proportion of small businesses in a community might better capture the presence of this kind of economic elite, but it was not available for the entire time period for all 244 cities.

38. I have argued that increased labor agitation inspired reform emergence, but, unfortunately, have no measure of this concept except indirectly through this measure of employment. The relationship between labor unrest and employment change is unclear. Some scholars find a negative cross-sectional relationship between union organizing and employment levels (Montgomery 1989; Blanchflower, Millward, and Oswald 1991). But other research has shown that there is no significant relationship between union development and growth in employment (Bronars and Deere 1993; Machin and Wadhwani 1991). Bronars and Deere (1993) argue that patterns of growth and union activity both reflect changes in the business cycle. They show that union activity is frequently preceded by strong systemic economic growth (Ashenfelter and Pencavel 1969 make a similar argument). If one accepts this argument and views the five-year change in employment as a measure of economic health, then one could tentatively suggest that a positive effect of this variable on reform emergence could indicate a positive relationship between union activity and reform consolidation.

39. I tested the inclusion of a variable noting the presence of a state-dictated literacy test as well. The variable was insignificant (though positive) and did not change the other results. This is most likely because the literacy test was much more widespread throughout the data set than the poll tax was. Even many machine cities faced literacy tests, which of course they commonly ignored. For this reason, I see the poll tax as a better measure of the presence of a state government supportive of reformers' ambitions.

40. These values were calculated using the "mfx" command in Stata, following the logistic regression.

41. This coefficient reaches statistical significance in the Cox model.

42. Another way to interpret the negative coefficients on the five-year change in renters and percent foreign stock would be that machines could not consolidate when low-income and immigrant populations were growing, perhaps because they would put too much pressure on the machine to share scarce resources. This interpretation would support Erie's (1988) theory that the main factor driving machine emergence was balancing municipal resources with voter demands.

43. These values were calculated using the "predict" command in Stata, following the logistic regression and then running a mean comparison of cases with an increase in the five-year change in the ratio of manufacturers to professionals to those with a negative value on this variable. Thus, all other variables are set at their actual values, not their mean values.

44. All of the variables in the Cox versions of the reform model reach statistical significance.

Chapter Five

1. See chapter 3 for a description of the governing coalition elites in each case.

2. City expenditures are the best proxy available for measuring transfers. Many, if not most, resource transfers are not recorded transactions, or at least not identifiable as such. Politicians do what they can to provide vague explanations of their actual machinations in office. In the case studies, I attempt to determine the demands of various sectors of the population and study the dominant coalition's responsiveness to these needs. I find

that as security increases, coalitions meet fewer demands. While the measure is rough, the results are robust.

3. Adding a control for the type of election (primary, general, or primary with no runoff) did not change the conclusions.

4. A number of scholars writing about Kansas City have suggested that the extent of electoral fraud was so great during the period of the machine's reign that it is difficult to draw any substantial conclusions about the level of turnout. For New Haven, the dates of the collapse of the machine are difficult to determine. I have selected 1969 as the decline date; this is the year in which the city was redistricted and African Americans won seats on the council for the first time. According to my guidelines, this represents the loss of a monopoly because the coalition in power lost both bias and control over the legislative branch. However, the city remained in the control of a weakened Democratic organization led by a very popular Italian mayor after this date. Turnout could have been suppressed because competition was low. Extending the bias period to 1989, when the city's first black mayor was elected, results in a different pattern—lower turnout during the bias period.

5. Only final elections for citywide offices are included in this regression. Data on the number of eligible voters or registered voters in individual districts was not available. This does not eliminate any election year for any city, but does have the effect of removing council races for reform cities after the end of the bias period.

6. Predicted values of turnout are 0.22 when bias period is set to zero and 0.16 when set to one; all other variables set at means. An interaction term for monopoly type and bias period is positive and significant, suggesting that machines actually see a significant increase in turnout when a monopoly is in power. This effect is wholly due to the cases of New Haven and Kansas City, which have unique properties, as explained above. When these cases are excluded, the effect is negative and the coefficient is not significant. To compare the magnitude of the effect for machine versus reform cities more clearly, I split the sample by regime type. The effect of the bias period is slightly larger (though not significantly so) for reform cities. This is an interesting side note on the effect of different biasing strategies and structures of dominance. Machines had weaker mechanisms for biasing the system and a hierarchical party structure that translated into a broader coalition and higher turnout than reformers enjoyed.

7. Predicted values are 0.21 when bias period is set to zero and 0.17 when set to one; all other variables set at means.

8. See chapter 3 for more detail on the coding of these neighborhoods.

9. The number of cases reduces due to missing data.

10. These data were collected and generously provided by Robert Lineberry.

11. Though Dawson died in 1970, his wards should still have been important to the machine base in the 1971 election.

12. All statistics are predicted values of the untransformed dependent variable. The variable of interest is set at minimum and maximum values. All other variables are set at their means, except Dawson's wards are set at zero.

13. No standardized data are available earlier than 1940. See the data appendix for a complete discussion of the collection.

14. For a similar argument about patronage at the state level, see Moynihan and Wilson (1964).

15. The category of education was not included because it is hard to know what to expect in patterns of education spending. In the South and West, education is not handled by city government during the analyzed period. Additionally, education may be seen as a service to homeowners or to working-class residents who cannot afford private school. See Pinderhughes 1987 for a description of the difficulty in analyzing education policies in Chicago.

16. I also reproduced this analysis using a factor analysis of margin of victory and incumbent success rate as an alternative definition of dominance. The patterns are identical though less significant in some cases due in part to a large reduction in observations (election data is only available for nine cities). Additionally, I tested a number of different methods to deal with the problem that the dependent variable is a proportion bounded by zero and one. For instance, I tested a logit transformation and running tobit analysis. The alternatives produce nearly identical outcomes, but each has problems. The logit transformation eliminates meaningful zeroes, and the tobit analysis made handling auto-correlation and panel dependence much more complicated. For ease of interpretation, the OLS regressions are presented.

17. Because the census did not ask about Latino identity until the 1970s, this measure likely excludes Latinos from the figure, an important consideration that might weaken the conclusions for the Western and Southwestern cities in the analysis. However, changes in the size of the Latino population are highly correlated with changes in the size of the total population and changes in the size of the low-income population, which is included here as the proportion of renters.

18. I also tested the analysis using year-fixed effects. The results are similar in all cases.

19. In the case of San Antonio, the city is coded as a machine city 1900–1939 and as a reform city 1940–86.

20. The average direct expenditure for reform cities in 1982 dollars is 154,647,700, and predicted values for the percent spent on sanitation are 9.4 percent when the reform bias is set at 0 and 15.5 percent when it is set at 1. For machine cities (without New York), the average direct general expenditure for the time period is 393,609,000, and predicted values for the percent spent on police and fire are 19.8 percent when machine bias is set at 0 and 23.3 percent when it is set at 1.

21. Results are from a regression of direct general expenditure per capita in 1982 dollars on the monopoly period and include all controls listed above.

22. This point is analogous to the price-setting power of a monopoly firm. While monopolists have power over price or output, they remain constrained by the market demand curve.

23. See Erie (1988) for aldermanic figures, and the 1970 United States census for city population figures.

24. Results are from an OLS regression using the same method and controls as in the spending analyses above.

25. Hise (1997) makes a similar argument about the development of Los Angeles. He finds that what most observers had viewed as unintended suburban sprawl was actually planned development meant to promote homeowning opportunities.

26. Davidson went on to explain that he did not want this job, so he "started backin'-off."

27. Analysis uses all controls discussed above.

28. The project was completed in 2006. Santa Clara Valley Water District, Lower Silver Creek Flood Protection Project, handout. Accessed online, September 12, 2006, at http://www.valleywater.org/media/pdf/watershed_monthly_progress_report_pdf/11–03%20-%20LSilver3.271Handout.pdf.

29. This is not something that the study points out. I drew this conclusion by analyzing the top ten concepts preferred by each set of respondents. The list was exactly the same for both groups, except for one concept. Anglo respondents chose the concept "a community involved in recycling, taking care of the land, not wasting things, living close together in a natural 'non-plastic' way" among their top ten while Mexican Americans selected "a suburb or subdivision with convenient access to highways, its own bus service to the city, specifically designed for people with children" instead.

Chapter Six

1. Scholars argue that the presence or expansion of a highly developed civil society also increases the probability of mobilization because community members come into contact with each other on a regular basis and are free to develop and consider alternative ideas (see Lipset, Trow, and Coleman 1956 and Acemoglu and Robinson 2006 for further explanation). A strong civil society can also offer potential challengers the space and resources to learn political skills. Since I have no measures of civil society, I cannot test this hypothesis.

2. An explanation of the selection criteria and monopoly coding of these cities can be found in chapters 1 and 4.

3. I also tested the effect of a change in the partisan makeup of a unified state government. Unfortunately, this happens so rarely that there was not enough variation to include this measure. Additionally, I chose not to include a measure of local civil service laws because this should be endogenous to machine strength.

4. I have data for every five years beginning in 1942 for each city. I interpolate values for the intervening years. Essentially, this variable captures a downward or upward trend in city revenue. I also created a five-year version of this variable to ensure that I was not capturing short-term fluctuations. The results are similar, but I present the one-year version because it allows me to evaluate more cases.

5. The census did not collect data on the foreign-stock population after 1970, so an analysis of the effect of this variable on reform collapse is virtually impossible because seven of nine cases collapsed after 1970.

6. In the models with dummy independent variables, the unstandardized log of the population is included as a control.

7. This example assumes that the probability of death is constant across individuals, but varies with time.

8. There is a selection bias problem with these data because only cities that hosted monopolies are analyzed. Most cities do not fall into this category. While it would make sense to model this selection directly, there is simply not enough data to do this. I use many of the same variables to predict monopoly emergence and decline, and the small number of cases with clear monopoly periods results in an inability to run complex models.

9. I also repeated the analyses allowing cities to reenter the data set after the collapse of the monopoly. The substantive results do not change. For theoretical reasons, I have chosen to present the results where I prohibit reentry. My analyses allow for two basic states: cities can be unmonopolized or monopolized. It is quite likely that once a city has

been monopolized, even if the regime collapses, the state to which the city returns is not exactly equal to the state the city was in prior to monopolization. It would be possible to complicate the model by adding additional types of states, but the evidence that I have collected and the theory which I present do not account for this diversity. Thus, the most appropriate model is the one presented.

10. I use the Efron method for dealing with ties. This method uses a weighted sum of the cases at risk when calculating the probability of exit and has been shown to be the best method in data sets with a small number of cases and large number of ties (see Hertz-Picciotto and Rockhill 1997 for analysis).

11. Plot points were generated by calculating the hazard ratio for all values of the independent variable of interest using exponentiated values of the coefficients presented in table 6.1. For ease of interpretation, the hazard ratio estimates are plotted against the nonstandardized values of each variable.

12. For an in-depth analysis of the relationship among local politics, coalition building, and federal urban policy, see Mollenkopf (1983).

13. Chapter 4 provides extensive narrative evidence of the class and ethnically based benefit distribution in all of these cities. The following discussion is meant as a summary version to explain the likely supporters of challenges to machines and reform regimes.

14. Mayor Jane Byrne did admit the presence of segregation in the schools and agreed to integrate public housing in response to a court order. She later recanted and reversed direction in both policy areas.

15. It is noteworthy that reformers also created this opportunity for discontented citizens by adopting the Populist direct democracy reforms (initiative, recall, and referendum) at the turn of the century in order to put themselves in power.

16. See Freedman 1988 for an analysis. Later, mayors found many other ways to provide public jobs to their supporters, but the use of public jobs for organizing the political party and generating party work was largely undermined by these decisions.

17. *Aranda v. Van Sickle*, 455 F.Supp. 625, D.C.Cal., 1976, July 15, 1976.

Chapter Seven

1. Email correspondence with David Crossley of the Gulf Tides Institute.

2. The counterfactual scenario is of course impossible to generate—would blacks be better rewarded if Daley faced strident competition? Maybe, but maybe not. It is perhaps obvious that the presence of a monopoly is not the only reason a group would continually lose in the distribution of government benefits.

3. This comports with what other scholars have found in modern city elections as well. See Wood 2002, for example.

4. San Antonio is coded as a reform city because the reform monopoly dominated more recently than the machine.

5. The Census data are from 1987, 1992, 1997, and 2002, and the ICMA data are from 1986, 1992, 1996, and 2001.

6. I control for the proportion of the population that is black, Latino, and Asian American; the proportion of the population under the poverty line and with a high school diploma (except in the analysis of college graduates); dummy variables for region and year; and total population or log of total population. I use the log of the total population in the analyses of median household expenditures and per capita taxes, and total population in all other analyses. I include a control for term limits in the political analyses. Errors are clustered by city.

7. This figure comes from an analysis of data collected by the ICMA in 1986. In this sample of cities, the mean turnout of eligible voters was 27 percent, with a standard deviation of 17 percent.

Appendix

1. For the years 1940–77, data were taken from the ICPSR file "County and City Data Book [United States] Consolidated File: City Data 1944–1977." Data for 1980 were taken from the ICPSR file "U.S. Dept. of Commerce, Bureau of the Census. COUNTY AND CITY DATA BOOK [UNITED STATES], 1983 [computer file]. ICPSR version." Washington DC: U.S. Dept. of Commerce, Bureau of the Census (producer), 1984. Ann Arbor: Inter-university Consortium for Political and Social Research (distributor), 1999.

2. It would be possible to compile data on the heritage of first- and second-generation immigrants from Spanish-speaking countries. To do this for all 244 cities for six censuses would have required resources that I simply did not have.

3. Notably, Amy Bridges provided me with election returns for Austin, Dallas, and San Antonio for nearly the entire period. I was able to request missing data from the registrars of voters in these cities. I attempted to get data for the remaining reform cities: Albuquerque, Berkeley, Phoenix, Richmond, and San Jose from other city politics scholars, but was unsuccessful. I also called registrars to find out if they could easily send me information, but this was not possible. In part because I had excellent access to political figures in San Jose, I decided to collect my own data in that city. This required reading through minutes from every city council meeting for the one-hundred-year period on microfiche and hand entering the results. Once this data collection was complete, my budget and time were exhausted. Election returns for Richmond, Virginia, are available beginning in 1926 in hardcopy at the University of Virginia, but I have not collected these data.

4. I was able to obtain Robert's Dahl's data for New Haven from Amy Bridges. She also supplied data on New York. Robert Lineberry provided me with data for Chicago. Searching through libraries and online resources I also found data for the entire period for Kansas City in a published collection (Johnson 1981) and for Philadelphia collected by the city government, available online at http://www.phila.gov/PHILS/Mayorlst.htm. Rather than selecting only four of these cases, I include them all in the analysis for a total of nine cities in the collection.

5. These five cities (Baltimore, Cincinnati, Kansas City, New York City, and San Antonio) all had machine monopolies. They are included in the regressions but are coded as nonmonopolies for the years I analyze.

REFERENCES

Abbott, Carl. 1987. *The new urban America: Growth and politics in sunbelt cities.* Chapel Hill: University of North Carolina Press.

Acemoglu, Daron, and James Robinson. 2006. *Economic origins of dictatorship and democracy.* Cambridge: Cambridge University Press.

Adrian, Charles R. 1952. Some general characteristics of nonpartisan elections. *American Political Science Review* 46 (3).

———. 1959. A typology for nonpartisan elections. *Western Political Quarterly* 12 (2): 449–58.

Adrian, Charles R., and Charles Press. 1968. Decision costs in coalition formation. *American Political Science Review* 62 (2).

Aldrich, John. 1995. *Why parties? The origin and transformation of political parties in America.* Chicago: University of Chicago Press.

Alesch, Daniel J., and Robert A. Levine. 1973. Growth in San Jose: A summary policy statement. Prepared for the National Science Foundation. Santa Monica: The Rand Corporation.

Alesina, Alberto, Reza Baqir, and William Easterly. 1999. Public goods and ethnic divisions. *Quarterly Journal of Economics* 114 (4): 1243–84.

———. 2000. Redistributive public employment. *Journal of Urban Economics*, Elsevier, 48 (2): 219–41.

Alford, Robert R., and Eugene C. Lee. 1968. Voting turnout in American cities. *American Political Science Review* 62 (3).

Allen-Taylor, J. Douglas. 1998. Watchin' the tidelands roll away. *Metro*, August 20–26. Accessed at *http://www.metroactive.com/papers/metro/08.20.98/cover/alviso-9833.html.*

Allswang, John. 1971. *A house for all peoples.* Lexington: University Press of Kentucky.

American Political Science Review. 1950. Toward a more responsible two-party system: A report of the committee on political parties. Vol. 44 (3), part 2, supplement. September.

Anderson, Martin. 1964. *The federal bulldozer: A critical analysis of urban renewal, 1949–1962.* Cambridge, MA: MIT Press.

Ansolabehere, Stephen, James Snyder, and Charles Stewart. 2000. Old voters, new voters, and the personal vote: Using redistricting to measure the incumbency advantage. *American Journal of Political Science* 44 (1).

Arbuckle, Clyde. 1985. *Clyde Arbuckle's history of San José: Chronicling San José's founding as California's earliest pueblo in 1777, through exciting and tumultuous history which paved the way for today's metropolitan San José; the culmination of a lifetime of research.* San José: Memorabilia of San José.

Argersinger, Peter H. 1985. New perspectives on election fraud in the gilded age. *Political Science Quarterly* 100 (4).

Ashenfelter, Orley, and John H. Pencavel. 1969. American trade union growth: 1900–1960. *Quarterly Journal of Economics* 83 (3): 434–48.

Associated Press. 2005. CIA leak prosecutor takes on Chicago machine: Fitzgerald leads investigation into Daley's political empire. Accessed on January 6, 2008, at http://www.msnbc.msn.com/.

Axelrod, Robert. 1970. *Conflict of interest: A theory of divergent goals with applications to politics.* Chicago: Markham.

———. 1972. Where the votes come from: An analysis of electoral coalitions, 1952–1968. *American Political Science Review* 66 (1).

Banfield, Edward, and James Q. Wilson. 1963. *City politics.* Cambridge, MA: Harvard University Press and MIT Press.

Banfield, Edward C. 1961. *Political influence.* Glencoe, IL: Free Press.

Barozzi, Louie. 2003. Personal interview by author.

Becerra, Hector. 2007. Lynwood defies order to hold recall. *Los Angeles Times,* July 3, part B.

Beck, Neal, and Jonathan Katz 1995. What to do (and not to do) with time-series cross-sectional data. *American Political Science Review* 89 (3).

Beddo, Carol. 2003. Personal interview by author.

Belenchia, Joanne. 1982. Latinos and Chicago politics. In *After Daley: Chicago politics in transition,* ed. Samuel Gove and Louis Masotti, 118–45. Chicago: University of Illinois Press.

Bennett, Stephen Earl, and David Resnick. 1990. The implications of nonvoting for democracy in the United States. *American Journal of Political Science* 34 (3).

Bernard, Richard M., and Bradley Robert Rice, eds. 1983. *Sunbelt cities: Politics and growth since world war II.* Austin: University of Texas Press.

Betsalel, Ken, and Jorge Chapa, eds. 1980. San Jose City Council elections, 1948–1978: Photocopies of *San Jose Mercury* news clippings. Berkeley, CA: Institute of Governmental Studies, UC Berkeley.

Biles, Roger. 1995. Edward J. Kelly: New deal machine builder. In *The mayors: The Chicago political tradition,* ed. Paul M. Green and Melvin G. Holli. Carbondale, IL: Southern Illinois University Press.

Blanchflower, David G., Neil Millward, and Andrew J. Oswald. 1991. Unionism and employment behaviour. *Economic Journal* 101 (407): 815–34.

Bogini, David. 2003. Personal interview by author.

Boix, Carles. 1999. Setting the rules of the game: The choice of electoral systems in advanced democracies. *American Political Science Review* 93 (3): 609–24.

Boix, Carles, and Susan C. Stokes. 2003. Endogenous democratization. *World Politics* 55:517–49.

Booth, John A. 1983. Political change in San Antonio, 1970–82: Toward decay or democracy? In *The politics of San Antonio: Community, progress, and power,* ed. David R. Johnson, John A. Booth, and Richard J. Harris. Lincoln: University of Nebraska Press.

Box-Steffensmeier, Janet, and Bradford S. Jones. 1997. Time is of the essence: Event history models in political science. *American Journal of Political Science* 41 (4).

Bradley, Donald, and Mayer L. Zald. 1965. From commercial elite to political administrator: The recruitment of the mayors of Chicago. *American Journal of Sociology* 71:627–47.

Bridges, Amy. 1984. *A city in the republic: Antebellum New York and the origins of machine politics.* New York: Cambridge University Press.

———. 1997. *Morning glories: Municipal reform in the southwest.* Princeton: Princeton University Press.

Bridges, Amy, and Richard Kronick. 1999. Writing the rules to win the game. *Urban Affairs Review* 34 (5).

Brierly, Allen Bronson, and David Moon. 1991. Electoral coalitions and institutional stability: The case of metropolitan reform in Dade County, Florida. *Journal of Politics* 53 (3).

Brischetto, Roberts, Charles L. Cotrell, and R. Michael Stevens. 1983. Conflict and change in the political culture of San Antonio in the 1970s. In *The politics of San Antonio: Community, progress, and power,* ed. David R. Johnson, John A. Booth, and Richard J. Harris. Lincoln: University of Nebraska Press.

Bronars, Stephen, and Donald Deere. 1993. Union organizing activity, firm growth, and the business cycle. *American Economic Review* 83 (1): 203–20.

Brooks, Robert C. 1917. Commission manager government in San Jose, Cal. *National Municipal Review* 6 (March).

Brown, M. Craig, and Charles N. Halaby. 1984. Bosses, reform, and the socioeconomic bases of urban expenditure, 1890–1940. In *The Politics of Urban Fiscal Policy,* ed. Terrence J. McDonald and Sally K. Ward. Beverly Hills: Sage.

———. 1987. Machine politics in America, 1870–1945. *Journal of Interdisciplinary History* 18:272–82.

Browning, Rufus, Dale Rodgers Marshall, and David Tabb. 1984. *Protest is not enough.* Berkeley: University of California Press.

Bryce, James. 1888. Rings and bosses. In *American Commonwealth,* vol. 2. London: Macmillan.

Buck, Thomas. 1958. Mayor to ask for new type of public housing: It could accommodate big families. *Chicago Daily Tribune,* January 15.

Buenker, John D. 1973. *Urban liberalism and progressive reform.* New York: Charles Scribner's Sons.

Bueno de Mesquita, Bruce, James Marrow, Randolph Siverson, and Alastair Smith. 2003. *The logic of political survival.* Cambridge, MA: MIT Press.

Burnham, W. Dean. Partisan division of American state governments, 1834–1985 [computer file]. Conducted by Massachusetts Institute of Technology. ICPSR ed. Ann Arbor: Inter-University Consortium for Political and Social Research (producer and distributor), 1985.

Cain, Bruce. 1985. Assessing the partisan effects of redistricting. *American Political Science Review* 79 (2).

Cain, Bruce E., John A. Ferejohn, and Morris P. Fiorina. 1987. *The personal vote: Constituency service and electoral independence.* Cambridge, MA: Harvard University Press.

Carlos, Ann M., and Jamie Brown Kruse. 1996. The decline of the Royal African Company: fringe firms and the role of the charter. *Economic History Review* 49 (2).

Caro, Robert. 1975. *The power broker: Robert Moses and the fall of New York*. New York: Random House.

Carson, Jamie, Erik J. Engstrom, and Jason M. Roberts. 2007. Candidate quality, the personal vote, and the incumbency advantage in Congress. *American Political Science Review* 101 (2): 289–302.

Casciano, Rebecca. 2007. How does being involved in electoral politics help a nonprofit community-based organization gain access to resources? A case study of a nonprofit CBO in Newark, New Jersey. Unpublished manuscript.

Cavanagh, Carlos. 1953. *Urban expansion and physical planning in San Jose, California: A case study*. MA thesis, University of California, Berkeley.

Chicago Tribune. 1931. Voice of the people. April 10.

Chicago Tribune. 1975. Mr. Daley's victory. April 3.

Childs, Richard S. 1965. *The first 50 Years of the council manager plan of municipal government*. New York: American Book–Stratford Press.

Christen, Francois G. 1973. Citizen preference for home, neighborhood, and city in Santa Clara County." Prepared for the National Science Foundation. Santa Monica: The Rand Corporation.

Christensen, Terry. 1997. San Jose becomes the capital of Silicon Valley. In *San Jose a city for all seasons,* ed. Judith Henderson. Encinitas, CA: Heritage Press. Supplemented excerpt available from http://www.sjsu.edu/depts/PoliSci/faculty/christensen/sj_history.htm.

Christian Science Monitor. 1938. San Jose city workers united in federation. February 5.

Cingranelli, David. 1981. Race, politics, and elites: Testing alternative models of municipal service distribution. *American Journal of Political Science* 25 (4).

Coate, Stephen, and Stephen Morris. 1995. On the form of transfers to special interests. *Journal of Political Economy* 103 (6): 1210–35.

Cohen, Adam, and Elizabeth Taylor. 2000. *American pharaoh*. Boston: Little, Brown and Company.

Cohen, Susan. 1985. The empire that Charlie built. *West Magazine (San Jose Mercury News)*, March 10.

Committee of Seventy. Seventy turns one hundred. Accessed on June 28, 2007, at *http://www.seventy.org/about/HistoryOfSeventy.html*.

Connolly, James. 1998. *The triumph of ethnic progressivism: Urban political culture in Boston, 1900–1925*. Cambridge, MA: Harvard University Press.

Cox, Gary, and Morgan Kousser. 1981. Turnout and rural corruption: New York as a test case. *American Journal of Political Science* 25 (4): 646–63.

Cox, Gary, and Mathew McCubbins. 1986. Electoral politics as a redistributive game. *Journal of Politics* 48 (2).

———. 2001. Public goods, targetable goods and electoral competition. Unpublished manuscript.

Cox, Gary W., and Jonathan N. Katz. 1999. The reapportionment revolution and bias in U.S. congressional elections. *American Journal of Political Science* 43 (3).

———. 2002. *Elbridge Gerry's salamander: The electoral consequences of the reapportionment revolution*. Cambridge: Cambridge University Press.

————. 2007. Gerrymandering roll calls in Congress, 1879–2000. *American Journal of Political Science* 51 (1): 108–19.

Curran, R. Garner. 1892. The amendments: Several very important questions to be voted on at the next election. *Los Angeles Times,* September 29.

Curry, Marshall. 2003. *Street fight* documentary.

Dahl, Robert. 1961. *Who governs? Democracy and power in the American city.* New Haven: Yale University Press.

Daily Defender (daily edition). 1957. Our segregated city. September 10.

Daily Defender (daily edition). 1960. Where a negro is needed. February 23.

Davidson, Chandler, and Luis Fraga. 1988. Slating groups as parties in a "nonpartisan" setting. *Western Political Quarterly* 41 (2): 373–90.

Davidson, Chandler, and Goerge Korbel. 1981. At-large elections and minority group representation: A re-examination of historical and contemporary evidence. *Journal of Politics* 43 (4).

Davidson, Charles W. 2003. Personal interview by author.

DiGaetano, Alan. 1988. The rise and development of urban political machines. *Urban Affairs Quarterly* 4:243–67.

Dixit, Avinash, and John Londregan. 1996. The determinants of success of special interests in redistributive politics. *Journal of Politics* 58 (4).

Dixon, Ruth B. 1966. Predicting voter turnout in city elections. MA thesis, University of California, Berkeley.

Dorsett, Lyle W. 1968. *The Pendergast machine.* New York: Oxford University Press.

Downs, Anthony. 1957. *An economic theory of democracy.* New York: Harper Collins Publishers.

Dupree, David. 1979. 3-point shot would have mixed affect. *Washington Post,* June 17.

Dye, Thomas R. 1969. Income inequality and American state politics. *American Political Science Review* 63 (1): 157–62.

Eakins, David, ed. 1976. *Businessmen and municipal reform: A study of ideals and practice in San Jose and Santa Cruz.* Sourisseau Academy for California State and Local History, San Jose State University Original Research in Santa Clara County History.

Ekdahl, Kristofer A. O. 2007. Reinventing the political machine: Modern politics in Newark and Philadelphia. Senior thesis, Princeton University.

Elkin, Stephen. 1987. *City and regime in the American republic.* Chicago: University of Chicago Press.

Ellsworth, Valerie, and Andrew Garbely. 1976. Centralization and efficiency: The reformers shape modern San Jose government. In *Businessmen and municipal reform: A study of ideals and practice in San Jose and Santa Cruz,* ed. David Eakins. Sourisseau Academy for California State and Local History, San Jose State University Original Research in Santa Clara County History.

Engstrom, Richard, and Michael McDonald. 1981. The election of blacks to city councils: Clarifying the impact of electoral arrangements in the seats/population relationship. *American Political Science Review* 75 (2).

Erie, Steven. 1988. *Rainbow's end: Irish Americans and the dilemmas of urban machine politics, 1840–1985*. Berkeley: University of California Press.

———. 2004. *Globalizing L.A.* Palo Alto: Stanford University Press.

Fairbanks, Robert. 1990. The good government machine: The citizens charter association and Dallas politics, 1930–1960. In *Essays on sunbelt cities and recent urban America*, ed. Robert B. Fairbanks and Kathleen Underwood. College Station, TX: Texas A&M University Press.

Fairbanks, Robert B., and Kathleen Underwood, eds. 1990. *Essays on sunbelt cities and recent urban America*. College Station, TX: Texas A&M University Press.

Farrell, Harry. 1992. *Swift justice*. New York: St. Martin's Press.

Fenno, Richard. [1978] 2003. *Home style: House members in their districts*. New York: Longman.

Finegold, Kenneth. 1995. *Experts and politicians: Reform challenges to machine politics in New York, Cleveland, and Chicago*. Princeton: Princeton University Press.

Forthal, Sonya. 1946. *Cogwheels of democracy: A study of the precinct captain*. New York: William-Frederick Press.

Fox, Kenneth. 1977. *Better city government: Innovation in American urban politics 1850–1927*. Philadelphia: Temple University Press.

Fraga, Luis Ricardo. 1988. Domination through democratic means: Nonpartisan slating groups in city electoral politics. *Urban Affairs Quarterly* 23 (4): 528–55.

Frasure, Lorrie, and Michael Jones-Correa. 2005. NIMBY's newest neighbors: Bureaucratic constraints, community-based organizing and the day laborer movement in suburbia. Paper prepared for Midwest Political Science Association Conference, Chicago.

Freedman, Anne. 1988. Doing battle with the patronage army: Politics, courts, and personnel administration in Chicago. *Public Administration Review* 48 (5): 847–59.

Fremon, David K. 1988. *Chicago politics ward by ward*. Bloomington: Indiana University Press.

Frohlich, Norman. 1975. The instability of minimum winning coalitions. *American Political Science Review* 69 (3).

Fuchs, Esther R. 1992. *Mayors and money: Fiscal policy in New York and Chicago*. Chicago: University of Chicago Press.

Fund, John. 2002. Newark, Zimbabwe? *Wall Street Journal* (Eastern edition), May 8.

Geilhufe, Nancy. 1979. *Chicanos and the police: A study of the politics of ethnicity in San Jose, California*. Society for Applied Anthropology monograph. no. 13. Washington DC: The Society for Applied Anthropology.

Gelb, Joyce. 1970. Blacks, blocs and ballots. *Polity* 3.

Gibson, Campbell. 1998 (June). Population of the 100 largest cities and other urban places in the United States: 1790 to 1990. Population Division working paper no. 27. Population Division, U.S. Bureau of the Census, Washington DC.

Gierzynski, Anthony, and David A. Breaux. 1993. Money and the party vote in state House elections. *Legislative Studies Quarterly* 18 (4): 515–33.

Gilbert, Charles E., and Christopher Clague. 1962. Electoral competition and electoral systems in large cities. *Journal of Politics* 24 (2).

Gilens, Martin. 2005. Inequality and democratic responsiveness. *Public Opinion Quarterly* 69 (5): 778–96.

Gimpel, James. 1993. Reform-resistant and reform-adopting machines: The electoral foundations of urban politics, 1910–1930. *Political Research Quarterly* 46 (2): 371–82.

Ginkel, John, and Alastair Smith. 1999. So you say you want a revolution: A game theoretic interpretation of revolution in repressive regimes. *Journal of Conflict Resolution* 43 (3): 291–316.

Good, David L. 1989. *Orvie: The dictator of Dearborn: The rise and reign of Orville L. Hubbard.* Detroit: Wayne State University Press.

Gordon, Daniel N. 1968. Immigrants and urban governmental form in American cities, 1933–1960. *American Journal of Sociology* 74 (2).

Gosnell, Harold F. 1933. The political party versus the political machine. *Annals of the American Academy of Political and Social Science* 169 (September): 21–28.

———. 1935. *Negro politicians: The rise of negro politics in Chicago.* Chicago: University of Chicago Press.

———. 1937. *Machine politics.* Chicago: University of Chicago Press.

Gottfried, Alex. 1955. The use of psychosomatic categories in a study of political personality. *Western Political Quarterly* 8 (2): 234–47.

———. 1962. *Boss Cermak of Chicago: A study of political leadership.* Seattle: University of Washington Press.

Gowran, Clay. 1955. Merriam charges election board bias: Rips Holzman as spokesman for opponent. *Chicago Tribune,* February 27.

Green, Paul M. 1984. The 1983 democratic mayoral primary: Some new players—same old rules. In *The Making of the Mayor: Chicago 1984,* ed. Melvin G. Holli and Paul M. Green. Grand Rapids: Eerdmans.

———. 1995a. Anton J. Cermak: The man and his machine. In *The mayors: The Chicago political tradition,* ed. Paul M. Green and Melvin G. Holli. Carbondale: Southern Illinois University Press.

———. 1995b. Mayor Richard J. Daley and the politics of good government. In *The mayors: The Chicago political tradition,* ed. Paul M. Green and Melvin G. Holli. Carbondale: Southern Illinois University Press.

Greenstein, Fred I. 1964. The changing pattern of urban party politics. *Annals of the American Academy of Political and Social Science* 353 (1): 1–13.

Grimshaw, William J. 1992. *Bitter fruit: Black politics and the Chicago machine, 1931–1991.* Chicago: University of Chicago Press.

Grofman, Bernard, W Koetzle, and T. Brunell. 1997. An integrated perspective on the three potential sources of partisan bias: Malapportionment, turnout differences, and the geographic distribution of party vote shares. *Electoral Studies* 16 (4): 457–70.

Groseclose, Timothy, and James Snyder. 1996. Buying supermajorities. *American Political Science Review* 90 (2): 303–15.

Hajnal, Zoltan, and Paul Lewis. 2003. Municipal institutions and voter turnout in local elections. *Urban Affairs Review* 38 (May): 645–68.

Hammer, Susan. 2003. Personal interview by author.

Handlin, Oscar. 1973. *The uprooted.* 2nd ed. Boston: Little, Brown.

Hanson, Royce. 2003. *Civic culture and urban change: Governing Dallas.* Detroit: Wayne State University Press.

Hardin, Russell. 1976. Hollow victory: The minimum winning coalition. *American Political Science Review* 70 (4): 1202–14.

Harper, Will. 2001. Playing favorites. *San Jose Metro.* March 29. Accessed at *http://www.metroactive.com/papers/metro/03.29.01/politicians-0113.html.*

Harrington, Joseph E. Jr. 1984. Noncooperative behavior by a cartel as an entry-deterring signal. *RAND Journal of Economics* 15 (3): 426–33.

Hawley, Willis D. 1973. *Nonpartisan elections and the case for party politics.* New York: Wiley.

Hayes, Janet Gray. 1980. Interview by Armando Acuna, Mark Saylor, and Philip J. Trounstine. March.

Hayes, Janet Gray. 2003. Personal interview by author.

Hays, Samuel P. 1964. The politics of reform in municipal government in the progressive era. *Pacific Northwest Quarterly* 55 (4).

Herberich, John, and Patricia Canon. 1976. The discovery of corruption as a public issue: The Good Government League and the machine in San Jose. In *Businessmen and municipal reform: A study of ideals and practice in San Jose and Santa Cruz,* ed. David Eakins. Sourisseau Academy for California State and Local History, San Jose State University Original Research in Santa Clara County History.

Hernandez, R. 2003. On politics: Hudson county amasses more power. *New York Times,* December 14.

Herring, Mary, and John Forbes. 1994. The overrepresentation of a white minority: Detroit's at-large city council, 1961–1989. *Social Science Quarterly* 75(2): 431–45.

Hershey, Marjorie Randon. 1973. Incumbency and the minimum winning coalition. *American Journal of Political Science* 17 (3).

Hershey, Majorie Randon, and Paul Allen Beck. 2003. *Party politics in America.* 10th ed. New York: Longman.

Hertz-Picciotto, Irva, and Beverly Rockhill. 1997. Validity and efficiency of approximation methods for tied survival times in Cox regression. *Biometrics* 53 (3): 1151–56.

Higgins, Caitlin. 2007. Bright lights, big city: The role of municipal institutions in translating preferences into policy. Senior thesis, Princeton University.

Hinckley, Barbara, 1972. Coalitions in Congress: Size and ideological distance. *Midwest Journal of Political Science* 16 (2): 197–207.

Hirsch, Arnold. 1983. *Making the second ghetto.* Cambridge: Cambridge University Press.

Hise, Greg. 1997. *Magnetic Los Angeles: Planning the twentieth-century metropolis.* Baltimore: Johns Hopkins University Press.

Hofstadter, Richard. 1955. *The age of reform.* New York: Random House.

Holden, Alice M. 1915. Commission and city manager government. *American Political Science Review* 9 (3): 561–63.

Holli, Melvin G. 1969. *Reform in Detroit: Hazen S. Pingree and urban politics.* New York: Oxford University Press.

Hopper, Stanley. 1975. Fragmentation of the California republican party in the one-party era, 1893–1932. *Western Political Quarterly* 28 (2).

Hunter, Floyd. 1953. *Community power structure*. Chapel Hill: University of North Carolina Press.

———. 1980. *Community power succession: Atlanta's policy-makers revisited*. Chapel Hill: University of North Carolina Press.

Inter-University Consortium for Political and Social Research. Time Series Data in Chicago, 1840–1973, by Wesley G. Skogan. ICPSR 7389.

Iverson, Torben, and Davis Soskice. 2006. Electoral institutions and the politics of coalitions: Why some democracies redistribute more than others. *American Political Science Review* 100 (2): 165–81.

Jackman, Robert. 1987. Political institutions and voter turnout in the industrial democracies. *American Political Science Review* 81 (2).

Jacobson, Gary C. 1997. *The politics of congressional elections*. New York: Longman.

Johnson, David R., John A. Booth, and Richard J. Harris, eds. 1983. *The politics of San Antonio: Community, progress, and power*. Lincoln: University of Nebraska Press.

Johnson, William A. 1981. *Kansas City votes, 1853–1979: Precinct election returns for the offices of president, governor, and Kansas City*. Committee for Urban and Public Affairs, University of Missouri, Kansas City.

Jones, Clinton B. 1976. The impact of local election systems on black political representation. *Urban Affairs Quarterly* 11.

Kahneman, Daniel, and Amos Tversky. 1979. Prospect theory: An analysis of decision under risk. *Econometrica* 47 (2): 263–92.

Karklins, Rasma, and Roger Petersen. 1993. Decision calculus of protestors and regimes: Eastern Europe 1989. *Journal of Politics* 55 (3).

Kaufmann, Karen M. 2004. *The urban voter: Group conflict and mayoral voting behavior in American cities*. Ann Arbor: University of Michigan Press.

Keegan, Anne. 1976. The common man pays respects to the common man. *Chicago Tribune*, December 22.

Keiser, Richard. 1997. *Subordination or empowerment? African American leadership and the struggle for urban political power*. New York: Oxford University Press.

———. 2003. Philadelphia's evolving bi-racial coalition. In *Racial politics in American cities*, 3rd ed., ed. Rufus Browning, Dale Rogers Marshall, and David H. Tabb. New York: Longman.

Kelley, Stanley Jr., Richard E. Ayres, and William G. Bowen. 1967. Registration and voting: Putting first things first. *American Political Science Review* 61 (2).

Kemp, Kathleen, and Robert Lineberry. 1982. The last of the great urban machines and the last of the great urban mayors? Chicago politics, 1955–77. In *After Daley: Chicago politics in transition*, ed. Samuel Gove and Louis Masotti, 1–26. Chicago: University of Illinois Press.

Key, V. O. 1935. Political machine strategy against investigations. *Social Forces* 14 (1): 120–28.

———. [1949] 1984. *Southern politics in state and nation*. Knoxville: University of Tennessee Press.

Keyssar, Alex. 2000. *The right to vote: The contested history of democracy in the United States*. New York: Basic Books.

270 References

Kleppner, Paul. 1985. *Chicago divided: The making of a black mayor.* DeKalb, IL: Northern Illinois University Press.

Knoke, David. 1982. The spread of municipal reform: Temporal, spatial and social dynamics. *American Journal of Sociology* 87 (6).

Koehler, David, and Margaret Wrightson. 1987. Inequality in the delivery of urban services: A reconsideration of the Chicago parks. *Journal of Politics* 49 (1): 80–99.

Kousser, J. Morgan. 1974. *The shaping of southern politics suffrage restriction and the establishment of the one-party south, 1880–1910.* New Haven: Yale University Press.

Krane, Dale, Platon N. Rigos, and Melvin B. Hill Jr. 2001. *Home rule in America: A fifty state handbook.* Washington D.C.: CQ Press.

Krebs, Timothy B. 1998. The determinants of candidates' vote share and the advantages of incumbency in city council elections. *American Journal of Political Science* 42 (3).

———. 2001. Political Experience and Fundraising in City Council Elections. *Social Science Quarterly* 82:537–51.

Krebs, Timothy B., and John P. Pelissero. 2001. Fund-raising coalitions in mayoral campaigns. *Urban Affairs Review* 37 (1): 67–84.

Kuran, Timur. 1991. Now out of never: The element of surprise in the East European revolutions of 1989. *World Politics* 44 (1): 7–48.

Lake, David, and Matthew Baum. 2001. The invisible hand of democracy: Political control and the provision of public services. *Comparative Political Studies* 34 (6).

Lambert, B., and S. Domash. 2004. Nassau aid went to campaign donors. *New York Times,* October 24.

Larsen, Lawrence H., and Nancy Hulston. 1997. *Pendergast!* Columbia, MO: University of Missouri Press.

Lascher, Edward L., Jr. 2005. Constituency size and incumbent safety: A reexamination. *Political Research Quarterly* 58 (2): 269–78.

Lee, Eugene. 1960. *The politics of nonpartisanship: A study of California city elections.* Berkeley: University of California Press.

Lewis, David E. 2008. *The politics of presidential appointments: Political control and bureaucratic performance.* Princeton: Princeton University Press.

Lewis, James, Tony Gierzynski, and Paul Kleppner. 1995. *Equality of opportunity? Financing 1991 campaigns for the Chicago city council.* Chicago: Chicago Urban League.

Lieske, Joel. 1989. The political dynamics of urban voting behavior. *American Journal of Political Science* 33 (1).

Lieske, Joel, and Jan William Hillard. 1984. The racial factor in urban elections. *Western Political Quarterly* 37 (4): 545–63.

Lipset, Seymour Martin, Martin Trow, and James Coleman. 1956. *Union democracy: The inside politics of the international typographical union.* New York: The Free Press.

Logan, John R., and Harvey L. Molotch. 1987. *Urban fortunes: The political economy of place.* Berkeley: University of California Press.

Lokey, Roy Eugene. 1974. Targeting in a municipal election: A case study in San Jose, California. MA thesis, San Jose State University.

Los Angeles Times. 1882. Electric light. January 5.

Los Angeles Times. 1888. Tired of bossism. June 30.

Los Angeles Times. 1916. Jap exclusion broached again. January 23.

Los Angeles Times. 1918. Hayes to run for governor. February 12.

Los Angeles Times. 1927. Unions boycott San Jose paper. September 19.

Los Angeles Times. 1933a. Mob breaks into jail: Hart killers seized. November 27.

Los Angeles Times. 1933b. The San Jose lynching. November 28.

Los Angeles Times. 1934. San Jose vigilantes organized. March 2.

Lukes, T. J., and G. Y. Okihiro. 1985. Japanese legacy: Farming and community life in California's Santa Clara valley. Cupertino, CA: California History Center, DeAnza College.

Lundstrom, Mack. 1993. Harvey Miller, 86, ex-SJ civic leader lawyer shaped political history. *San Jose Mercury News,* May 7.

Machin, Stephen, and Sushil Wadhwani. 1991. The effects of unions on organisational change and employment. *Economic Journal* 101 (407): 835–54.

Martin, Harold H. 1961. The new millionaires of Phoenix. *Saturday Evening Post,* September 30.

Marwell, Nicole. 2004. Privatizing the welfare state: Nonprofit community-based organizations as political actors. *American Sociological Review* 69 (2): 265–91.

Matthews, Glenna. 2003. *Silicon Valley, women, and the California dream: gender, class, and opportunity in the 20th century.* Stanford: Stanford University Press.

Mayhew, David. 1974. *Congress: The electoral connection.* New Haven: Yale University Press.

———. 1986. *Placing parties in American politics.* Princeton: Princeton University Press.

McCaffery, Peter. 1992. Style, structure, and institutionalization of machine politics: Philadelphia, 1867–1933. *Journal of Interdisciplinary History* 22 (3): 435–52.

———. 1993. *When bosses ruled Philadelphia: The emergence of the republican machine, 1867–1933.* University Park: Pennsylvania State University Press.

McDonald, Terrence J. 1985. The problem of the political in recent American urban history: Liberal pluralism and the rise of functionalism. *Social History* 10: 324–45.

———. 1994. Introd. to *Plunkitt of Tammany Hall: A series of very plain talks on very practical politics,* by William L. Riordan. Boston: Bedford Books of St. Martin's Press.

McEnery, Tom. 2003. Personal interview by author.

McGuire, Martin C., and Mancur Olson Jr. 1996. The economics of autocracy and majority rule: The invisible hand and the use of force. *Journal of Economic Literature* 34 (1).

Mehler, Neil. 1976. Kelly, Dunne vie for party leader's post. *Chicago Tribune,* December 28.

Meier, Kenneth J., and Thomas M. Holbrook. 1992. "I seen my opportunities and I took 'em": Political corruption in the American states. *Journal of Politics* 54 (1).

Meier, Kenneth J., Joseph Stewart Jr., and Robert E. England. 1991. The politics of bureaucratic discretion: Educational access as an urban service. *American Journal of Political Science* 35 (1): 155–77.

Meltzer, Allan, and Scott Richard. 1981. A rational theory of the size of government. *Journal of Political Economy* 89 (5).

Merritt, Sharyne. 1977. Winners and losers: Sex differences in municipal elections. *American Journal of Political Science* 21: 731–43.

Merton, Robert K. 1957. *Social theory and social structure*. New York: The Free Press.

Miller, Zane L. 1968. *Boss Cox's Cincinnati: Urban politics in the progressive era*. Oxford and New York: Oxford University Press.

———. 1982. Bosses, machines, and the urban political process. In *Ethics, machines, and the American urban future,* ed. Scott Greer. Cambridge, MA: Schenkman Publishing Company.

Minnite, Lorraine. 2007. The politics of voter fraud. Washington DC: Project Vote.

Mladenka, Kenneth. 1980. The urban bureaucracy and the Chicago political machine: Who gets what and the limits of political control. *American Political Science Review* 74 (4): 991–98.

Mollenkopf, John. 1983. *The contested city*. Princeton: Princeton University Press.

Montgomery, Edward. 1989. Employment and unemployment effects of unions. *Journal of Labor Economics* 7 (2): 170–90.

Morton, Rebecca. 1987. A group majority voting model of public good provision. *Social Choice and Welfare* 4 (2): 117–31.

Moynihan, Daniel P., and Nathan Glazer. 1970. *Beyond the melting pot*. Cambridge, MA: MIT Press.

Moynihan, Daniel Patrick, and James Q. Wilson. 1964. Patronage in New York state, 1955–1959. *American Political Science Review* 58 (2).

Munoz, Carlos Jr., and Charles Henry. 1986. Rainbow coalitions in four big cities: San Antonio, Denver, Chicago and Philadelphia. *PS: Political Science & Politics* 19 (3): 598–609.

Munro, William B. 1933. The boss in politics—asset or liability? *Annals of the American Academy of Political and Social Science* 169: 12–20.

New York Times. [1857] 1877. Tammany election funds; where some of them come from. How the corporation attorney's office is worked for electioneering purposes. August 27.

New York Times. 1917. The golden prime of Tammany. October 28.

New York Times. 1931. Walker hails big bill; Hears a song of "tony"; Veres about Cermak, democratic nominee, are read to New York's mayor. February 25.

New York Times. 1976. The mayor. December 22.

Nobles, Melissa. 2000. *Shades of citizenship: Race and the census in modern politics*. Stanford: Stanford University Press.

Nordheimer, Jon. 1969. Lee's bowing out pleases New Haven democratic chief. *New York Times,* July 13.

Norrander, Barbara J. 1989. Ideological representativeness of presidential primary voters. *American Journal of Political Science* 33 (3).

O'Connor, Len. 1975. Daley cracks election whip with 100,000 sure votes. *Chicago Tribune,* April 10.

O'Conor, Charles. 1871. The ring robbers. *New York Times,* October 20.

Oliver, J. Eric, and Shang E. Ha. 2007. Vote choice in suburban elections. *American Political Science Review* 101 (3): 393–408.

Olson, David, 1967. Austin: The capital city. In *Urban politics in the southwest,* ed. Leonard E. Goodall. Tempe: Arizona State University Press.

O'Neill, Hugh. 1970. The growth of municipal employee unions. *Proceedings of the Academy of Political Science* 30 (2): 1–13.

Orr, Marion. 2003. The struggle for black empowerment in Baltimore. In *Racial politics in American cities,* 3rd ed., ed. Rufus P. Browning, Dale Rogers Marshall, and David H. Tabb. New York: Longman.

Orum, Anthony. 1987. *Power, money, and the people: The making of modern Austin.* Austin: Texas Monthly Press.

Ostrogorski, M. 1910. Democracy and the party system in the United States: A study in *extra-constitutional government.* New York: Macmillan Company.

Parenti, Michael. 1970. Power and pluralism: A view from the bottom. *Journal of Politics* 32 (3).

Peterson, Paul E. 1981. *City limits.* Chicago: University of Chicago Press.

Pinderhughes, Dianne. 1987. *Race and ethnicity in Chicago politics: A reexamination of pluralist theory.* Chicago: University of Illinois Press.

———. 1994. Racial and ethnic politics in Chicago mayoral elections. In *Big city politics, governance, and fiscal constraints,* ed. G. E. Peterson. Urbana, IL: University of Illinois.

Pitti, Stephen J. 2003. *The devil in Silicon Valley: Northern California, race, and Mexican Americans.* Princeton: Princeton University Press.

Polinard, J. L., Robert Wrinkle, Tomas Longoria, and Norman Binder. 1994. *Electoral structure and urban policy: The impact on Mexican American communities.* Armonk, NY: M. E. Sharpe.

Posner, Richard A. 1975. The social costs of monopoly and regulation. *Journal of Political Economy* 83 (4): 807–28.

Poughkeepsie Journal. 2006. Valley's dead cast their votes. October 29.

Preston, Michael B. 1982. Black politics in the post-Daley era. In *After Daley: Chicago politics in transition,* ed. Samuel K. Gove and Louis Masotti. Chicago: University of Illinois Press.

Prewitt, Kenneth. 1970. *The recruitment of political leaders: A study of citizen politicians.* Indianapolis: Bobbs-Merrill.

Przeworski, A. 1986. Some problems in the study of transition to democracy. In *Transitions from Authoritarian Rule,* ed. G. O'Donnell and P. C. Schmitter, 40–63. Baltimore: Johns Hopkins University Press.

Przeworski, Adam, Michael Alvarez, Jose Antonio Cheibub, and Fernando Limongi. 2000. *Democracy and development: Political institutions and well-being in the world, 1950–1990.* Cambridge: Cambridge University Press.

Rae, Douglas. 2003. *City: Urbanism and its end.* New Haven: Yale University Press.

Rakove, Milton L. 1975. *Don't make no waves: An insider's analysis of the Daley machine.* Bloomington: Indiana University Press.

Ranney, Austin, and Willmoore Kendall. 1954. The American party system. *American Political Science Review* 48 (2).

Reed, Thomas H. 1931. Notes on municipal affairs. *American Political Science Review* 25 (3): 671–82.

Reid, Joseph D., and Michael M. Kurth. 1988. Public employees in political firms: Part A, the patronage era. *Public Choice* 59 (3): 253–62.

Reitman, Alan, and Robert B. Davidson. 1972. *The election process: Voting laws and procedures.* Dobbs Ferry, NY: Oceana Publications.

Riker, William. 1962. *The theory of political coalitions.* New Haven: Yale University Press.

Riordan, William L. 1994. *Plunkitt of Tammany Hall: A series of very plain talks on very practical politics.* Boston: Bedford Books of St. Martin's Press.

Robbins, Maro. 2004. Politicos' lawyers rip bribery case indictments; attorneys for Prado and Martin say allegations meant to inflame jury. *San Antonio Express-News,* July 14.

Rogers, Paul. 1999. The man behind S. J.'s rapid growth former city manager set stage for valley's boom and sprawl. *San Jose Mercury News,* December 30.

Rosales, Rodolfo. 2000. *The illusion of inclusion: The untold political story of San Antonio.* Austin: University of Texas Press.

Ross, Bernard H., and Myron A. Levine. 2001. *Urban politics: Power in metropolitan America.* 6th ed. Itasca, IL: Peacock Publishers.

Royko, Mike. 1971. *Boss: Richard J. Daley of Chicago.* New York: Signet Press.

Rozhon, Tracie. 1981. '60s dream of renewal fades with time. *New York Times,* January 11.

Ruhil, Anirudh V. S. 2003. Structural change and fiscal flows: A framework for analyzing the effects of urban events. *Urban Affairs Review* 38 (3): 396–416.

Salter, John T. 1935. *Boss rule: Portraits in city politics.* New York: McGraw-Hill Book Company.

Sanders, Heywood. 1991. The creation of post-war San Antonio: Politics, voting, and fiscal regimes, 1945 to 1960. Paper prepared for the annual meeting of the Southwestern Social Science Association, San Antonio, TX.

San Jose City Charter. Accessed on August 6, 2007, at http://www.sanjoseca.gov/clerk/charter.htm.

San Jose Commission on the Internment of Local Japanese Americans. 1985. *With liberty and justice for all: the story of San Jose's Japanese Community.*

San Jose Mercury News. 1950a. It's official: Hamann new city manager. March 7.

San Jose Mercury News. 1950b. No city candidate biographies. March 7.

San Jose Mercury News. 1962a. 4 city charter changes on Tuesday ballot. November 3.

San Jose Mercury News. 1962b. 84,207 eligible to vote in city charter ballot. February 18.

San Jose Mercury News. 1962c. New charter rejected in light vote. February 21.

San Jose Mercury News. 1964a. Incumbents win by over 2–1 margin. July 15.

San Jose Mercury News. 1964b. The Mercury recommends. July 12.

San Jose Mercury News. 1965. Charter ok: Theater too. March 14.

San Jose Public Library. 2003. Branch Facilities Master Plan.

Santa Clara County Housing Task Force. 1977. Housing: A call for action. Santa Clara County Planning Department, October.

Schaffner, Brian, Matthew Streb, and Gerald Wright. 2001. Teams without uniforms: The nonpartisan ballot in state and local elections. *Political Research Quarterly* 54 (1).

Schelling, Thomas. 1985. *Micromotives and macrobehavior.* New York: Gordon and Breach.

Schill, Michael H., and Susan M. Wachter. 1995. The spatial bias of federal housing law and policy: Concentrated poverty in urban America. *University of Pennsylvania Law Review* 143 (5): 1285–1342.

Schneider, Mark, and Paul Teske. 1993. The antigrowth entrepreneur: Challenging the "equilibrium" of the growth machine. *Journal of Politics* 55 (3).

Schoennauer, Gary. 2003. Personal interview by author.

Schreiber, Edward. 1968. Shoot arsonists: Daley appoints committee to investigate riots: Conlisk rebuked over inaction in disorders. *Chicago Tribune,* April 16.

Scott, Thomas. 1968. Diffusion of urban governmental forms as a case of social learning. *Journal of Politics* 30:1091–1108.

Shannon, W. V. 1969. Age of the bosses. *American Heritage* 29 (June): 27–31.

Sharp, Elaine B., ed. 1999. *Culture wars and local politics.* Lawrence: University Press of Kansas.

Shaw, Michael, Doug Moore, and Paul Hampel. 2005. All are guilty in vote fraud trial. *St Louis Post-Dispatch,* June 30.

Shefter, Martin. 1976. The emergence of the political machine: An alternative view. In *Theoretical perspectives on urban politics,* ed. Willis D. Hawley et al. Englewood Cliffs, NJ: Prentice Hall.

———. 1978. The electoral foundations of the political machine: New York City, 1884–1897. In *The history of American electoral behavior,* ed. Joel H. Silbey, Allan G. Bogue, and William H. Flanigan. Princeton: Princeton University Press.

Shepsle, Kenneth A. 1974. On the size of winning coalitions. *American Political Science Review* 68 (2).

Simpson, Dick. 2001. *Rogues, rebels, and rubber stamps: The politics of the Chicago city council from 1863 to the present.* Boulder: Westview Press.

Simpson, Dick, Ola Adeoye, Daniel Bliss, Kevin Navratil, and Rebecca Raines. 2004. The new Daley machine: 1989–2004. Paper presented at the City Futures Conference.

Skerry, Peter. 1995. The black alienation: African Americans vs. immigrants. *New Republic* 212:19–20.

Sorauf, Frank J. 1960. The silent revolution in patronage. *Public Administration Review* 20 (1): 28–34.

Spalding, John. 1964. Recall issue goes on ballot Tuesday. *San Jose Mercury News,* July 12.

Spielman, Fran. 2006. Daley's 56 percent approval rating has him smiling: But 70% don't believe he didn't know about corruption. *Chicago Sun Times,* February 16.

Stanford Environmental Law Society. 1970. *San Jose: Sprawling city.* Stanford: Stanford University.

Starbird, George. 1972. *The new metropolis.* San Jose: Rosicrucian Press.

Stave, Bruce M., John M. Allswang, Terrence J. McDonald, and Jon C. Teaford. 1988. A reassessment of the urban political boss: An exchange of views. *History Teacher* 21 (3): 293–312.

Steffens, Lincoln. 1902. *The shame of the cities.* New York: Hill and Wang Publishing.

Stein, Lana. 1991. *Holding bureaucrats accountable: Politicians and professionals in St. Louis.* Institute for Social Science Research. Tuscaloosa: University of Alabama Press.

Stein, Lana, and Arnold Fleischman. 1987. Newspaper and business endorsements in municipal elections: A test of the conventional wisdom. *Journal of Urban Affairs* 9:325–36.

Stokes, Susan. 2007. Is vote buying undemocratic? In *Elections for sale: The causes and consequences of vote buying,* ed. Frederic Charles Shaffer. Boulder and London: Lynn Reinner Publishers.

Stone, Clarence. 1989. *Regime politics: Governing Atlanta, 1946–1988.* Lawrence: University Press of Kansas.

———. 1996. Urban political machines: Taking stock. *PS: Political Science & Politics* 29 (3): 446–50.

Stone, Harold, Don Price, and Kathryn Stone. 1937. City manager government in Austin, Texas. A report submitted to the Committee on Public Administration of the Social Science Research Council, Washington DC.

———. 1940. *City manager government in nine cities.* Chicago: Public Administration Service.

Summers, Mary, and Philip Klinkner. 1990. The election of John Daniels as mayor of New Haven. *PS: Political Science & Politics* 23 (2).

Teaford, John. 1984. *The unheralded triumph: City government in America, 1870–1900.* Baltimore: Johns Hopkins University Press.

Teibout, Charles. 1956. A pure theory of local expenditures. *Journal of Political Economy* 64 (5): 416–24.

Thorpe, Robert. 1938. Council-manager government in San Jose, California. MA thesis, Stanford University.

Tomz, Michael, J. Wittenberg, and Gary King. 2003. CLARIFY: Software for interpreting and presenting statistical results. Version 2.1. Accessed March 13, 2006, at http://gking.harvard.edu/stats.shtml#clarify.

Trounstine, Jessica, and Melody Ellis Valdini. 2007. *The context matters: The effects of single member vs. at-large districts on diversity.* Unpublished manuscript.

Trounstine, Jessica L. 2006. The demise of urban democracy. *Journal of Politics* 68 (4): 879–93.

Trounstine, Mary. 2003. Personal interview by author.

Trounstine, Philip J. 1985. Who should have the clout to run San Jose? *San Jose Mercury News,* November 3.

———. 1995. His career was based on diligence, attention to detail and wariness. *San Jose Mercury News,* September 11.

———. 2003. Personal interview by author.

Trounstine, Philip J., and Terry Christensen. 1982. *Movers and shakers: The study of community power.* New York: St. Martin's Press. Excerpt available at *http://www.sjsu.edu/depts/PoliSci/faculty/christensen/flashback.htm.*

Tsebelis, George. 2002. *Veto players: How political institutions work.* Princeton: Princeton University Press.

Uhlaner, Carole. 1995. Rational turnout: The neglected role of groups. *American Journal of Political Science* 33 (2).

Ward, Geoffrey C., and Ken Burns. 2000. *Jazz: A history of America's music*. New York: Knopf.

Washington Post. 2002. The mayor pays a price. Editorial, August 16.

Weber, Max. 1946. *Essays in sociology*. New York: Oxford University Press.

Welch, Susan, and Timothy Bledsoe. 1988. *Urban reform and its consequences*. Chicago: University of Chicago Press.

White, Andrew. 1890 [1969]. The government of American cities. *Forum*. Repr. in E. Banfield, ed. *Urban Government*. New York: Free Press.

Whyte, William Foote. 1955. *Street corner society: The social structure of an Italian slum*. Chicago: University of Chicago Press.

Williams, Lance, and Chuck Finnie. 2002. Federal probe of assessor in S. F. *San Francisco Chronicle*, May 11.

Williams, Oliver, and Charles Adrian. 1959. The insulation of local politics under the nonpartisan ballot. *American Political Science Review* 53 (4).

Wolfinger, Raymond. 1972. Why political machines have not withered away and other revisionist thoughts. *Journal of Politics* 34 (2): 365–98.

———. 1974. *The Politics of Progress*. Englewood Cliffs, NJ: Prentice-Hall, Inc.

Wolfinger, Raymond E., Benjamin Highton, and Megan Mullin. 2005. How postregistration laws affect the turnout of registrants. *State Politics and Policy Quarterly* 5 (Spring): 1–5.

Wolfinger, Raymond E., and Steven J. Rosenstone. 1980. *Who votes?* New Haven: Yale University Press.

Wolman, Harold, John Strate, and Alan Melchior. 1996. Does changing mayors matter? *Journal of Politics* 58 (1).

Wood, Curtis. 2002. Voter turnout in city elections. *Urban Affairs Review* 38 (2).

Wright, John, and Arthur Goldberg. 1985. Risk and uncertainty as factors in the durability of political coalitions. *American Political Science Review* 79 (3): 704–18.

Wyman, Roger. 1974. Middle-class voters and progressive reform: The conflict of class and culture. *American Political Science Review* 68 (2).

Yu, Connie Young. 1991. *Chinatown, San Jose, USA*. San Jose: San Jose Historical Museum Association.

Zaller, John. 1998. Politicians as prize fighters: Electoral selection and the incumbency advantage. In *Politicians and party politics*, ed. John G. Geer, 125–85. New York: Palgrave Macmillan.

Zikmund, Joseph II. 1982. Mayoral voting and ethnic politics in the Daley-Bilandic-Byrne era. In *After Daley: Chicago politics in transition*, ed. Samuel K. Gove and Louis Masotti. Chicago: University of Illinois Press.

Zink, Harold. 1930. *City bosses in the United States: A study of twenty municipal bosses*. New York: AMS Press.

INDEX

Page numbers in italics indicate tables.

Acemoglu, Daron, 232
Adamowski, Benjamin, 192, 200
Adeoye, Ola, 222, 226, 228, 229
affirmative action, 219
African Americans: ability to gain control of cities, 11; annexation of community in Phoenix, 59; in Austin, 166, 169; benefits in Pittsburgh, 157; challenge to reapportionment, 212; in Dearborn, 223; demand for integration, 162; disenfranchisement of, 32; exclusion from reform governments, 80; gerrymandering and, *57*; Kelly's pursuit of, 70, 164–65; loyalty to the Republican Party, 71, 88, 248n6, 249n4; mobilization against Chicago machine, 172, 200–201, 209–10, 214–15; monopolistic governments' hindrance of, 109; new Daley regime and, 228–29; in New Haven, 194; opposition to Daley administration, 40, 41; opposition to reform charters, 76, 78, 112; opposition to reform coalition in Dallas, 112, 202; Pendergast's pursuit of, 71, 249n5; police brutality and, 167; political effectiveness of, 96–97; political gains in machine-run cities, 198, 209–10; political gains in reform cities, 196, 204; populations in Southwestern cities, 76; in public housing projects, 161–62, *163*; representation of in Chicago, 199; segregation of in Chicago, 139, 161–62, 192–93, 199–200, 259n15; share of benefits, 159, 259n2; support of Cermak, 67, *69*; urban renewal and, 162–64; voter turnout under Dawson, 146–47, *147;* Washington's election in Chicago and, 218–19. *See also* integration; segregation

Albany, New York: civil service in, 206; core group of supporters in, 249n2; distribution of benefits in, *157, 160*; electoral fraud in, 248n7; home rule in, 72; Irish in public offices, 156; period of monopoly control, *180, 184*; response to threats of mobilization in, 194; treatment of immigrants before consolidation, 165

Albuquerque, New Mexico: core group of supporters in, *78*; distribution of benefits in, 166; factions in governing coalition, 211; opposition coalition in, 202, 204; period of monopoly control, *180;* public services in, 166; strategic annexation in, 59; voter turnout during monopoly control, *143*

Aldrich, John, 64
Alesina, Alberto, 253n26
Alien Land Law (California), 79
alien suffrage, 53, 55, 62, 115, 142
Allswang, John, 6, 68, 71, 98, 249nn3–4
American Federation of Labor (AFL), 202
American Federation of State, County, and Municipal Employees, 202
American Political Science Review, 92
annexation: basis of decisions concerning, 159; challenge to in San Antonio, 212–13; collapse of monopolies and, 179, *187,* 190, 195; denied to Tammany Hall, 210; problems arising from, 165–68; strategic annexation, *32, 33,* 58–59. *See also* development